TRINIDAD AND TOBAGO

Democracy and Development in the Caribbean

Scott B. MacDonald

PRAEGER

PRAEGER SPECIAL STUDIES • PRAEGER SCIENTIFIC
New York • Westport, Connecticut • London

Library of Congress Cataloging-in-Publication Data

MacDonald, Scott B.
  Trinidad and Tobago.

  Bibliography: p.
  Includes index.
  1. Trinidad and Tobago — Politics and government.
2. Trinidad and Tobago — Economic conditions.
3. Trinidad and Tobago — Social conditions. I. Title.
F2119.M33   1986   972.98'3   86-639
ISBN 0-275-92004-6 (alk. paper)

Copyright © 1986 by Praeger Publishers

All rights reserved. No portion of this book may be reproduced, by any process or technique, without the express written consent of the publisher.

Library of Congress Catalog Card Number: 86-639
ISBN: 0-275-92004-6

First published in 1986

Praeger Publishers, 521 Fifth Avenue, New York, NY 10175
A division of Greenwood Press, Inc.

Printed in the United States of America

The paper used in this book complies with the Permanent
Paper Standard issued by the National Information Standards
Organization (Z39.48-1984).

10 9 8 7 6 5 4   3 2 1

This book is dedicated to the memory of my father, Dr. Alvin R. MacDonald and my father-in-law, Michael Scott, who provided much of the inspiration to finish it. It is also dedicated to my wife, Kateri; my mother, Anita MacDonald; friend and mentor, Albert Gastmann; my mother-in-law, Anne Scott; and Suriname, our cat.

Contents

1. INTRODUCTION: DEMOCRACY AND DEVELOPMENT	1
Notes	17
2. THE COLONIAL HERITAGE: PLANTATION SOCIETY, WHITE SUPREMACY, AND THE EMERGENCE OF THE AFRO-CREOLE MIDDLE SECTORS	22
Introduction	22
The Plantation System: From Spanish Colonization to the East Indian Arrival	23
Changes in the Socioeconomic System at the Close of the Century	28
Trinidad and Tobago—The Unified Colony	29
White Supremacy	30
The Emergence of the Afro-Creole Middle Sectors	32
The Politicalization of the Afro-Creole Middle Sectors	36
The Water Riot of 1903	39
The Trinidad Workingmen's Association	40
Conclusion	42
Notes	42
3. THE INTERWAR AND WAR YEARS: EXPERIMENTATION WITH POLITICAL PARTIES	45
The Changing Political Economy	46
The 1919 Riots and Revival of the TWA	48
Cipriani and the Trinidad Labour Party	50
The Turbulent 1930s and the Decline of Cipriani	55
Moderating the Labor Movement	60
The War Years: The Influence of the U.S. Occupation	63
Conclusion	66
Notes	67
4. THE MAZE OF COLOR, 1946-56	71
The 1946 General Elections: The Left's Failure to Capture Power	72
The Docker's Strike, Butler's Sour Grapes, and Constitutional Reform	76
The 1950 General Elections	80
The Maze of Color and the Middle Sectors	83
The Knox Street Quintet	84
The Capitalist Path	85
Poverty, Race, Population, and Unemployment	89
Federation and Constitutional Reform	92
Notes	95

5. ERIC WILLIAMS AND THE BIRTH OF THE PNM, 1955-56 — 98
- Williams and the Influence of Childhood — 98
- From Oxford to the Anglo-American Commission — 100
- Forerunners of the People's National Movement — 102
- Casting Down the Bucket — 104
- The 1956 Elections: The Issues and the Opposition — 105
- Notes — 111

6. CONSOLIDATION OF POWER, 1956-61 — 113
- The Federal Issue and the Changing Caribbean — 114
- The Democratic Labour Party — 116
- The Federal Elections of 1958 — 118
- The Road to Independence and Constitutional Reform — 120
- Leftward Bound — 122
- The Turn to the Right — 127
- The 1961 Elections: Accommodation — 130
- Demise of the Federation and Independence — 136
- Conclusion — 139
- Notes — 139

7. THE CHALLENGE OF INDEPENDENCE, 1962-69 — 145
- The Accommodationist Middle-Class Alliance — 145
- End of the Alliance — 147
- Economic Difficulties and the Alienation of Labor — 148
- DLP Disunity and the 1966 Elections — 151
- The Deepening Economic Crisis — 155
- Conclusion — 158
- Notes — 159

8. THE SHADOW OF AUTHORITARIANISM, 1969-76 — 161
- Trinidad and Tobago's Time of Troubles — 162
- The Authoritarian Temptation, 1970-72 — 166
- The 1971 General Elections — 170
- The Middle Sectors and Localization of the Economy, 1972-76 — 173
- The New Middle Class and Interlocking Directorates — 177
- Development of a New Opposition — 179
- The General Elections of 1976 — 181
- Conclusion — 185
- Notes — 186

9. THE MIDDLE CLASSIZATION OF TRINIDAD AND TOBAGO, 1976-83 — 190
- Trinidad's Economic Miracle — 191
- The Consumer Revolution, Corruption, and the Crisis in Agriculture — 193

The Last Years of the Doctor, 1980-81	195
The 1981 General Elections: Middle Sector Fragmentation	201
The 1983 Municipal Elections: A Wave of the Future?	205
Conclusion	209
Notes	210
10. CONCLUSION	214
Notes	218
SELECTED BIBLIOGRAPHY	221
INDEX	229
ABOUT THE AUTHOR	231

1

Introduction: Democracy and Development

Outside of the Caribbean, there are few areas in the Third World that may be regarded as having a preponderance of open political systems where electoral competition is strong, a loyal opposition exists, and change of government is peaceful and regular, while at the same time, governments seek to improve the standard of living for their citizens.[1] In contrast, the great majority of African, Asian, and Latin American nations that have achieved substantial economic growth are governed by authoritarian regimes or have recently experimented with that form of government. Democracies are the exception, not the rule in the Third World. Successful economic development, where it has occurred, has largely been associated with closed and controlled political systems in which the opposition is either proscribed or co-opted. If democracies along Western lines are the exception rather than the norm, why then do parliamentary democracies like that of Trinidad and Tobago survive? It would appear, from a global viewpoint, that the odds are against the survival of democratic regimes. Yet in the Commonwealth Caribbean, at least, the norm is democratic in the political realm and capitalist in the economic.

This study of Trinidad and Tobago is designed to explore why that nation has had a relatively successful experiment with democracy. The hypothesis advanced is that some Third World nations, in particular those in the Commonwealth Caribbean, can have democratic political systems hand-in-hand with capitalist economic development due to a "package" of factors. It is proposed that in Trinidad and

Tobago this package includes a democratic-minded middle class (multi-racial in nature), a sizable state sector in the economy, the existence of oil, and accepted, yet controlled, foreign investment. The two-island state has clearly followed the conservative-moderate path of development as contrasted to the more radical paths pursued in Grenada (1979-83), Jamaica (1972-80), Cuba under Castro, Nicaragua under the Sandinistas since 1979, and Guyana under Forbes Burnham. While political problems existed that functioned to push the government to play a more active role in the economy and the authoritarian temptation clearly existed in the political realm, Trinidad's development, in a comparative sense, has been successful, and the parliamentary system has not been abandoned, hence confirming this study's hypothesis.

In the following chapters, the evolution of these factors will be examined in a historical approach that encompasses the colonial period, the movement to independence, and the postindependence struggle to maintain positive economic development and democracy, which have sometimes worked at odds. The emphasis of this study is in the postindependence period and ends at the 1983 municipal elections in which the ruling Peoples' National Movement (PNM) lost—its first loss in any major elections since 1958. Throughout, the focus will be on the role of the middle sectors, their interrelationship with the state and multinational corporations. Above all, the Trinidadian middle class is the main factor in the establishment and, ultimately, the maintenance of the democratic political system and the defender of a Third World variant of capitalism.

Given that these findings are valid for Trinidad and Tobago, can conclusions derived from them be extended to other Caribbean societies, both Commonwealth and non-Commonwealth? This matter is not exhaustively explored here, but some preliminary and tentative suggestions are advanced in the final chapter.

In researching this study, use was made of the available theoretical literature on development and particularly of that literature prepared by Caribbean scholars who have focused on the Caribbean reality. Research on Trinidad and Tobago, however, led to the conclusion that, for the most part, literature is flawed. Moroever, investigators would do well to reexamine the now almost forgotten and, to an extent, casually discredited work of John J. Johnson whose early appreciation of the "middle sectors" in development appears to have real usefulness (with revisions), at least when applied to Trinidad and Tobago.

John J. Johnson's *Political Change in Latin America: The Emergence of the Middle Sectors* is a classic work in the "salvation through the middle class" vein. The author argued that Latin America was advancing toward a political system founded upon the concepts of liberal Western democracy. The key to the advance to democratic government, according to Johnson, was in the middle sectors, which were characterized by six attributes: they were overwhelmingly urban; they not only had well above-average educations, but also firmly believed in universal public education; they were convinced that the future of their nations was inextricably tied to industrialization; they were nationalistic; they believed that the state should actively intrude in the social and economic areas; and they recognized that the family had weakened as a political unit in the urban centers and, consequently, had given their support to the development of political parties.[2]

Johnson tested his thesis on five Latin American nations—Argentina, Brazil, Chile, Mexico, and Uruguay—which he maintained were moving to a more democratic phase of political development. By historical examination he reasoned that each nation had made important political and social changes in recent decades. Moreover, "These five nations . . . will set the pattern of tomorrow for the present feudally held Dominican Republics, the socially retarded Paraguays, the poverty stricken Haitis, and the strife-torn Venezuela's which so often capture the headlines."[3] The optimism manifested by Johnson was also reflected in other works of the time, such as Tad Szulz's *Twilight of the Tyrants* and Robert Alexander's *Today's Latin America*. At the close of the 1950s and in the early 1960s, the advance of democracy in Latin America and the Caribbean was indeed promising as dictatorships came to an end in Colombia (1957), Venezuela (1958), Cuba (1959), and the Dominican Republic (1961).

From the vantage point of the late 1950s and early 1960s, Johnson's *Political Change in Latin America* appeared to be an accurate assessment. However, the coup in Brazil in 1964 signaled the dawn of a new age of military regimes and the discredit of the Johnson thesis. The studies of Juan Linz, Alfred Stepan, and Guillermo O'Donnell concurred in demonstrating that the Brazilian and later the Argentine (1966), Peruvian (1968), Chilean (1973), and Uruguayan (1974) middle sectors were allied with the military or favorable to it before the coups.[4] The opening of the political system to the popular sectors, the workers and the peasants, the ability of populist politicians to appeal to the lower classes, promised to disrupt any kind of economic development that favored the middle class, hence the alliance with the armed forces.

Johnson's middle sector thesis not only proved to have serious shortcomings with regard to Latin America, but also in Europe where a long analytical and historical tradition links the rise of fascism and nazism to the middle sectors.[5] The failure to transfer democratic institutions, in most cases, to former colonial nations in Africa and Asia, where many newly independent states succumbed to native tyrannies in a variety of forms and degrees, further discredited the Johnson thesis, supposedly demonstrating its invalidity. For many scholars it became a forgotten piece of literature belonging to a more optimistic era.

Johnson's greatest contribution, in many aspects, was to stir more serious investigation of the relationship between the role of the middle classes and the development process. Therefore, in utilizing Johnson's middle sectors thesis, six major revisions are necessary to make it applicable to Trinidad and Tobago's particular political, social, and economic evolutions. These revisions are to define clearly what the middle sectors are; to deemphasize the urban factor; to identify groups or subgroups within the middle sectors; to take into consideration plural societies; to define fully the relationship between the middle sectors and the international economic system; and to define adequately the scope of the state's role in the economy.

One of the most evident shortcomings of *Political Change in Latin America* was Johnson's failure to define fully the "middle sectors," which were described as "politically ambitious middle groups," largely urban, educated, committed to industrialization, nationalistic, sympathetic to state intervention in the economy, and active in political parties. Although a distinction was emphasized between the middle classes and sectors, the latter was never fully identified. Consequently, the definition of the middle sectors is the first major revision.

In the examination of Trinidad and Tobago, the definition of middle classes and middle sectors will be synonymous. The operational term *middle sectors* or *middle classes* will refer to the politically ambitious middle groups that are characterized by the crucial aspects of urbanization (although there can be a rural middle class), class restratification, movements toward national unification, technological innovation, and the spread of "Westernized" education.[6] This definition cuts across all color barriers, although certain racial groups may be represented by greater numbers.

The second revision is to deemphasize the urban factor. Johnson's work is heavily urban oriented, concentrating on the large city life of Rio de Janeiro, São Paulo, Mexico City, Buenos Aires, Santiago, and Montevideo. The approach is understandable to a point since the middle sectors are largely an urban phenomenon. However, such a perspective is inadequate in two ways: the study develops an overly urban viewpoint and, more importantly, there is no understanding of the "bridge linking the citified middle sectors with the remainder of the structure of which they form a part."[7] A logical deduction is that the middle sectors should function as a stimulus, inducing further change in the nation's political system. Johnson's urban thrust and failure to link rural developments, especially the mobilization of the peasant or rural proletariat, left an important force uncovered. A further reason for deemphasizing the urban factor is the existence of a rural middle class or classes, which in largely agricultural societies often play a significant role.

The third revision is the need to identify groups or subgroups that exist within the middle sectors. Johnson, following Lasswell, made considerable use of elites, almost suggesting that the middle sectors are one well-organized group, dynamic and progressive. It is difficult to consider the middle classes or middle sectors as anything but a number of groups within one loosely defined "class." As Leonard Binder noted in an article on Iran, "the modern middle class is not politically or socially homogenous. There is a modern middle class and a traditional middle class; a commercial middle class, an intellectual middle class, a professional middle class, and a managerial middle class, and a middle class of the minorities and foreigners; there is an urban middle class and a rural middle class."[8]

In another study of the Middle East conducted by James A. Bill and Carl Leiden, four middle-class groups were identified: the bureaucratic, the bourgeois, the cleric, and the professional middle class.[9] The first three have been characterized as traditional and usually allied to the forces that support the status quo, imposed stability, and promoted Islam. The last group, however, "is a threat to the traditional socio-political system in the Middle East," since some of its members demand political development and "refuse to relate to the ruling class in terms of subservience and deference."[10]

Unlike Johnson, a number of Middle East scholars have made an important distinction between groups within the middle sectors: they are aware that within the middle sectors groups may be progressive as well as traditional and may seek to hinder development as well as promote it.[11] Of these, the new middle class (or modern middle class) has caused a degree of controversy and has been a noticeable phenomenon in both the developing and developed nations.[12]

Johnson's Latin American middle sectors, in many aspects, are Bill and Leiden's professional middle class. The latter recognize that, while being progressive, largely urban, well educated, nationalistic, and active in political parties, the class denoted suffers from "deep fissures" caused in part by the "blandishments of bribery and personal aggrandizement."[13] In examining Trinidad and Tobago, it will be necessary to be aware of different and sometimes opposing groups within the middle class.

To further clarify the distinctions within the Trinidadian middle sectors, the term *new bourgeois*, as advanced by David G. Becker in a study on Peru, will be utilized.[14] This group, which emerged in the decades following World War II, especially in the 1960s and 1970s, was composed of managers and technical specialists "whose members are based in both the private and public sectors."[15] Allied to this group are the "transformed middle classes," defined as middle-level professionals, technicians, and administrative supervisors. Following Johnson, the importance of education remains a constant, as emphasized by Becker and by Selwyn Ryan's study on Trinidad and Tobago in which the evolution of the Afro-Creole middle classes is traced from formation to independence to nationhood.[16] The same factor is reflected in other studies on Trinidad by Ivar Oxaal, Bridget Brereton, and Yogenda K. Malik.[17] While these studies have made some analysis of middle-class participation in the development process, the focus has usually been limited to either the preindependence period or the 1960s with little or no work on the 1970s and early 1980s, something this work will cover. Finally, most writers on Trinidad and Johnson ignore the process of "embourgeoisement" in which the most unionized members of the workforce are able to negotiate for higher wages than nonunionized labor. In a sense, a modern sector working class with bourgeois attitudes and behavioral and consumeristic patterns emerges and, as in Trinidad, forms a segment of the lower middle sectors.[18]

The fourth revision entails increased recognition that the multiplication of groups within the middle class becomes even more complex when examined within the context of a plural society. Plural societies were described by J. S. Furnivall as two or more elements or social orders living side by side without mingling in the political unit.[19]

For many societies, both developed and developing, the challenge of cultural plurality has been an important factor in the survival of the nation-state. Anthony D. Smith notes, "the fact is that very few of the world's states are ethnically homogeneous, and many of them are distinctly polyethnic in composition."[20]

Furnivall's definition, which appeared in 1939, is not completely adequate in characterizing nations with fairly large minorities, like the United States, Canada, and France, in which a "mingling" in the political unit has occurred and democratic governments have continued to function. However, in many nations, such as Ireland, Nigeria, and Sri Lanka, cleavages caused by cultural differences have resulted in riots, pogroms, terrorist attacks, and sometimes civil war. In other instances, cultural diversity has fragmented ideological alliances and cut across class lines dividing societies vertically as well as horizontally. In the genesis of societal fragmentation, political systems have usually undergone serious transformations, reflecting, in large part, societal polarization. It is in nations suffering from these problems that Furnivall's definition has a degree of credibility.

Crawford Young grouped cultural differentiation into five categories: ethnic, race, caste, religion, and region.[21] Of these, ethnicity is probably the most encompassing as it "may include language, territory, political unit or common cultural values or symbols."[22] Linked to ethnic differences, factors such as economic power and political influence are crucial in any consideration of a nation's life. For the West Indies and Trinidad and Tobago in particular, ethnicity and race are important features in political and economic development.

Trinidad and Tobago share with Guyana and Suriname similar factors in their national evolution: an ethnically and racially mixed population of Afro-Creoles, East Indians, Chinese, Europeans, and Lebanese-Syrians; colonial rule that superimposed Western, Christian values and social mores on a mixed population; and an economic dependence on one or more commodities, such as sugar or bauxite, which has been the major source of employment and national revenue. After achieving independence each nation developed differently, the latter two characterized by ethnic polarization, parliamentary breakdown, and eventually the establishment of authoritarian rule. Politics in Guyana and Suriname were ethnically and racially divided between the East Indian and Afro-Creole communities. In such situations, the political winner took all, excluding, when possible, members of the other ethnic group from positions of authority. Afro-Creole dominance in Guyana and Suriname, where the East Indians are the largest minority, outnumbering the Afro-Creoles, has resulted in the massive emigration of East Indians to the Netherlands, the United Kingdom, and the United States, further disrupting development and heightening communal tensions. Also, due to the tense situation and lack of employment opportunities, a large number of Afro-Creoles have also left the region.

The emergence of the "black power" doctrine during the 1960s and early 1970s, born of the long-standing frustration of U.S. blacks, had an impact in the Caribbean. In a sense, black power became an ideology of racial solidarity and identity, founded upon the intellectual tradition of the earlier Pan-African and Paris-based négritude movements, which had as their leading advocates, W. E. B. Dubois, Aimé Césaire, Marcus Garvey, Julius Nyerere, and Leopold Senghor. As Young indicates "the idea of negritude took form, asserting a common cultural tradition and unique virtues associated with Black identity, but the essential origins of African racial self-awareness lie in the factors stated by Dubois and Nyerere: a common subjugation, collective incorporation by Europeans into institutionalized subordination, linked to an ideology of racial superiority."[2,3] This ideology made inroads in postcolonial societies in the Caribbean's eastern tier where the rising East Indian birthrate was gradually overtaking the Afro-Creole, and ethnic competition over jobs and political positions was becoming more acute as the East Indians moved upward on the social scale.

The political turmoil that characterized Trinidad and Tobago in the early 1970s was, in part, caused by black power, while rising inflation and unemployment were the major sources of frustration. The Arab Oil Embargo (1973-74), however, provided Trinidad and Tobago with an important lever of prosperity that "softened" the impact of ethnic tensions, while the very radicalization of the period "pushed" the Afro-Creole and Indo-Trinidadian middle sectors together in their support for the Williams government, which favored capitalist development programs. In a sense, class interests began to supercede ethnic and racial differences, especially since the East Indians in Trinidad were unable to maintain a middle-class-led Indian party, unlike their counterparts in the Guianas.

In Guyana and Suriname the fortunes of bauxite, sugar, and rice failed to insure economic progress, and political behavior was increasingly marked by ethnic polarization and political intimidation. Rising oil prices aggravated the situation. While Trinidad and Tobago had a degree of economic prosperity and political stability, Guyana and Suriname suffered declining economic fortunes and strong cultural divisions.

In Trinidad and Tobago the parliamentary system and the Westminster tradition have survived despite ethnic differences between the equally sized Afro-Creole and East Indian communities. The cases of Guyana and Suriname offer a contrast, and all three nations demonstrate that the diverse ethnic communities that constitute their plural societies are likely to differ markedly in their political development. Johnson's approach failed to address such issues, and consequently it is necessary to examine the relationship between ethnic relations and political and economic development. *Political Change in Latin America* would offer little to explain the ethnic polarization of Guyana or Suriname or the demise of their native middle sectors as a political force. Moreover, a serious flaw would have been evident in a similar approach to Trinidad and Tobago. In understanding Trinidadian development, all factors—ethnic, racial, political, religious, and economic— have to be scrutinized. As Malcolm Cross notes, "It is impossible to understand the recent historical changes within Trinidad without looking at economic forces. For one thing the presence of a comparatively black, coloured, and Indian middle class has, incidently, led to a greater disjunction between racial and economic divisions."[2,4]

The fifth revision of the Johnson thesis is the relationship between the middle sectors and the international economic system. Johnson portrayed the middle sectors as favoring industrialization and the mixed economy and, through cultural linkages, looking to the West for models and inspiration. It is implied that the middle sectors favor and actively participate in an economic relationship that is set within the framework of the capitalist global economic system. The rise of capitalism was, in fact, bolstered by the middle classes' position vis-à-vis other social groups and made it, according to Johnson, a positive agent of change in moving toward democratic government.

Johnson's research implied much, but it fell short of actually examining how a society and, in particular, how the middle sectors were influenced by the changes in the international economic system. Trinidad and Tobago's political and social formation can hardly be understood without an examination of economic forces. The same could be said for any nation. Trinidad and Tobago's fertile soils and raw materials usually functioned as a buffer against some of the more severe disturbances in the global economic system, which, in turn, helped the advancement of a national middle class.

Through the evolution of the international economic system, Trinidad and Tobago developed linkages to the dominant forces in that system, first England and then the United States, in the twentieth century. This is easily demonstrated by the fact that the United States is Trinidad and Tobago's largest trade partner.[25] The decline of U.S. economic might in the late 1970s was also reflected in trade patterns with Trinidad and Tobago: although North American trade dominated, Port of Spain began looking to other nations for technological aid and joined other Third World nations in the movement to create a New International Economic Order (NIEO). As the 1980s began, the Japanese had helped establish a Trinidadian automobile industry, and trade agreements were made with the European Economic Community through the Lomé Conventions. It is important to stress, however, that U.S. involvement will almost certainly remain dominant, maintained through large corporations involved in the energy sector and organizations like the U.S. Chamber of Commerce.

In dealing with the stronger powers in the international political economy, the role of the middle sectors requires some investigation. Are the Trinidadian middle sectors nationalistic, regarding foreign investment as a tool for the development of their country, or are they the proverbial "running dogs of capitalism," seeking to empty the country of its wealth and exploit the workers?

One of the earliest and clearly most influential voices of the dependency school, Raúl Prebisch, an Argentine banker-economist, argued that a new bourgeoisie, commercial and industrial in nature, was in the process of emerging in the 1960s. This new group, like Johnson's middle sectors, was a supporter of national interests in the face of foreign penetration into the domestic economies of developing nations. As Prebisch wrote, "And new forces are emerging, chiefly from the middle strata of society, which have expanded considerably. It is mainly from these middle strata that the men who are striving to transform the Latin American economy are coming to the fore."[26] Rómulo Betancourt, president of Venezuela (1945-48 and 1959-64), made a similar observation of a new middle class in his nation: "It is opposed to the intervention of foreign capital in the national economy and favors industrialization, agrarian reform, and those methods of social betterment that tend to reinforce the position of Venezuelan consumers and to create an internal market for national products."[27] The emphasis with Prebisch and Betancourt was anti-imperialist and nationalist, but not opposed to capitalism, an important distinction from more radical dependency theorists.

According to other dependency theorists, foreign capitalists are hegemonic by nature, are disruptive of social groups, and are seeking to influence the wealthy or upper classes in the Third World. Multinational corporations (MNCs), in particular, are responsible for the fragmentation of existing social groups since they encourage the development of what Celso Furtado calls the "managerial middle class."[28] This group tends to demand concessions for its own benefit rather than for society as a whole, while finding foreign firms as supportive allies. Financially secure and influential because of their disproportionately large incomes from successful involvement in industry, members of the managerial middle class have advocated tax reductions and promoted legislation for trade concessions and import licenses. It is argued that this "alliance" between a native middle class and foreign business has resulted in unbalanced economic development and repressive, nondemocratic military regimes that ignore the mass of the people.

Furtado regarded the entire process as the "development of underdevelopment." The solution was to be found in autonomy, which meant a restructuring of relations with multinational corporations: greater controls were urged for foreign investment, and the agricultural sector was to be revitalized and made more productive in order to meet internal needs and markets.

A more radical critique of the middle class and its relationship with the international economic system is found with Marxist dependency theorists, André Gunder Frank, James Petras, and the late Guyanese scholar, Walter Rodney.[29] To this group, underdevelopment and dependency were increased by the diffusion of knowledge, organization, values, technology, managerial skills, and capital from the "core" nations of the capitalist world economy to the peripheral and dependent states of Africa, Asia, and Latin America. In other words, the capitalist system reinforced itself in the periphery, and part of that reinforcement came from native middle sectors. As Frank states, "underdevelopment in a dependent region such as Latin America cannot be understood except as the product of a bourgeois policy formulated in response to class interests and class structure, which in turn was determined by the dependence of the Latin American satellite on the colonialist, imperialist metropolis."[30]

To radical dependency theorists, the Third World was exploited by the international forces of capitalism: MNCs from the core, the native middle sectors, and the military in the periphery. Rarely are there cases where Third World nations, such as Trinidad and Tobago or Barbados, benefit from contact with the industrialized metropolis. Business is perceived as "bad," seeking to exploit worker and peasant, while creating an outflow of national capital that hinders any indigenous development. In this situation, the managerial middle class or "lumpenbourgeoisie is an active tool of foreign industry and commerce."[3][1]

The emergence of the dependency school of analysis from Latin America was echoed in the Caribbean in the 1960s and 1970s. In Jamaica the New World Group was an important consolidation of the forces at work in the first decade of independence in much of the Commonwealth Caribbean. Among its members were Norman Girvan, Trevor Munroe, Lloyd Best, James Millette, Clive Thomas, and George Lamming.

The core concern of the New World Group was the necessity of making the people of the Caribbean aware of the threat of neocolonialism. Lamming, a leading West Indian literary figure, argued that neocolonialism undermined the significance of political independence and maintained a system of controls that was not local. In a sense, independence meant no more than a change of elites, with the "Afro-Saxons," those of mixed African and European blood or those who became assimilated fully into Western culture with ties to the corporate world, becoming substitute middlemen. As Lamming notes with regard to this situation: "Here is a humiliation that goes deep; a humiliation which no abstract independence can heal. No change of flag or anthem can stem this spiritual bleeding of men who have nothing to celebrate but a raise in salary. . . . The vocabulary of politics has changed but the politics of their lives remains the same."[3][2]

Much of what the New World Group wrote corresponded to Frantz Fanon's two most important books, *Black Skin, White Masks* and *The Wretched of the Earth*. In these works, the political thought of Fanon, a Martinican by birth, has lived on past the author's short life of 36 years. His writings, although not entirely on the Caribbean, are topical to the discussion of the character of the middle sectors and its relationship with the international political economy.

In *The Wretched of the Earth*, a book that has had some impact on the Caribbean left, Fanon analyzed the national middle class, arguing that its historical mission is that of an intermediary between the independent underdeveloped nation and the MNCs. Industries may be nationalized after independence is achieved, but Fanon felt that was for the purpose of making the foreign companies deal with the middle class. Moreover, nationalization does not mean a better distribution of resources as the bourgeoisie perceive state control of the economy as the way to "transfer into native hands of those unfair advantages which are a legacy of the colonial period."[33] The path to "liberation" was only achieved by force. As Fanon commented, "At the level of individuals, violence is a cleansing force. It frees the native from his inferiority complex and from his despair and inaction; it makes him fearless and restores his self-respect."[34]

From these thoughts many Caribbean radicals derived the conviction that violent revolution was necessary to oust the colonial power. In this viewpoint the middle class also stands as an obstacle to true liberation, even after independence: the role of the middle class as an intermediary impinges on development since the unfair relationships between the state and foreign companies have survived political independence. The middle class, therefore, also must be removed by violence.

For most radical dependency theorists, the much lauded solution for underdevelopment and capitalist domination has been revolution along socialist lines and a move out of the capitalist world order. An unspoken assumption is that the middle class must be eliminated as in Cuba or, much more radically, Kampuchea under the Khmer Rouge.

In fact, of course, not all contact between the capitalist metropole and the periphery has been negative; multinational corporations, the middle classes, and military cannot be blamed for all Third World problems. Foreign investors, dependent on markets and buyers, do not want to bankrupt the nations with which they do business. While unequal exchanges have occurred and MNCs produce goods for people with higher incomes, they also offer benefits: employment, access to international markets, and technology transfer. Moreover, the much lauded socialist model of development, which emphasizes independence from the capitalist world system and central planning and a greatly reduced private sector, has not been notably successful. Socialist nations such as Poland and Vietnam have not found clear and quick remedies to underdevelopment through central planning: both have problems in their balance of payments and have witnessed domestic discontent over goods distribution, bureaucratic inflexibility, and bottlenecks.[35] Even the Soviet Union has had its share of economic difficulties as exemplified by distribution allocation problems, production shortfalls, and an inability to meet consumer demand.

Socialism in the developing world and East Europe has not shown the world a development model without outside aid and some form of political repression. Soviet assistance to Cuba and Vietnam has made those nations among the highest aid receivers in the world. Nor has membership in the Council for Mutual Economic Assistance (COMECON) resulted in tremendous changes in Cuba's economic structure, as it is still dependent on sugar.

Radical dependency theorists point to the increased life expectancy, the eradication of malnutrition, and improved educational standards as proof of the success of the Cuban socialist model in the Caribbean and Latin America. At the same time, they ignore the fact that other nations, such as Trinidad and Tobago, Barbados, Panama, Costa Rica, and the Dominican Republic, have also made improvements in health education and per capita income by pursuing "capitalist" models. Also, many Marxist dependency theorists, living in capitalist societies in which recent experiences are nondemocratic, prefer to ignore the fact that democracies exist in the Third World where national middle classes are supportive of national development. They denigrate history to a rise and fall of import-export trade, portraying Third World populations as hapless victims without any dynamism of their own. Ultimately, radical dependency theorists, like Johnson in *Political Change in Latin America*, lack the understanding that the middle class can be a progressive force as well as a negative force in the development process and that the middle sectors comprise more than one group.

The last major revision to *Political Change in Latin America* concerns the role of the state in the economy, something already briefly noted in the discussion of the middle sectors and their relationship with the international economic system. Although Johnson indicated the importance of state involvement in the economy due to the urging of the middle sectors, exactly what he meant in terms of actual implementation of programs and strategy was left hazy. What was clear was that he felt the state should promote industrialization, which did occur to varying degrees in Argentina, Brazil, Chile, Mexico, and Uruguay.[36] In Johnson's work the equation was simple: industrialization promoted by the state equaled economic growth with distribution (through trickle down), which in turn equaled stability and democratic political development. To a certain extent, there was both cause and effect in the equation as vigorous GDP growth, stemming from the industrializing economy, promoted democracy and also followed from it.

In examining Trinidad and Tobago, the state plays a dominant role in the management of the economy, especially in the oil sector. The state's role, however, is not limited only to the promotion of industry. While Johnson noted that the middle sectors of Latin America had moved away from laissez-faire capitalism, in supporting and shaping the "managerial" state, he did not fully grasp the full scope of statist intervention in economic affairs that had already emerged. Alfred Stepan notes:

> A major, nearly world-wide trend since the 1930s has been the steady growth of the state in political life. In the industrialized world, the emergence of the managerial state to combat the crisis of capitalism during the depression, the widened scope of executive power in World War II, and growing state regulative and welfare functions since the war, have all contributed to the expansion of the state. In the Third World, it is even clearer that most development plans call for the state to play a major role in structuring economic and social systems.[37]

In many cases, as in Trinidad and Tobago, the state has become involved in exchange regulation, the control of marketing channels of raw materials, and the monitoring of credit conditions as well as the erection and removal of tariff and nontariff barriers. State subsidies are also allocated to various nonindustrial sectors such as agriculture, forestry, and fishing. Moreover, many nations have adopted five-year plans. These are much more than a mere framework for the allocation of resources for economic investment. As B. L. C. Johnson notes, "Usually they are also the vehicles for an expression of the nation's ultimate social and economic goals and thus a reflection of its ideology."[38] He also notes there can be subtle changes in time on emphasis in priorities and even in ideological objectives, something that *Political Change in Latin America* makes no allowance for.

Another element in the discussion involves determining how extensive the state role in the economy should be. To the classical school of economists who emerged in England in the 1700s (Adam Smith, David Ricardo, and John Stuart Mill), the state's role should be minimal.[39] The key to growth of the nation-state was the expansion of markets, and market size was expanded by the development of the world market, hence the need for free trade. Free trade, of course, was a rejection of mercantilism.

The mercantilists had recognized the growing power of the national economy in the late 1600s and early 1700s and favored the intervention of the state in economic activity to maximize national wealth.[40] Under mercantilism wealth was measured by precious metals, a large amount of which was earned by war (i.e., England and the Netherlands warring on Spain and its overseas colonies, as in the New World) and by the exploitation of colonies. Johnson failed to indicate where he stood: did he feel the middle sectors favored the free trade approach or did they look to mercantilism, or even more likely did they stand somewhere in between, advocating the development of national industries with certain protective barriers until that product could stand the test of the international marketplace.

Lloyd Best, a Trinidadian economist, indicates the importance of this discussion to the Caribbean:

> The Caribbean is the *locus classicus* of mercantilism. The first three hundred years of its economic life have provided perhaps the purest example of this philosophy in operation. Economic activity in the region was governed not so much by external as by metropolitan demand and the structures of production, consumption and trade simply followed suit. There being no interest in and possibility of matching domestic demand and supply, any economic integration of the Caribbean was automatically ruled out since each sub-unit of the region was more or less similarly organized and run.[41]

Best felt the system had perpetuated itself and that the "policy of *laisse-faire* which, in the 19th century (1840-1940), displaced that of mercantilism, set up many conflicts of adjustment but in the end left the old structure largely intact."[42] Development in the Caribbean context, therefore, meant transforming the traditional order. To do so, Best proposed that manufacturing industries, aided by government initiatives, would create jobs and incomes domestically. Essential to these new industries was regional integration. While not as essential to the larger scale economies of the Latin American countries that Johnson investigated, integration makes considerable sense in the Caribbean due to the small size of island economies. As Best wrote, "Without internal integration the flow of output would be to the metropolis and not to the region—except insofar as it is a metropolitan decision to integrate the region through firms operating in several territories."[43] This viewpoint is also shared by William Demas, another Caribbean economist, who notes, "I shall argue that underdevelopment and self-sustained growth cannot be considered in isolation from the size of a particular country."[44]

Considering what Best and Demas indicate, two new elements are observable in revising Johnson's variable of state intervention in the economy. These two points are the extent of intervention with regard to the historical background of mercantilism and free trade and the importance of size. Mercantilism built up linkages to the metropole that have not been easily broken or transformed. Part of that economic system was the plantation, which Trinidad has steadily moved away from. Size also limited what could be done with the economy. However, in transforming these developments to the benefit of the Third World country, the state, at least in the case of Trinidad and Tobago, has functioned as the major force in restructuring at least part of the overall system that it deals with.

For this study the state role in the economy is regarded as essential in not only the promotion of industry, but also in the shaping of the political terrain in which the marketplace exists. Also taken into consideration is that size is a factor, calling for different strategies from those utilized in the larger Latin American countries examined by Johnson. Moreover, it should be emphasized that the private sector has an important place in the economy and should not be shunted aside, especially if that nation wants to remain within the capitalist system. In a sense, what developed in Trinidad and Tobago, was state capitalism that existed alongside the private sector, much as it has in Venezuela. Integration, however, is more important in the Caribbean scenario, as reflected by Trinidad's membership to the Caribbean Community (CARICOM), a regional trading bloc based on the same concepts as the European Economic Community.

In making revisions on the Johnson thesis, a solid framework of analysis has been created for a case study on Trinidad and Tobago. Due to the current political and economic situation in the Caribbean, one of international conflict and competition, it is helpful to understand how the democratic capitalist model can succeed (at least in one country.[45] As a recent State Department study notes, "Elections by themselves cannot remake society or solve every problem."[46] There is clearly much more to be taken into consideration, and this case study seeks to cover those other factors.

In the following chapters, the reason that Trinidad and Tobago has had a relatively successful experiment with democracy will be examined. The hypothesis advanced is that democratic-capitalist development has occurred in the two-island state due to a package of factors that include a democratic-minded middle class (multiracial in nature), a sizable state sector in the economy, the existence of oil, and controlled foreign investment. The next chapter provides a comparative framework, which is needed to demonstrate Trinidad and Tobago's relative success, and sets the stage for the development of the case study.

NOTES

1. To the Caribbean should be added the new states of the South Pacific, such as Fiji, Vanatu, and Tuvalu. See Arnold Leibowitz, *Colonial Emancipation*

in the Pacific and the Caribbean (New York: Praeger, 1976); Robert Norton, *Race and Politics in Fiji* (New York: St. Martin's Press, 1977); Patrice Boer, "Paradise Threatened by the 20th Century?" *Manchester Guardian Weekly*, September 1983, pp. 12, 14; and by the same author, "Tonga and Fiji—Racial Tensions and a Generation Gap," *Manchester Guardian Weekly*, September 12, 1983, pp. 12, 14. Mauritius in the Indian Ocean would also fit into the democratic category. See Bernard Iehembre, *L'île Maurice* (Paris: Editions Karthala, 1984) and Adele Smith Simmons, *Modern Mauritius: The Politics of Decolonization* (Bloomington: Indiana University Press, 1982).

2. John J. Johnson, *Political Change in Latin America: The Emergence of the Middle Sectors* (Stanford: Stanford University Press, 1958), p. 5.

3. Ibid., p. viii.

4. Alfred Stepan, *The Military in Politics: Changing Patterns in Brazil* (Princeton: Princeton University Press, 1971); Guillermo A. O'Donnell, *Modernización y Golpes Militares* (Buenos Aires: Institute Torcuate di Tella Centro de Investigaciónes de Administracion Publica, 1972); Juan Linz and Alfred Stepan, *The Breakdown of Democratic Regimes* (Baltimore: Johns Hopkins University Press, 1978).

5. Literature on this is extensive, and the following is only a small selection: Robert Gellately, *The Politics of Economic Despair: Shopkeepers and German Politics, 1890-1914* (London: Sage, 1974); Herman Lebovics, *Social Conservatism and the Middle Classes in Germany, 1914-1933* (Princeton: Princeton University Press, 1969); R. Dahrendorf, "Recent Changes in Class Structure," in S. R. Grauband, ed., *A New Europe* (Boston: Harvard University Press, 1964); R. Dahrendorf, *Class Conflict in Industrial Society* (Stanford: Stanford University Press, 1959) and R. Dahrendorf, *Society and Democracy in Germany* (Garden City, N.Y.: Anchor Books, 1965); Richard Grunberger, *The 12-Year Reich: A Social History of Nazi Germany* (New York: Ballantine Books, 1971); Erich Fromm, *Escape from Freedom* (New York: Avon Books, 1941, 1965); and for an overall discussion about the lower middle classes, see Peter Stearns, *European Society in Upheaval: Social History Since 1800* (London: Collier-MacMillan, 1967).

6. George I. Blanksten, "In Quest of the Middle Sectors," *World Politics*, no. 2 (January 1960): 325. Further descriptions may be found in B. B. Misra, *The Indian Middle Classes: Their Growth in Modern Times* (London: Oxford University Press, 1961), pp. 12-13.

7. Blanksten, "Quest of the Middle Sectors," p. 326.

8. Leonard Binder, "Iran's Potential as a Regional Power" in P. Y. Hammond and S. S. Alexander, eds., *Political Dynamics in the Middle East* (New York: American Elsevier, 1972), p. 375.

9. James A. Bill and Carl Leiden, *Politics in the Middle East* (Boston: Little, Brown, 1974, 1979), pp. 117-33.

10. Ibid., p. 126.

11. For further studies on the Middle East's middle classes, see Morroe Berger, *The Arab World Today* (Garden City, N.Y.: Doubleday, 1962), pp. 271-

72; Manfred Halpern, *The Politics of Social Change in the Middle East and North Africa* (Princeton: Princeton University Press, 1963), pp. 51-78; H. A. R. Gibb, "Social Reform: Factor X," in Walter Z. Laqueur, ed., *The Middle East in Transition* (New York: Praeger, 1958), pp. 3-11; James A. Bill, *The Politics of Iran: Groups Classes and Modernization* (Columbus, Ohio: Charles E. Merrill, 1973), pp. 53-72; and William A. Rugh, "Emergence of a New Middle Class in Saudi Arabia," *Middle East Review*, 27 (Winter 1973): 7-20.

12. Ezra Vogel concluded that a new societal order was emerging in postwar Japan in which the "old middle class" of small businessmen and landlords was gradually being replaced by a "new middle class" of white-collar employees of large business corporations and government bureaucracies. Ezra Vogel, *Japan's New Middle Class: The Salary Man and His Family in a Tokyo Suburb* (Berkeley: University of California Press, 1963), p. 4.

13. Bill and Leiden, *Politics in the Middle East*, p. 127.

14. David G. Becker, *The New Bourgeoisie and the Limits of Dependency: Mining, Class, and Power in "Revolutionary" Peru* (Princeton: Princeton University Press, 1983).

15. Ibid., p. 5.

16. Selwyn Ryan, *Race and Nationalism in Trinidad and Tobago: A Study of Decolonization in a Multiracial Society* (Toronto: University of Toronto Press, 1972).

17. Bridget Brereton, *A History of Modern Trinidad* (London: Heineman Educational Books, 1981) and by the same author, *Race Relations in Colonial Trinidad, 1870-1900* (New York: Cambridge University Press, 1979); Ivar Oxaal, *Black Intellectuals Come to Power: The Rise of Creole Nationalism in Trinidad and Tobago* (Cambridge, Mass.: Schenkman, 1968); and Yogenda Malik, *East Indians in Trinidad: A Study in Minority Politics* (London: Oxford University Press, 1971).

18. Stephen Glazier, in a private discussion at the University of Connecticut, October 25, 1983, agreed with this development. See his "Research Report: Cultural Pluralism and Respectability in Trinidad," *Ethnic and Racial Studies* 6 (July 1983): 351-55. David Renwick, formerly the editor of the *Trinidad Express* and now the Trinidad-based associate editor of *Caribbean and West Indies Chronicle* and *Insight-Caribbean Newsletter*, concurs with this viewpoint in his country survey of Trinidad and Tobago in *Latin America and Caribbean 1983* (Saffron Walden, Sussex, England: World of Information, 1983), p. 261.

19. J. S. Furnivall, *Netherlands India* (Cambridge: Cambridge University Press, 1939), p. 446. Also see his *Colonial Policy and Practice* (Cambridge: Cambridge University Press, 1948) and "Burma: Independence and After," *Asian Horizon* 2 (1949).

20. Anthony D. Smith, *The Ethnic Revival in the Modern World* (Cambridge: Cambridge University Press, 1981), p. 9.

21. Crawford Young, *The Politics of Cultural Pluralism* (Madison: University of Wisconsin Press, 1979), pp. 47-65.

22. Ibid., p. 48.

23. Ibid., p. 51. For further reading on the negritude movement see Susan Frutkin, *Aimé Césaire: Black Between Worlds* (Miami: University of Florida Press, 1973).

24. Malcolm Cross, "On Conflict, Race Relations and the Theory of the Plural Society," *Race* 12 (1978): 490.

25. *Direction of Trade Statistics Yearbook 1984* (Washington, D.C.: International Monetary Fund, 1984), pp. 369-70.

26. Raúl Prebisch, *Change and Development—Latin America's Great Task* (New York: Praeger, 1971), p. 152.

27. Quoted in Paul Sigmund, *Models of Political Change in Latin America* (New York: Praeger, 1971), pp. 240-41.

28. Celso Furtado, *Obstacles to Development in Latin America* (New York: Anchor Books, 1967), p. 107.

29. André Gunder Frank, "Sociology of Development and Underdevelopment of Sociology," *Catalyst* 3 (Summer 1967): 20-73; James Petras, *Politics and Social Structure in Latin America* (New York: Monthly Review Press, 1970); Walter Rodney, *How Europe Underdeveloped Africa* (Washington, D.C.: Howard University Press, 1974); and Stanley J. Stein and Barbara H. Stein, *The Colonial Heritage of Latin America: Essays on Economic Dependence in Perspective* (New York: Oxford University Press, 1970).

30. André Gundar Frank, *Lumpen-Bourgeoisie; Lumpendevelopment: Dependence, Class and Politics in Latin America* (New York: Monthly Review Press, 1972), p. 1.

31. Ibid., p. 5. According to Petras, the Latin American middle classes are largely responsible for the "inevitable choking off of economic development by the diversion of potential investment capital toward the achievement of Western middle-class standards of living," and this "raises serious doubts about the validity of Western political, economic and social models for underdeveloped countries." *Politics and Social Structure*, p. 51.

32. George Lanning, "Introduction," *New World Quarterly* 2 (1966): 68.

33. Frantz Fanon, *The Wretched of the Earth* (New York: Grove Press, 1968), p. 150.

34. Ibid., p. 73.

35. Nora Beloff, "COMECON Blues," *Foreign Policy*, no. 31 (Summer 1978): 159-79; and Alexander Casella, "Dateline Vietnam: Managing the Peace," *Foreign Policy*, no. 30 (Spring 1978): 170-91. Even Democratic Kampuchea, the ultimate example of departing from the capitalist global system, was dependent on a certain amount of foreign aid. See Craig Etcheson, *The Rise and Demise of Democratic Kampuchea* (Boulder: Westview Press, 1984), chaps. 7, 8.

36. There is an extensive literature of the state in the economy, and this is only a small menu: W. Baer and M. Gillis, eds., *Export Diversification and the New Protectionism: The Experience of Latin America* (Champaign: University of Illinois Press, 1981); T. Bruneau and P. Faucher, eds., *Athoritarian Capitalism*:

Brazil's Contemporary Economic and Political Development (Boulder: Westview Press, 1981); K. P. Erikson, *The Brazilian Corporative State and Working Class Politics* (Berkeley: University of California Press, 1977); Peter Evans, *Dependent Development* (Princeton: Princeton University Press, 1979); Peter Smith, *Labyrinths of Power: Political Recruitment in Twentieth-Century Mexico* (Princeton: Princeton University Press, 1979); Van R. Whiting, Jr., "State Intervention in Brazil and Mexico: Theoretical Considerations for a Comparative Study," paper presented at the Twelfth World Congress of the International Political Science Association, August 9-14, 1982, Rio de Janeiro.

37. Alfred Stepan, *The State and Society: Peru in Comparative Perspective* (Princeton: Princeton University Press, 1978), p. 3.

38. B. L. C. Johnson, *Development in South Asia* (New York: Penguin Books, 1983), p. 38.

39. This is obviously a shortened description. For a fuller discussion see Daniel Fusfeld, *The Age of the Economist* (Oakland, N.J.: Scott, Foresman, 1977), pp. 23-55.

40. G. Bannock, R. E. Baxter, and R. Rees, *The Penguin Dictionary of Economics* (Harmondsworth, England: Penguin Books, 1977), p. 197.

41. Lloyd Best, "Current Development Strategy and Economic Integration in the Caribbean," in Sybil Lewis and Thomas Mathews, eds., *Caribbean Integration: Papers on Social, Political and Economic Integration* (Rio Piedras, Puerto Rico: Institute of Caribbean Studies, 1967), p. 58.

42. Ibid.

43. Ibid., p. 68.

44. William Demas, *The Economics of Development in Small Countries With Special Reference to the Caribbean* (Montreal: Centre for Developing-Area Studies, McGill University Press, 1965), p. 3.

45. Anthony Payne, *The International Crisis in the Caribbean* (Baltimore: Johns Hopkins University Press, 1984), p. 1.

46. U.S. Department of State, *Democracy in Latin America and the Caribbean*, Current Policy no. 605 (August 1984), p. 3.

2

The Colonial Heritage: Plantation Society, White Supremacy, and the Emergence of the Afro-Creole Middle Sectors

INTRODUCTION

From the early colonization of Trinidad and Tobago in the 1500s by the Spanish through the British conquest in 1797 to the advent of the oil industry in the early twentieth century, the plantation dominated the development of the island and helped influence the formation of its political, social, and economic institutions. The same could be said of Tobago with the caveat that the smaller island of the unitary state never fully recovered from the long decline of King Sugar.

By the early nineteenth century, Trinidad and Tobago's society was led by a white upper class of Spanish, French, and English descent. To this ruling class, based on the economic foundations of the plantation system and merchant firms, the ideology of white supremacy justified the lack of representative political institutions embodied in the Crown Colony model of colonial rule. Despite the emergence of a "Westernized" Afro-Creole middle class and emancipation in 1834, plantation agriculture continued to play a major role in shaping society as it perpetuated the existence of an agro-proletariat in the imported and indentured East Indian population.

It is the purpose of this chapter to analyze briefly the three major elements of Trinidad and Tobago's early political economy—the ideology of white supremacy, the Crown Colony system, and the plantation—against which the Afro-Creole middle sectors militated and ultimately overcame in their struggle for equality. As Crawford Young notes of the interrelationship of these elements, "The maintenance of a loose colonial overrule for more than a century after the abolition of slavery permitted the consolidation of the racial stratification which had its roots in the initial plantation system."[1] Along these lines, access to education and to employment in the civil service, as Johnson emphasized in his examination of Latin America, was crucial in the emergence of the middle sectors and their eventual concern with political advancement.

THE PLANTATION SYSTEM: FROM SPANISH COLONIZATION TO THE EAST INDIAN ARRIVAL

It was not until the last decades of the eighteenth century that Spain decided to develop Trinidad. Since its discovery in 1498, the island had been an almost forgotten outpost of the empire, with large tracts of unused land. The stimulus for development, however, was not from within the empire nor from the island; rather it came from what other nationalities were accomplishing with their Caribbean possessions. In the decline of Spanish power, the English, French, and Dutch penetrated the West Indies, established colonies, and experimented with various crops. Eventually, the "plantation revolution," based upon the intensive, nearly monocultural production of sugar swept the non-Hispanic islands such as St. Kitts, Barbados, and Guadeloupe.

The New World plantation system combined African labor and European management, capital, and technology. Situated in the Americas and utilizing Asiatic and American plants, the plantation system was, as Sidney Mintz notes, "an absolutely unprecedented social, economic and political institution, and by no means simply an innovation in the organization of agriculture."[2] In effect, the high organizational basis of the plantation helped revolutionize agriculture in the Caribbean. By the 1760s both England and France owned sugar islands and held sway over sizable empires in the Western Hemisphere. Trinidad, only loosely held by Spain and relatively untouched, became a highly regarded piece of real estate to the English and French who were seeking new lands for sugar production.

Sensitive to English and French intentions, Spain belatedly sought to develop Trinidad into a lucrative sugar colony. The Spanish, however, lacked labor, capital, expertise, and settlers. Eventually Spanish authorities turned to French planters from other Caribbean islands when, in December 1776, they granted foreign Catholics the privilege of settling in Spanish colonies. The immigration of the French and their slaves was to have important and long-lasting consequences on Trinidad and Tobago's political, social, and economic evolution.

The settlement of the French in Trinidad in the 1780s and 1790s created an entirely new society. Although Trinidad's population was religiously homogeneous, being Catholic, linguistically it was predominantly French, but officially Spanish. Aspects of both cultures were accepted as a degree of tolerance prevailed even in terms of race relations, which allowed some upward social mobility for those of European and African mixed blood. In terms of development, the French influx helped improve the economy, placing an emphasis on plantation agriculture, especially that of sugar, which significantly increased the number of Africans brought to the island as slaves.

The profits of the sugar industry, paradoxically, proved to attract not only the French, but also the English, who captured the island in 1797. The British invasion of Trinidad brought a new period of political and social formation. The influx of newcomers, mainly English and Scots, with a small group of Germans, was largely Protestant and English speaking. Many of those of what was called the "English" party were merchants, lawyers, doctors, government officials, and small shop owners, and their presence in Trinidad was not always appreciated by the Spanish and French Creoles, who regarded the latecomers as intruders.

Aware that an official imposition of the Protestant religion and English laws would create considerable tension, the earlier British governors had carefully maintained a balance between the two national and religious communities, hence, in effect, guaranteeing the island's cultural plurality. The English governors also had to face the political realities of the situation: a small group of Englishmen and Scots, supported by a small military force, ruled a population largely French and African in origin. The history of many West Indian islands had been one of constant changes of ownership and bitter conquests. Considering that the early English possession of Trinidad was by no means firm, a delicate balance was maintained between the communities by the gradual implementation of the Crown Colony system of government. In this, Trinidad was an experimental colony, the first territory under English rule to have the Crown Colony form of government.

In adding Trinidad to the British Empire, London was confronted with the problem of how to rule its new acquisition. Many decision makers felt that limited self-government, based upon constitutions granted by the monarchy and with electorates composed of landholders, had been one cause of the American Revolution.[3] Similar experiments in the West Indies, in particular those islands conquered from the French, Grenada and St. Lucia, had also been troublesome for ministers seeking to shape them to the goals of the British Empire.[4]

Although the arrival of English and Scottish merchants in Trinidad stimulated a demand for representative government along the lines of the British Parliament, the authorities were apprehensive over ruling a predominantly non-British population and ignored these demands. This was especially true under the island's first English governor, Colonel Thomas Picton, who became a staunch friend of the French Royalist planters, who in turn sought to maintain their position as the most favored class to the exclusion of the "free people of color." It should be noted that before 1797 Trinidad had the largest free Afro-Creole population in the Caribbean, some of whom were landed. Any widening of the island's political system would have to include this group—something that the English government and most upper-class French Creole planters strongly opposed. The white middle class on the island, largely composed of small merchants and members of the civil service, was small, and the rights of the free Afro-Creole community was of no concern to them.

Upon the occupation of the island, Picton was instructed to govern the island in accordance with Spanish law. Under the Spanish system the governor was the most powerful political actor, being chief executive and chief judge. His power, however, was limited by a number of built-in checks such as the royal *audencia* in Caracas, a "court of residence" at the close of each administrative term, and the *cabildo*, or municipal council, of Port of Spain, which functioned as an advisory board to the governor and had the power to select *alcaldes*, or judges, for the lower courts amongst its ranks. Moreover, the *cabildo* was able to protest to the government against any of the governor's actions that it regarded in the disinterest of the colony.

The British gradually changed the structure of the government as the *cabildo* was replaced by a Council of Advice, which was presided over by the governor who selected the members. This governmental organ remained in operation until 1831 when it was replaced by the Legislative Council, which was made up of six unofficial nominated members (nominated by the governor and community leaders) and six civil servants. In the latter body, the governor was the chief executive and had power over who sat in the council. Significantly, the formation of the Legislative Council was only part of the refinement of the Crown Colony system that had been established to eliminate the hazy power of Spanish institutions, to silence the vocal English merchants (small firms) who demanded representative government, and to keep power out of the hands of those of African and mixed African-European descent, especially after emancipation.

The Crown Colony was, in many aspects, an autocratic form of government headed by a governor who, ruling in the monarch's name, had almost unlimited power. In theory he was the impartial, yet special, protector of the unrepresented masses. In reality he usually shared the planters' general political and social views, which was mirrored in policy. A governor who sought to implement policies that went against the planters found his tenure of office difficult, but not impossible. While the upper classes had access to the island's chief executive, the majority of the population remained without political representation. This undemocratic system of government was to remain largely unchanged from 1831 to 1924, when considerable political tension began to surface.

Certain political freedoms existed in Trinidad that helped create a foundation for the later experiment with democracy despite the autocratic nature of the Crown Colony system. First and foremost, the metropole gradually moved toward the abolition of the slave trade and slavery itself in 1838 over the resistance of the planters. In England an alliance of abolitionists and large capitalists coalesced to terminate the system of slavery, which became increasingly uneconomic due to heavy industrialization in the metropole and the emergence of sugar beet cultivation.[5] Hence, the changing economic situation in England benefited the Afro-Creole community in Trinidad and Tobago as the institution of slavery was ended.

The other political freedoms that emerged during the same period, the early 1800s, included a high level of freedom of speech, which, although muted from time to time, persisted. At least five institutions were involved, in one form or another, in providing a forum for groups or individuals to espouse their causes: the Chamber of Commerce, the churches, the municipalities, public meetings, and the press.[6] The newspapers, in particular, were critical of various government policies and often sought to mobilize popular support behind certain issues. Public opinion, to a limited degree, served to influence the affairs of the colony, a tradition that was to continue into the twentieth century.

While one part of Trinidadian society gradually moved toward a unified Western system of government and norms in the early 1800s, a recently arrived component found itself politically isolated and economically dependent on the plantation. This component was the

East Indian. The five institutions that allowed the Afro-Creole community a certain amount of say in the colony's life had little meaning to this group. Moreover, an East Indian middle class would be much slower to emerge due to its later arrival to the island and the conditions under which it initially lived.

The planters experienced shortages of labor with emancipation. The Afro-Creoles left the plantations, some becoming small-scale farmers and others drifting into the urban areas in search of work. Consequently, the planters were forced to recruit workers first from the surrounding islands, then from Madeira, and, with the failure of those two sources, from Asia. The quest for cheap labor brought the planters to China and India. These two countries, with their large and impoverished populations, were perceived as labor pools for Trinidad and other sugar colonies, such as Mauritius and Réunion in the Indian Ocean and Fiji in the South Pacific as well as British Guiana and Suriname in the Caribbean.[7]

The importation of Chinese and Indians (referred to as East Indians to distinguish them from those in Asia and also from native American Indians) brought two groups of people to the island that were alien to any previous societal groups in the Caribbean. The Chinese came in small numbers but were able to move rapidly away from agriculture and, by the 1870s, had become part of the European-dominated society through intermarriage and the pursuit of middle-class professions. In contrast, the East Indians, who came in substantial numbers, remained outside the colonial society largely because they attempted to maintain their traditional way of life and did not accept the prevailing white European social mores.

Between 1845 and 1917, with a short break from 1848 to 1851, a total of 143,939 Indians arrived in Trinidad to work as indentured labor on the sugar estates.[8] The majority came from north India and were Hindu. There was also a small representation of Muslims. Significant to Trinidad's development was that the greater number of East Indians remained in the colony after the period they were contracted for. By 1871 the East Indians accounted for 25 percent of the total population, and by 1901 the number had increased to 33 percent.[9]

One of the lasting contributions the East Indians made in Trinidad's history was in agriculture. In the crucial years following emancipation, East Indian labor helped expand the acreage of land under sugar cultivation, especially in the 1840s. By the 1860s they had become the backbone of Trinidad's plantation workforce. As Bridget

Brereton noted, by 1872 the Indians constituted 75.3 percent of the total sugar estate labor, and by 1895 the figure had risen to 87 percent; although a substantial proportion were indentured, 44.7 percent in 1872, most free East Indians remained in agriculture.[10] By doing so, the East Indians isolated themselves from the colony's political centers in the urban areas, especially Port of Spain, another factor in their slow emergence as a politically aware group.

CHANGES IN THE SOCIOECONOMIC SYSTEM AT THE CLOSE OF THE CENTURY

Although East Indians proved to be a good source of cheap labor, not all planters were able to afford the costs entailed. The prolonged economic crisis in the Caribbean, beginning in the 1820s and worsening in the 1840s, was complicated by the influx of bounty-fed European beet sugar on the British market in the 1860s.[11] From 95.1 percent of total world sugar production in 1839, cane production steadily declined to 69.5 percent in 1865 to a critical low of 37.7 percent in 1889.[12] Production in Trinidad followed the global pattern.

In Trinidad many planters were forced to leave the sector, the majority being French Creoles. Ultimately, the sugar industry was left to the English Creoles and large metropole-based firms operating their estates through local agents. As sugar became the domain of the English, a number of French Creoles turned to the cultivation of cocoa. Thereafter, that crop became the foundation of new French Creole prosperity. Requiring less labor and capital investment, cocoa regained its importance in the island's economic life, especially since prices were consistently high between 1870 and 1918. Moreover, during the depression of the 1880s and 1890s in the sugar industry, the vastly increased demand for chocolate in England enabled cocoa to outstrip sugar and molasses as the most important export of the colony.[13]

The changes in Trinidad's economic structure in the later half of the nineteenth century were not, in many aspects, drastic. Although sugar was to decline, cocoa replaced it, maintaining the dominance of agriculture in the colony's economic life. At the same time, these structural changes and the accompanying depressions caused the small white middle class to contract, creating openings for an Afro-Creole middle class. Moreover, the East Indians and French Creoles remained tied to the land, which isolated them from much of the island's political life occurring in Port of Spain, the capital.

By the close of the nineteenth century, the Indo-Trinidadians had become a peasantry linked to the English capitalists in sugar and, to a lesser extent, the French Creoles in cocoa. The Afro-Creole population was divided between the lighter-skinned urban middle sectors and the black popular sectors, which were in the process of becoming urbanized and tied to employment in nonagricultural areas.

TRINIDAD AND TOBAGO—THE UNIFIED COLONY

Tobago's development was markedly different from Trinidad's. While Trinidad had been a forgotten colonial backwater throughout most of Spanish rule, Tobago was one of the most fought over islands in the Caribbean: between 1632 and 1676 the Dutch alone made six attempts to settle the island.[14] One reason for the fierce international competition was the fertility of the soil. As one would-be settler commented, "It is more fruitful than any of the Caribbees, there being not a hill which may not be planted; there is abundance of ginger, sugar-canes, indigo, cassia, fistula, cocoa, and roacou trees for dyeing orange, cocoanuts, oranges, lemons; tobacco and rice will grow there."[15]

Under the English (and the French), Tobago demonstrated its potential as the island began to produce sugar, cotton, and other crops. In 1770 the first ships laden with sugar left the island. By 1780, 1,157 tons were exported, and in 1799, the peak of production, 8,890 tons were sent to England, a sum that was considerably higher than those of Trinidad, Dominica, or British Guiana.[16] From 1809 to 1827 Tobago's economy became monocultural, and the export of sugar remained substantial. After that, however, the days of "King Sugar" were numbered as the slaves were emancipated in 1834, the protective tariffs on sugar in England were removed in the 1840s, and a severe hurricane in 1847 destroyed cane fields, sugar mills, and estate houses. Furthermore, constant use of land caused soil fertility loss.[17] By the 1870s Tobago's economy had deteriorated considerably, and, after a series of attempted administrative unions with other islands, the island was made a charge of Trinidad in 1888. The union was hardly comfortable due to tensions stemming from fundamental differences: Trinidad was a richer and geographically larger colony, had better linkages to the metropole, and therefore was better suited to survive the economic problems of the late nineteenth century.

There are other differences to consider. Trinidad had relatively sizable towns, such as Port of Spain, San Fernando, and Arima, but

Scarborough, the capital of Tobago, was just a small harbor and a main street. The remaining "towns," Plymouth and Roxborough, were even smaller. The existence of more and larger urban areas in Trinidad certainly can be regarded as a factor in the emergence of the middle sectors. Simply stated, more of political significance happened in Port of Spain than in Scarborough. By 1889 the latter was not even the capital of the colony, while the former was.

Related to urbanization was the improvement of educational facilities. In Port of Spain, Queen's Royal College and St. Mary's College were founded, and the sons of the upper and middle classes attended school. Island scholarships, offered to a few poor, but academically deserving individuals, functioned to expand contact with the greater world, adding to the size of the middle sectors. Tobago, with fewer funds at its disposal, had a smaller number of schools, and, although literacy was comparatively high, it was the result of active churches. Public education remained in a poor state, which was one underlying cause, among many, for the lack of a middle class in Tobago.

On both islands a peasantry emerged that was also a part-time proletariat linked to estate production of either sugar, cocoa, or coconuts. This trend, it should be emphasized, was much more evident in Trinidad due to the survival of sugar estates operated by large metropole-based firms. Moreover, in Tobago the peasant population was homogeneous, being of African descent and Protestant. In Trinidad that societal group was divided by race with a mixture of Afro-Creoles, East Indians, Chinese, and Latin Americans from Venezuela and Colombia. Divisions also existed along religious lines: Christians, Hindus, and Muslims. In a sense, Crown Colony government, in its authoritarian fashion, smoothed over many of the contrasts between the two islands and ethnic communities—at least on the surface. It also functioned to tie these two islands in the Caribbean to the metropole by a commercial system that exploited the colony for the benefit of the mother country. Although England gradually shifted from the dictates of mercantilism to economic policies founded upon the concepts of free trade, the Crown Colony system allowed that change to occur in the unitary colony of Trinidad and Tobago regardless of the consequences.

WHITE SUPREMACY

At the close of the nineteenth century, Trinidad and Tobago's society was divided along several lines and dominated by the ideology of white supremacy, which was European in origin, reflecting the racist thinking of local and metropolitan whites.[18] Social Darwinism, in vogue in Europe and North America, categorized the darker-skinned peoples of the world as "inferior" and behind the whites in evolution. This theory was especially leveled against those of African descent and, in the Caribbean, also the East Indians.

The view of the black as a "primitive savage," supported by "scientific" arguments, was often reflected in the works of those who visited the Caribbean, such as J. A. Froude and Anthony Trollope. In general, West Indian blacks were regarded as indolent, docile, and brutish.[19] One of the most damaging books was Spencer St. John's *Hayti: or, The Black Republic* (1889), which was widely read and had an influence in consolidating the white supremacist position that those with darker skins were inferior and that blacks should not be allowed to have any form of representative government. As St. John comments, "I know what the black man is, and I have no hesitation in declaring that he is incapable of the art of government, and that to entrust him with framing and working the laws for our islands is to condemn them to inevitable ruin."[20]

St. John's analysis was what many West Indian whites felt and feared—that representative government would one day be granted and any meaningful franchise would immediately include a large number of black voters, which in turn would mean the end of white supremacy. Haiti was constantly used as an example of what black rule would bring: chaos, bloodshed, intermittent civil wars and revolutions, economic decline, and the elimination of whites. This type of reasoning served as a justification for the continuation of the Crown Colony, which was dominated by wealthy whites, usually planters and large merchants.

In Trinidad racial divisions existed, but the white supremacist view was not as entrenched or as harsh in its appraisal of the black.[21] Furthermore, an educated and articulate mixed African-European and black middle class was quick to challenge racial discrimination while defending their right to legal equality. Hence, although racism existed in Trinidad at the close of the nineteenth century and was the foundation of political order, it was not as blatant as in other colonies. White supremacist ideology held sway, but its base was weak due to the early diffusion of the white upper classes into various national groups, the greater degree of racial tolerance practiced by the French and Spanish Creoles, and the desire of the small Afro-Creole middle class to move ahead.

Trinidad's colonial experience had created a three-tiered society with the small white elite at the top, followed by an Afro-Creole middle class and the black popular sectors. To this could be added the Chinese, who moved into the middle sectors, along with the Portuguese. In this society the dominant values were European and increasingly English. White European culture, which included Christianity, was the accepted goal for those aspiring to move up the social scale. The adoption of European clothing and mannerisms and, most important, the European ideal of attaining a good education were the correct and understood path to assimilation. Assimilation in turn increased opportunities to become middle class and move further from the stigma of working the land, a perception held before and after emancipation.

In contrast to the rest of society, the majority of East Indians made no attempt to assimilate themselves but rather kept their own customs and traditions. Their separateness also meant that they largely existed outside of Trinidad and Tobago's Creole society, while being an important economic force. The East Indian population was divided within itself between Muslims and Hindus, which in some aspects fit well with a larger society divided at all levels: between the English and French-Spanish Creoles in the white upper classes; between those of African descent from Barbados, Africa, and the Eastern Caribbean in the middle sectors; and those of the popular sectors between Afro-Creoles and a smaller group of Spanish-speaking peons from Colombia and Venezuela. As Brereton concludes, "Class, colour, caste and race combined to create an immensely complex pattern of human relationships in late nineteenth-century Trinidad."[22]

THE EMERGENCE OF THE AFRO-CREOLE MIDDLE SECTORS

The gradual Afro-Trinidadian middle sector movement into colonial politics entailed the acceptance of European social attitudes, referred to as the process of assimilation. This pattern had evolved in Trinidad well before emancipation as the free colored and black middle sectors were divided into two major groups by cultural identification: the French free colored who had come to the island before 1797 and the free English colored who came after that date were the two groups that formed a middle strata in colonial society.

Both groups were urbanized, but the French Afro-Creoles cherished aristocratic traditions, respected birth and breeding, intermarried amongst their own, had possession of land in the countryside, and spoke French. Under the Spanish this group had been entitled to a number of rights: the 1783 Cedula and the terms of capitulation (1797) had given the free colored a legal status almost equivalent to that of the whites.[23]

Governor Picton, who had feared the French Republicans among them, and his successor, Woodward, who regarded them as a potential source of disorder, had gradually taken away their rights by implementing a number of discriminatory regulations that excluded them from officerships in the militia, taxed their social functions, and allowed corporal punishment for minor misdemeanors. The loss of these privileges forced the free colored, French and English, to organize and agitate for their restoration. It should be emphasized that the majority of those involved in the movement for equality were light-skinned Afro-Creoles and that the struggle was for the rights of the free colored, not the rights of the enslaved black population.

By the 1820s, the free colored, led by doctors and lawyers educated in Europe, conducted a strong public campaign on the island and in England for full civil and political equality with the whites. Many of those in this group were students of the Enlightenment, and, consequently, they found the quasi-authoritarian nature of the Crown Colony system unacceptable. This emerging middle sector group, in a sense, was part of the colony's professional and administrative life and had skills that identified them with the white elites and disassociated them from the laboring sectors, especially the slaves. Moreover, the lower classes were largely illiterate and had no sense of the cause in progress and good government.[24]

The two major figures of the free colored campaign were Dr. John Baptiste Philip, the son of a wealthy planter, and Francis De Ridder, the son of a Dutch planter and a black slave. Both were educated in Europe, the former returning to Trinidad to become a respectable professional with an appreciation of English culture and literature and the latter, a more dynamic person, going to the colony on a religious mission and becoming politically involved in the French Afro-Creole community's struggle for equality with its white counterparts.[25]

The loss of privileges, initiated by the British government, was a serious setback that was directly linked to status. Moreover, it implied a reverse in the process of assimilating white Western-Hellenic civilization and modernity. To many of the free colored, there was a fear of "slipping back" and being associated with the black slaves who, it was perceived and maintained by white supremacist ideology, symbolized the uncivilized and barbaric traditions of Africa.

In 1823 a delegation led by Dr. Philip went to England and met with the colonial authorities, which resulted in the repealing of many of the discriminatory laws in 1826. It was difficult for the colonial authorities to exclude Trinidad's free colored entirely, considering that in 1823 they numbered some 13,347—close to a third of the colony's population and one of the largest free colored communities in the Caribbean at the time.[26] The struggle continued until 1829 when an order of the King in Council was issued removing all legal restrictions on civil and political rights and placing the free colored in a position, at least in theory and under English law, of total legal equality with the whites.[27] This, in part, may be regarded as one of the earlier reasons for the successful evolution in the democratic-capitalist system in Trinidad since recourse to the king, as a higher level of authority, gave the Afro-Creole middle sectors some faith in the British system. Although the Crown Colony form of government was not appreciated, justice (in a sense) had been served.

While unofficial discrimination continued, the position of the free colored benefited from the economic crisis of the times. By 1832 large numbers of white merchants and artisans had left Trinidad, and, with their departure, the free Afro-Creoles moved into their positions or, more importantly, began seeking jobs in the civil service.[28] Emancipation also helped push this group up the social ladder as they already had a tradition of freedom and had the advantage of being in a number of middle-class professions. Interestingly, once the early free colored movement achieved its proclaimed objectives, which was followed by the abolition of slavery, it was a spent political force; the concern of this group became financial security and class standing, especially since the black Afro-Creole population began its long migration to the towns.

The free colored who were assimilated into English culture had also emerged in the period before emancipation. Significant expansion of the Afro-Creole middle sectors, colored and black, however, occurred after 1838 as both groups rose in society through education and the civil service.[29] The English freemen included native-born Afro-Creoles as well as British West Indians, mainly from Barbados and Grenada, who had immigrated to Trinidad after slavery was abolished.

The Trinidadian Afro-Creoles often spoke a form of local patois (mixed Spanish, French, and English), which was not easily understood by English authorities. Consequently, the colonial government recruited a large number of Barbadians, who usually spoke the king's English, over Afro-Trinidadians, hence creating a civil service and police force largely staffed with British West Indians and more assimilated Trinidadians. According to the census report for Trinidad in 1891, British West Indians provided a significant proportion of the professional and clerical working groups in the colony: teachers, 22 percent; clergy, 15 percent; civil engineers, 19 percent; public officers and clerks, 26 percent; druggists, dispensers, and midwives, 34 percent; postal and prison officers, 67 percent; and nurses and wardsmen, 59 percent.[30] At the same time, the British West Indians were important in skilled work sectors, comprising 40 percent of all craft workers and mechanics, 46 percent of all carpenters, and 68 percent of all shoemakers.[31]

The Afro-Creole middle sectors, both native Trinidadians and West Indians, were seeking to improve their status by education and hard work, as reflected by their growing numbers. The latter, in particular, had made sacrifices to come to Trinidad, an island richer than most in the British Caribbean. In many aspects, the work ethic of the newcomers, anxious to find an occupational niche, stimulated the middle sectors to expand further.

The urban areas, with educational facilities superior to those of the countryside, were the core of a new societal movement, especially since the sugar and cocoa regions did not offer suitable employment to the educated colored, which the towns did. While urbanization, access to education, and immigration helped augment this new middle class of the Afro-Creoles, the realm of "big business" remained in white hands.[32] The whites continued to hold the colony's economic and political power, although they made certain accommodations with the urbanized Afro-Creole middle sectors that could have functioned to modify that group's political aggressiveness until the late 1800s.

Since the advance of middle-class Afro-Creoles into the white-collar occupations of teaching, civil service, law, journalism, clerical work, pharmacy, and medicine was founded upon access to education, education became the most important form of employment open to the Afro-Creole population.[33] Many of the growing professional class of African descent came from families where a parent was a teacher. As a consequence of the middle class's emphasis on education, educational opportunities were extended to their class at a much faster rate than they were to the lower classes. This, in effect, widened the cultural and educational gap between the urbanized colored and black middle sectors and the rural black peasantry and agro-proletariat. The cost of education was also a barrier to the poorer blacks to whom it was indispensable if any social mobility were to be achieved.[34]

Projection of an urban Afro-Creole group into a middle status above the large body of blacks, yet beneath the much smaller white elite, generated a degree of frustration at the discrimination evident in Trinidad and Tobago's colonial society. British colonialism, which often helped perpetuate the snobbery and arrogance of a small group of colonial administrators and European Creoles, paradoxically, was also responsible for the establishment of an educational system that would eventually produce a politically aware Afro-Creole opposition to the Crown Colony.

THE POLITICALIZATION OF THE AFRO-CREOLE MIDDLE SECTORS

The political leadership of the Afro-Trinidadian middle sectors was largely composed of lawyers, many of whom had been educated in Europe and had become highly assimilated. Colored and black lawyers, such as Michael Maxwell Philip, solicitor general (1869-88), and L. P. Pierre, the Afro-Creole stipendiary magistrate, were articulate advocates for equality and more representative government. Under the leadership of such individuals, one of the earliest middle-class political organizations was the Legislative Reform Committee. This coalition of Afro-Creole professionals, French Creole cocoa interests, and English merchants was formed in the 1850s and lasted, in one form or another, to 1914.[35] The principal issues that unified the members were their resistance to state-sponsored East Indian immigration and their feeling that British colonial officials exercised many of the powers that Creoles were entitled to.[36] While advocating a restructuring of the political system that favored a localization of power, the Legislative Reform Committee was not for universal suffrage and was far from being a mass party, nor did it ever have widespread support from the colony's population.

A number of prominent individuals of African descent were members of the Legislative Reform Committee. Among those was C. P. David, a black solicitor, who was the organization's secretary from 1892 to 1895, Henry Alcazar, a lawyer and four-term mayor of Port of Spain, and Vincent Brown, another lawyer and mayor of Port of Spain. Despite the vocal reformist nature of these men, they were gradually drawn into working with the colonial government: Brown was made solicitor general and later attorney general; Alcazar became an unofficial member of the Legislative Council in 1894; and David became the first black unofficial member in 1904.[37]

Although clearly opposed to the Crown Colony government, the political leadership of the Afro-Creole middle classes operated within the system, and the system in turn made minor concessions. When the give and take of politics between the colonial government and the middle sectors began to tighten in the latter decades of the 1800s, the attraction to work within the system's framework diminished, and new organizations arose, reflecting discontent with the assimilation process.

One of the few avenues open to the Afro-Creole middle class was the Port of Spain Municipal Borough Council. The Borough Council was responsible for public services such as the financial management of the city's hospital, education, and registration of births and deaths. To gain a seat on the council, one had to be elected. C. R. Ottley notes that in 1886 only 52 of the 700 electors went to the polls.[38] In essence, the management of the capital's day-to-day affairs was left to the Borough Council, which was largely the domain of the urbanized and educated middle sectors of African descent.

The whites, controlling the Legislative Council, left the Borough Council to the nonwhite middle class as part of the give and take of colonial politics. In 1864 the Borough Council and the colonial government became embroiled in a dispute over a debt incurred. Financing became difficult and the city was forced to borrow from private citizens and increase rates for certain public services. With costs incurred from the expansion of the educational system, damages from the Carnival Riot of 1880, the installation of phones in 1883, and numerous other projects, the Borough Council was almost bankrupt by the 1890s. Despite pleas for assistance, the colonial government refused to aid the ailing municipal organization.

Commencing in the early 1890s, agitation for reform in both the colonial government and the Borough Council gained momentum, especially with the decline in the opportunities for unofficial representation on government bodies.[39] In 1898 the colonial authorities, under the guidance of Sir Joseph Chamberlain, the secretary of state for the colonies, abolished the Borough Council, and the unofficials lost their majority in the Legislative Council. The former body was replaced by a more subservient Board of Commissions, and the latter was restructured as new official members (directly appointed by the governor) were added to create a permanent official majority. Previously, the unofficials had been in a majority and, although relatively powerless before the governor's power, could make certain issues tension-filled. These political and administrative restructurings were all part of Chamberlain's policy to deny granting any representative institutions to those colonies where the majority of the people were not European.

The secretary of state's policy was part of an authoritarian pattern of colonial rule, and his highly unpopular tactics alienated not only some of the wealthier planters who sat in the Legislative Council, but also the moderates and radicals in the white and Afro-Creole middle sectors, who in turn began to look to the black masses as a political tool to be used for changing policy. In this atmosphere, the Ratepayers Association (RPA) was founded in 1901. The RPA, although limited to a membership of less than 200, became the first common ground for both the white and Afro-Creole middle-class moderates and radicals opposed to Chamberlain's authoritarian policies. It differed from the Legislative Reform Committee, which was a moderate, almost conservative, group seeking change within the system. The RPA, in contrast, was a more action-oriented organization and became, for a brief period, an important force in the colony's politics. Before advancing further, however, it is necessary to examine another trend that overlapped and influenced Trinidad's political life in the 1900s.

At the core of Afro-Creole middle-class politicization was the paradoxical question of identity—the rejection, on the one hand, of white supremacist ideology and, on the other hand, the acceptance that West Indian culture was a part of the greater Hellenic-Christian civilization. The former stimulated the formation of the Pan-African movement among black intellectuals, such as Trinidadians H. S. Williams, C. L. R. James, and George Padmore, who linked the black West Indian experience to the past accomplishments and culture of sub-Saharan Africa. In its questioning of the supremacy of Western culture, Pan-Africanism emphasized the positive and common aspects of the black experience in the Atlantic Triangle of Africa, South America, and the circum-Caribbean region.[40]

To the claims that people of African descent were "stupid," "barbaric," and, in general, "subhuman," a number of Afro-Creole Trinidadians counterattacked. Even before the establishment of the Pan-African movement in London in 1897, J. J. Thomas, a successful black teacher and author, wrote a classic rebuttal of white supremacist ideas extolled in Froude's *The English in the West Indies* (1888).[41] Written in 1889, Thomas's *Froudacity: West Indian Fables by James*

Anthony Froude replied to that Englishman's attacks on the largely Afro-Creole middle-class Legislative Reform movement. Thomas comments, "The gentlemen of Trinidad, who are struggling for political enfranchisement, are not likely to heed, except as a matter for indignant contempt, the obtrusion by our author of his opinion that 'they best let well alone.' "[42]

Thomas also criticized those English civil servants who came to the colony for a few years, earned considerable salaries, and then left as "birds of passage." He regarded them as a negative factor in Trinidad's development as they felt they had a divine right to rule any territory because they were white Anglo-Saxons. The critical attacks on the myth of white supremacy had an impact on the urbanized Afro-Creoles as it gave them some cause to have pride in their race's past. Consequently, several short-lived Pan-African associations were established on the island, and the awareness of race gradually became more pronounced.

THE WATER RIOT OF 1903

Although the expressed purpose of the Ratepayers Association was to petition against the rising costs of public services, the underlying political motive was to organize an opposition to the highhandedness of Chamberlain, who was responsible for the destruction of the limited political participation allowed through unofficial membership in the Legislative Council and in the Borough Council.

The RPA gradually began putting pressure on the colonial government. The particular issue it chose to give battle was the introduction into the Legislative Council of the Waterworks Ordinance of 1903, "as it provided a focal point for grievances which included the demarcation between central and municipal government, rates and government finance and, of course, the issue of representation."[43] Public meetings and massive demonstrations outside the Red House, the seat of the Legislative Council, disrupted the process of government, ultimately culminating in widespread riots in which the police opened fire on the crowd killing at least 16 and wounding many others. The police, outnumbered and unable to restore order, could not prevent damage to the governor's mansion and the burning of the Red House. The civil upheaval was brought to a conclusion only with the intervention of British troops from Barbados.

The Water Riot of 1903 brought important changes to Trinidad and Tobago's political scenario. Significantly, the metropole was forced to respond to events on the island as Chamberlain moved quickly to co-opt the opposition by allowing the restoration of the Borough Council to be debated and making some of the RPA's leaders members of the Legislative Council where they would be easier to watch. Eventually, between 1914 and 1917, the Borough Council was restored, a process that kept many middle-class politicians active and within the system.

Regarded as a victory for the opposition to Crown Colony government, the next target was the Legislative Council. Over this, the opposition divided between the majority of the Afro-Creole middle class, which favored working within the system after the 1903 riot, and a radical minority that observed direct action and an alliance with the popular sectors as the means of achieving the desired changes. It was acknowledged that the black masses involved in the Water Riot of 1903 were there for the excitement, not because of firmly held political convictions. In a sense, the middle-class moderates and radicals had used the urbanized lower classes as an effective tool to enact changes in the political system. The moderates, having gotten much of what they wanted, turned back to the principle that evolution rather than revolution was the path to a suitable future, while the acceptance of European values continued. The radicals, in contrast, were more activist in outlook and sought to mobilize an emerging black working class.

THE TRINIDAD WORKINGMEN'S ASSOCIATION

The radical Afro-Creole middle-class group's attempt to create a worker-middle-class alliance occurred before 1903 and resulted in the Trinidad Workingmen's Association (TWA). Founded in 1897, it was based upon the English Workingmen's Association, formed in the wake of the Industrial Revolution. The TWA's early leadership was lower middle class and colored. Its first president, Walter Mills, was a pharmacist, and among its ranks were carpenters, masons, laborers, and tailors.

The TWA functioned as a trade union and political pressure group, seeking to improve working conditions and the insanitary conditions in the urban sectors where the working class lived, reduce taxes on foodstuffs and agricultural tools used by laborers, improve transportation, introduce savings banks, and increase the opening of Crown lands. Like the legislative Reform Committee and the RPA, it favored constitutional reform and was strongly opposed to state-aided East Indian immigration, which "increased the competition for starvation wages paid on sugar estates."⁴⁴ Unlike the Legislative Reform Committee and the RPA, the TWA's major objective was to bring elective government to Trinidad and Tobago in which the working classes would have the vote.

As a pressure group, the TWA met resistance from the government, which often quietly consigned the organization's letters to the trash bin. The unsuccessful waterfront strike of 1902 and the Water Riot of 1903 were serious setbacks for the young organization. From 1903 to 1906 the TWA was inactive, and its membership dwindled to a mere 223 from the 1,000 ascribed to it in 1900.⁴⁵

Although the revival of the TWA in 1906 was brief, lasting until the outbreak of World War I, it was not without some significance. The issue of reestablishing the Borough Council had led Alfred Richards, an Afro-Creole apothecary, to reform the organization. Some assistance to the TWA came from a "corresponding" affiliated group in the British Labour Party, which provided for some representation in the metropole. In 1912 Joseph Pointer, a member for the Aftercliffe division in Sheffield and a junior labour whip in Parliament, visited Trinidad and helped to organize and expand the TWA. Pointer even attempted to include the East Indians, but this was a failure due to their reluctance to become involved in the island's politics and their apprehension of the Afro-Creoles.

Important organizational and political support from English labor groups considerably enhanced the TWA. In 1913 it agitated for the restoration of the Borough Council alongside of the colony's other groups. By 1914, however, the association was almost destroyed by factional struggles between the moderates, led by Richards who favored gradual change, trusting in petitions, delegations, and public meetings, and the radicals, led by J. S. de Bourg, who argued that only the threat of disorder would induce the government to take action on the worker's behalf. By December 1914 Richards resigned and the TWA temporarily disappeared as a political organization. It appeared that the radical middle-sector experiment with a working class alliance was a failure.

With the outbreak of World War I, political activity in the colony halted. The Afro-Creole middle sectors, however, had begun the process of politicalization as they experimented with early forms of political organizations and questioned their role in society.

CONCLUSION

By World War I, Trinidad and Tobago's society was divided by race, religion, caste, and geography. Tobago was administratively part of the colony, yet its historical evolution had created a largely homogeneous population of African descent. In contrast, Trinidad's population was multiethnic. While the East Indians sought isolation from the "polluting" influences of Western civilization, the Afro-Creoles sought assimilation, making them aware of the system's inequalities. Education, based in part on the ideas of the Enlightenment, created a desire to enact change. Related to this was the rejection of white supremacist ideology, which had long sought to justify the perpetuation of unrepresentative government and maintain the wealthy white elite above all other colonial groups.

In a Johnsonian sense, the Afro-Creole middle sectors that evolved in the nineteenth century were urbanized, placed an emphasis on education, and, in general, supported the capitalistic system as long as they benefited from it. The concept of massive state intervention in the economy and the need to industrialize were not really factors at this point, as they would be in the mid-twentieth century. By World War I, the emerging Afro-Creole middle sectors had made the transition from the relatively conservative Ratepayers Association to the more radical TWA. The significance was that the gradual movement to political parties had begun.

NOTES

1. Crawford Young, *The Politics of Cultural Pluralism* (Madison: University of Wisconsin Press), p. 86.

2. Sidney Mintz, "Forward to Ramiro G. Sanchez," *Sugar and Society in the Caribbean: An Economic History of Cuban Agriculture* (New Haven: Yale University Press, 1944), p. xiv.

3. See Helen Taft Manning, *British Colonial Government After the American Revolution 1782-1820* (Hamden, Conn.: Archon Books, 1966).

4. James Millette, *The Genesis of Crown Colony Government, Trinidad, 1783-1810* (Curepe, Trinidad: Moko Enterprises, 1970), p. 7.

5. This argument is taken up by Eric Williams, *Capitalism and Slavery* (Chapel Hill: University of North Carolina Press, 1944).

6. C. R. Ottley, *The Trinidad Callaloo, Life in Trinidad from 1851-1900* (Diego Martin, Trinidad: Crusoe, 1978), p. 111.

7. For the Indian experience overseas, see Robert Norton *Race and Politics in Fiji* (New York: St. Martin's Press, 1977); Michael Moynagh, *Brown or White? A History of the Fiji Sugar Industry 1873-1973* (Canberra: Australian National

University, 1981); Adele Smith Simmons, *Modern Mauritius: The Politics of Decolonization* (Bloomington: Indiana University Press, 1982); and Bridget Brereton and Winston Dookeran, eds., *East Indians in the Caribbean* (Millwood, N.Y.: Kraus International Publications, 1982).

8. G. M. Takasingh, "The Establishment of the Indians in Trinidad, 1870-1900," Ph.D. dissertation, University of the West Indies, St. Augustine, Trinidad, 1976, pp. 8-9, 49.

9. M. Ramesar, "The Impact of the Indian Immigrants on Colonial Trinidad Society," *Caribbean Quarterly* 22 (1976): 6-7.

10. Bridget Brereton, *Race Relations in Colonial Trinidad, 1870-1900* (New York: Cambridge University Press, 1979), p. 178.

11. On the bad economic conditions of the early and mid-1800s, see Anthony de Verteuil, *The Years Before* (Trinidad: Imprint Caribbean, 1981).

12. Noel Deerr, *The History of Sugar* (London: Chapman and Hall, 1949-50), p. 490.

13. Donald Wood, *Trinidad in Transition* (London: Oxford University Press, 1968), p. 100.

14. See Cornelius Ch. Goslinga, *The Dutch in the Caribbean and in the Wild Coast 1580-1680* (Gainesville: University of Florida Press, 1971), chap. 17.

15. "1667 Memorial of the island of Tobago, now called New Walcheren, how it is situate, and of what advantage it may be to the state of the United Provinces", *Colonial Papers*, vol. 21, no. 171 (London, Her Majesty's Stationery Office).

16. Deerr, *The History of Sugar, Volume 2*, pp. 200-2.

17. David L. Niddrie, *Tobago* (Gainesville: Litho Press, 1980), p. 135.

18. Brereton, *Race Relations*, p. 193.

19. J. A. Froude, *The English in the West Indies or, The Bow of Ulysses* (New York: Charles Scribners and Sons, 1888), p. 183; Anthony Trollope, *The West Indies and the Spanish Main* (London, 1860), p. 225; W. A. Paton, *Down the Islands* (London, 1887), pp. 211-14; and J. H. Stark, *Guide Book and History of Trinidad* (London, 1887), p. 76.

20. Spencer St. John, *Hayti: or, The Black Republic* (London, 1889), p. xi.

21. L. A. A. De Verteuil, *Trinidad* (London, 1858), pp. 25, 175.

22. Brereton, *Race Relations*, p. 212.

23. Verteuil, *The Years Before*, p. 11.

24. John J. Johnson, *Political Change in Latin America: The Emergence of the Middle Sectors* (Stanford: University of Stanford Press, 1958), p. 16.

25. Carl Campbell, "The Rebel Priest: Francis De Ridder and the Fight for Free Coloureds' Rights in Trinidad, 1825-32," *Journal of Caribbean History* 15 (1981): 90.

26. John T. Harricharan, *The Catholic Church in Trinidad, 1498-1852* (Trinidad: Imprint Caribbean, 1981), p. 90.

27. Verteuil, *The Years Before*, p. 17.

28. Harricharan, *Catholic Church in Trinidad*, pp. 91-104.

29. Verteuil, *The Years Before*, p. 204.

30. Marianne Ramesar, "Patterns of Regional Settlement and Economic Activity by Immigrant Groups in Trinidad, 1851-1900," *Social and Economic Studies* 25 (September 1976): 205.

31. Ibid.

32. Brereton, *Race Relations*, p. 128.

33. Ibid.

34. Carl Campbell, "Charles Warner and the Development of Education Policy in Trinidad, 1838-70," *Journal of Caribbean Studies* 10 and 11 (1978): 70.

35. Selwyn Ryan, *Race and Nationalism in Trinidad and Tobago: A Study of Decolonization in a Multiracial Society* (Toronto: University of Toronto Press, 1972), p. 25.

36. Ibid.

37. B. Samaroo, "C. P. David: A Case in the Emergence of the Black Man in Trinidad Politics," *Journal of Caribbean History* 3 (November 1971).

38. C. R. Ottley, *The Story of Port of Spain* (Diego Martin, Trinidad: Crusoe, 1962, 1970, 1978), p. 81.

39. A. J. Stockwell, "Hugh Clifford in Trinidad 1903-1907," *Caribbean Quarterly* 24, (March-June 1978): 10.

40. O. Carlos Stoetzer, "Dreams of Integration," *Caribbean Review* 12 (April/May/June 1978): 29.

41. Froude wrote, "The West Indian Negro is conscious of his own defects, and responds more willingly than most to a guiding hand. . . . The poor black was a faithful servant as long as he was a slave. As a free man he was conscious of his inferiority at the bottom of his heart and would attach himself to a rational white employer with at least as much fidelity as a spaniel. . . ." Quoted in Eric Williams, *History of the People of Trinidad and Tobago* (London: André Deutsch, 1964), p. 32.

42. J. J. Thomas, *Froudacity* (London: New Beacon Books, 1889, 1969), p. 91.

43. Stockwell, "Hugh Clifford in Trinidad," p. 11. Also see K. O. Laurence, "The Trinidad Water Riot of 1903: Reflections of an Eyewitness," *Caribbean Quarterly* 15 (December 1969): 5.

44. Brinsley Samaroo, "The Trinidad Workingmen's Association and the Origins of Popular Protest in a Crown Colony," *Social and Economic Studies* 21 (June 1972): 207.

45. Ryan, *Race and Nationalism*, pp. 26-27.

3

The Interwar and War Years: Experimentation with Political Parties

The interwar and war years (1919-45) were important in the development of the middle sectors due to the rapid, basic transformation of Trinidad's state and class structures, accompanied and in part carried through by the politicalization of the Afro-Creole working class. That working class emerged during this period as the two-island colony changed from an agrarian society, dependent on sugar and cocoa, to a semi-industrial society, increasingly dependent on the exploitation of oil. This is not to say that agriculture disappeared: a sizable agricultural sector, albeit of fluctuating and declining fortunes, survived and was, in part, responsible for the long tenure of East Indians to the land and their almost total absence in the political spectrum. With the end of indentureship in 1917, however, the growing awareness that Trinidad was their future, pushed the East Indian middle class into politics, which had in the late nineteenth century been the arena of competition between the Afro-Creole middle sectors and the white upper class.

As the demand for greater political liberties became stronger, alongside the growing labor movement, the white upper class and the Afro-Creole and Indo-Trinidadian middle sectors fragmented between those opposed to change and those favoring it. The former appealed to the colonial authorities to slow the pace of political restructuring, and the latter appealed for a quicker pace. The latter, mainly the Afro-Creoles, also sought to develop an alliance with the emerging working class to advance their cause of democratization. In this, A. A.

Cipriani, a white Corsican Creole, became an important leader, heading the Trinidad Labour Party and attempting to be a "bridge" between the Afro-Creoles and East Indians who were growing mutually suspicious of each other. Above the entire struggle was the British Colonial Office, which drew heavily upon a long history of gradual change from above in its own country. That gradualist approach to political development was strongly challenged by the joint (although not entirely coordinated) impetus of the bourgeouis-worker alliance in Trinidad. The disturbances of 1934-35 and the riots of 1937, in particular, shook the colonial system in the islands, causing serious introspection by all parties. The purpose of this chapter is to examine these trends and their impact on the progression of democratic capitalism in Trinidad and Tobago.

THE CHANGING POLITICAL ECONOMY

Although the Great War temporarily suspended political activity in the West Indies, the conflict in Europe set in motion several forces. Three important changes occurred during the war in Trinidad and Tobago.[1] The first was the structure of the economy. Lond dependent on the export of sugar and cocoa, the colony's economy was similar to most British Caribbean colonies: by the 1890s and the first decades of the twentieth century, the sugar industry was characterized by declining productivity and falling prices.[2] The sugar and cocoa booms of the war years were brief interludes as production of the former plummeted from 70,891 tons in 1917 to 45,256 tons in 1917,[3] and, beginning in 1917, similar figures for the latter are evident.[4] Unlike other Caribbean colonies, such as Dominica and Grenada, Trinidad was able to move away from a dependence on agricultural exports to oil.

In 1865 Walter Darwent, a U.S. civil engineer, and a group of Port of Spain merchants established the Paria Oil Company, and, with the discovery of oil in 1866, the colony's oil industry was founded. Expansion of the industry, however, was slow, and it was not until the British Admiralty evinced an interest in converting the British Navy from coal to oil firing in the latter half of the nineteenth century that large-scale exploration and development commenced.[5] Commercial quantities were discovered in 1907, and in 1909 the Trinidad Oilfields, Limited, was formed to exploit the newly discovered reserves.[6]

Despite the development of the industry in the first decade of the twentieth century, the major oil "rush" began when Winston

Churchill, then first lord of the admiralty, formally announced that the British Navy had converted to oil.[7] In this change of policy, Trinidad, a secure British possession, was perceived as a reliable source of fuel for the Royal Navy. From that point forward, the Trinidadian oil industry underwent tremendous expansion. In 1910 alone, some 30 companies were granted loans to develop the colony's oil sector.[8] By 1914 Trinidad's oil production was an essential asset to Britain's military, being its major source of oil fuel throughout World War I. The industry continued to expand following the conflict, with the output increasing from 125,112 barrels in 1910 to 2,003,027 in 1920.[9]

The second and related change was the emergence of a black working class, employed largely in the urban areas and in the oil fields, which became increasingly conscious of the inequalities in Trinidad's society. This group emerged because of the accelerated expansion of the economy made possible by the development of viable agricultural and industrial sectors.[10] The boom years of the 1890s and first 15 years of the 1900s created more job opportunities than before and allowed the new and upwardly mobile-aspiring worker a greater chance of capital accumulation. The changes in the colony's economic fortunes led, as Sahadeo Basdeo noted, "to a heightened interest in educational opportunities and general self-improvement; the result of this was an increased awareness of political and social affairs."[11] This increased awareness in turn raised the question of the distribution of the colony's wealth, especially since a few people, mainly of European descent, held the leading positions in industry, commerce, agriculture, and government.[12] An important added stimulus to the politicalization of this class was the return to the colony of members of the British West Indies Regiment.[13] Many people of working class background returned from military service profoundly influenced by new ideas on democracy, workers' action, and personal freedoms, which they would seek to convert into a reality in their homeland.

A third change indirectly caused by World War I, but caused more directly by structural economic transformations, was the termination of the system of indentured East Indian labor. Pressure from a rising nationalist movement in India, which regarded indentureship as degrading and the marked decline of export agriculture in Trinidad, indicated that the system was in poor shape. The dangers of wartime shipping and the need to recruit large numbers of Indians into the military also contributed to the decline of the system. By 1917, when indentureship was officially ended, most East Indians had already completed their term and had remained on the estates as wage earners, forming an agro-proletariat. A smaller group turned to small-scale farming.

Crucial to the development of democratic capitalism along Johnsonian lines was the emergence of an East Indian middle class, composed of Western-educated lawyers, doctors, and small business people. Largely rural, the Indo-Trinidadian middle sectors only became involved in politics in 1898, when the East Indian National Association (EINA) was formed to protest the Immigration Ordinance of 1897. However, the EINA remained peripheral and could largely be characterized as a "middle-class pressure group" with ties to similar organizations in England.

A more radical group, the East Indian National Congress (EINC), was founded in 1909 due to the dissatisfaction with the EINA's lack of action. Like the older organization, however, its membership was also middle class. While the EINA looked to Indian interest groups in the metropole, the EINC looked to India for inspiration. The Indian National Congress, in particular, was highly regarded. In a sense, the newer group represented the beginnings of a nationalism in the East Indian middle sectors. That nationalism, however, was ill-defined and backward looking, in that it looked back to India for inspiration and did not fully address the reality of Trinidadian politics. At this point, the emphasis was clearly on "Indianess," not East Indianess and certainly not Trinidadian nationalism.

THE 1919 RIOTS AND REVIVAL OF THE TWA

The difficult economic conditions which came at the close of the war led to the revival of the Trinidad Workingman's Association as frustrated former servicemen sought a political voice in the colony's affairs. Embittered over high inflation, the difficulty in finding employment, rising prices for food and clothing, and resentment of the war profits of the "stay-at-home" capitalists, the former soldiers helped restructure the TWA into a powerful activist organization. This was reflected in the new leadership that emerged in the TWA's elections in 1918. A mixture of middle-sector and working-class radicals came to power: these included the secretary, James Braithwaite (a Barbadian longshoreman), J. S. de Bourg (a black Grenadian-born lawyer), and William Bishop (a Guyanese journalist and teacher). Under their leadership, the TWA sought to rescue the working class from the difficult economic conditions as well as to advance political reforms. In May 1919 a team of the TWA secured concessions for the workers of the Trinidad Asphalt Company, an important victory that boosted the organization's status among laborers, leading to an increase in membership and the foundation of two new branches.[14]

The TWA's increased activity coincided with and benefited from the tense atmosphere in the colony, stemming from growing labor-management strife and a heightening of racial sensitivity caused by the resentment of the former servicemen who had experienced racial discrimination during their tour of duty. A number of race riots in England, which included the murder of a Trinidadian sailor, added another factor in the Afro-Creoles' growing animosity vis-à-vis the white upper class.[15] Moreover, the visit of F. E. M. Hercules, secretary of the Society of Peoples of African Origin, to Trinidad in September 1919 helped give impetus to greater race consciousness among the black popular sectors.[16]

The emerging antiwhite radicalism was felt in the upper class when British sailors were assaulted in Port of Spain in July 1919. The white community turned to the colonial authorities, demanding that British troops help maintain law and order on the island. Because a small number of East Indians participated in the troubled events of 1919, the perception that the rest of society had risen against the white community was reinforced.

The main catalyst to the riots of 1919 and early 1920 was the longshoremen's strike. The longshoremen of Port of Spain, hard hit by inflation and rising prices, and influenced by contact with overseas radical ideas, ranging from pan-Africanism to socialism, went on strike in November 1919, demanding higher wages and an eight-hour workday.[17] As much of the stevedore leadership was also part of the TWA, that organization was brought into negotiate with the shipping companies. The companies, however, refused to discuss the matter, and scab labor was hired to work the docks. On December 1 the dockworkers stormed the waterfront, closing down the harbor. From there the strikers marched through the streets of Port of Spain where they were joined by city council employees and East Indian sweepers and cartermen.[18] Businesses were forced to close, and the colony's capital was temporarily held by the demonstrators.

Under pressure from the colonial government, the shipping companies negotiated with the TWA and made several concessions. The victory at the bargaining table, however, led to new strikes on a colonywide basis as workers in the major urban areas demonstrated their support for the longshoremen. Significantly, these expressions of solidarity were limited to the urban and industrial workers, the latter located in the southern oil belt. The majority of demonstrators were also Afro-Creoles, although minor disturbances were recorded in East Indian areas. The disturbances also had an impact in Tobago, the long-neglected ward, as estate workers struck and marched into Scarborough; the police killed one of the strike's leaders before restoring order with the aid of British troops.

The 1919-20 riots were an important watershed in Trinidadian politics as Afro-Creole urban and industrial workers, in an alliance with middle-class radicals in the TWA, brought the colony to a standstill and clarified the divisions between the political forces in the colony. The conservatives, supported by the colonial government, became aware of their lack of support from the rest of the population and became more conscious that they were a small white minority in a predominantly nonwhite society. Their response was twofold: one, they looked to the metropole to maintain the status quo, with troops if necessary, and, two, white businessmen formed a volunteer force, the Colonial Vigilantes, to protect their property.

Whereas 1919 was the year of radical ascendency in Trinidad's politics, 1920 became the year of the "Thermidorian Reaction." The conservatives and alarmed moderates in the government, with the security of British troops, struck back. The leadership of the TWA was a major target as many of its leaders were foreign born, including the secretary, Braithwaite, and were deported back to their home islands. Therefore, in the aftermath of the 1919-20 riots, the government crackdown allowed the white upper classes to regain their hold over the island's political life. That hold was considerably weakened, however. Although the TWA's leadership had been decimated, the strikes, the concessions made by the shipping companies, and the "martyrdom" of its most prominent figures swelled the ranks of the organization and gave it a popular image with the Afro-Creole workers.

CIPRIANI AND THE TRINIDAD LABOUR PARTY

The personality of Captain Arthur A. Cipriani, without a doubt, left its imprint on the political development of Trinidad and Tobago. From a family of Corsican planters, he became politically aware during the 1914-18 period when he served as commander of the British West Indies Regiment.[19] After a long dispute with the colonial government over whether West Indian troops should have the right to fight for the British Empire, Cipriani and the British West Indies Regiment were sent to Egypt where they functioned as labor battalions.[20] The resentment over such treatment made him aware of the discrimination in the British Empire, while wartime duty improved his leadership abilities.

Upon his return to Trinidad, Cipriani was elected in 1919 as the president of the Soldiers and Sailors Union because the largely Afro-Creole ex-soldier membership had confidence in him. During the same year, "the captain," as he was often called, also joined the TWA on the insistence of W. Howard Bishop, who had become its secretary. Within the TWA it was felt that by placing a white man in the leadership the gap between Afro-Creoles and East Indians could be bridged. The need for such a bridge was especially necessary as the EINA and EINC regarded themselves as the "Indian counterparts to the Workingmen's Association."[21] Moreover, as Ryan notes, it was beneficial to have a neutral ethnic type as part of the TWA's leadership as well as for the colonial population as a whole: "whiteness was still a highly regarded attribute, and Cipriani's charisma owed as much to whiteness as it did to his other leadership qualities."[22]

In 1921 Cipriani became chairman of the TWA's Advisory Board and Management Committee. By 1924 he was the association's president and, by far, the colony's most popular figure, regarded as the "champion of the barefoot man." Although perceived as a radical by conservatives, Cipriani also appealed to the Afro-Creole middle sectors, which helped to place him on the colony's first elected Legislative Council in 1925, a position he was continuously elected to until his death in 1945.

By the election of 1925, several changes had occurred in the colony's political life that were linked to the rise of Cipriani. Following the upheaval of 1919-20, radical members of the Afro-Creole middle sectors, with the support of the TWA, renewed the campaign for a more representative political system. The creation of elective members in Grenada's Legislative Council in the early 1920s added strength to these demands. A new Legislative Reform Committee was also established, composed largely of lighter-skinned Afro-Creole moderates. The real struggle for constitutional reform, however, was led by the radicals in the TWA as Bishop went to London where he met with the colonial undersecretary, Major E. F. L. Wood, and sympathetic labour party members of Parliament.[23] Through these metropolitan contacts, the matter was brought before Parliament, which sent Wood to investigate conditions in the West Indies in 1921.

The Wood Report, published in 1922 by the British Colonial Office, acknowledged that Trinidad was ready for limited political reform.[24] Wood felt that constitutional reforms were inevitable and that slowness to implement them would reap only negative dividends. Accordingly, there were several reasons for widening the political system. As Wood wrote:

> The wave of democratic sentiment has been powerfully stimulated by the war. Education is rapidly spreading, and tending to produce a coloured and black intelligentsia, of which the members are quick to absorb elements of knowledge requisite for entry into the learned professions. They return from travel with minds emancipated and enlarged, ready to devote time and energy to propaganda among their own people. Local traditions of representative institutions reinforce these tendencies.[25]

Wood was aware of the radical politicalization of the working-class movement but strongly argued that "the educated and intelligent minority of today is powerful enough to mould the thought of the majority of tomorrow."[26]

Due to Wood's recommendations, modest reforms were implemented as the Legislative Council was expanded to 26 members; 12 were to be appointed officials, and 13 would be unofficial members.[27] The remaining member of the council was the governor, who functioned as a de facto prime minister, retaining his vote and having the routine backing of the "official party," which nearly always gave him a majority of one.

The question of expanding the franchise was difficult and complicated by the racial and ethnic divisions in Trinidad and Tobago's society. The East Indian majority, represented by the EINA, opposed any change, arguing that an elective system would harm Indians because of their relative lack of education.[28] The EINA felt that more nominated representatives should be added to protect their group's concerns in the colonial government. The East Indian National Congress, in contrast, advocated for elected members and communal representation for East Indians to prevent the possibility of their being outvoted since it was anticipated that few of their number would qualify to vote.

Most East Indians feared that electoral reform and the widening of the franchise would, in part, be based upon language, meaning that it was necessary to speak and write English to vote. The substantial majority of the East Indian community spoke Hindi and had only a rudimentary grasp of English. A small Christianized minority, who had become assimilated into the colony's Western culture, had emerged as part of the "national" middle class. Their influence in the colony's affairs was small, but any new legislation would be to their benefit and not necessarily to the rest of the East Indian community.

The predominantly Afro-Creole middle-sectors-dominated Legislative Reform Committee opposed communal representation, which would require each ethnic group to have members appointed, by proportion of numbers, to the Legislative Council. The governor would have the power of selecting those individuals he thought best represented each community's interests. Those in the Reform Committee felt this type of system would weaken their influence and enhance that of the emerging East Indian middle class.[29]

Although not brought into the open, the Trinidadian middle class was sharply divided in its approach to politics: the constitutional reform issue became a question of race relations with each community fearing each other more than the small white elite that ruled.[30] The colonial authorities finally decided against communal voting, apprehensive that it would perpetuate differences between the major ethnic groups and stand as an obstacle to eventual national integration.

Although the rejection of communal voting could be perceived as a victory for the Afro-Creole middle sectors, the final decisions concerning who could vote was limited, largely excluding the black working class and the majority of East Indians. Qualifications were confined to those who had high incomes or owned substantial property. The franchise was for both sexes, although men had to be 21 and women 30, and all voters were required to speak English. The qualifications for office holders were even more stringent: candidates were required to have even more substantial holdings and wealth and must have resided in their constituency for one year or own real estate there of $24,000 in value or from which they derived an annual income of $19,000.[31] Furthermore, only male candidates able to read and write English were eligible for election.[32] One last qualification was that members of the Legislative Council were not paid, which limited the franchise to the wealthy and landed. The constitutional changes of the early 1920s, in effect, helped maintain conservative white power since the right to vote was granted to the upper and middle classes, constitutionally making the whites and those of mixed European-African descent into the new political elite.

The general elections of 1925, the product of the reforms, were the first of their kind held in the colony, and personalities and race were the major factors. The most exciting contest was in Port of Spain where Major Randolf Rust ran against Cipriani. Rust, a wealthy businessman, represented the white ruling class: his positions were pro-government and pro-status quo. During the campaign he labeled his opponent as a "bolshevik" and argued that government should be run by businessmen. Rust's campaign was ineffective as he was badly beaten by Cipriani.

Cipriani's successful campaign was due to the aid of the TWA and the support of the Afro-Creole middle sectors. As Ryan notes, "Despite the hostility of the established press and the limited nature of the franchise, Cipriani had undoubtedly proven to be the favorite of the Trinidad masses.... But it was also clear that he had the support of the non-white middle class as well."[33]

Cipriani's 1925 victory marked his rise to power as a national figure while also helping him consolidate control over the TWA. Although the Legislative Council was "nothing more than a debating assembly," it provided Cipriani with a visible forum from which to push for workers' compensation, a minimum wage, an eight-hour workday, and regulations prohibiting child labor.[34] He also advocated for compulsory education, condemned the neglect of public works, and favored better salaries for teachers. Simply stated, Cipriani's role in the Legislative Council was to articulate the TWA's reform program and, when possible, to pass legislation in the workers' interest.[35] Very much the public man, the captain captured the attention of the Afro-Creole popular sectors and segments of the East Indian population. As Ryan stated, "He was the instrument by which large numbers of individuals who had previously experienced no attraction towards one another came to develop feelings of national kinship and identification."[36] All these factors contributed to Cipriani's becoming the undisputed leader of the TWA.

Under Cipriani, the TWA expanded its membership, establishing new branches in Trinidad and, significantly, 13 in Tobago by 1928.[37] This expansion included not only black industrial and urban workers, but also members of the East Indian community, an important step toward creating a "national" organization. Among those East Indians recruited into the TWA were Sarran Teelucksingh, who was the only Indian elected to the Legislative Council in 1925, Timothy Roodal, elected in 1928, F. E. M. Hosein, a candidate in 1928 (also former leader of the East Indian National Congress), and Adrian Cola Rienzi. Both Teelucksingh and Roodal became presidents of the San Fernando branch in 1925. Although these men were visible and influential in the TWA, East Indian membership remained small in the predominantly Afro-Creole organization.

The TWA's ties to the British Labour Party, cemented by Cipriani's trips to London, were an important part in his policies and ideology.[38] While his ideology was radical, it was not revolutionary as he was a socialist along Fabian lines, favoring evolution over revolution. More than once he proclaimed that he was not a Marxist, reflecting, in part, many of the political characteristics of the mainstream British Labour Party that came to power in January 1924.[39] Under the leadership of Ramsey MacDonald, also the prime minister, the Labour Party accepted the logic of gradualism and rejected the thought that the immediate object of holding power was to nationalize the means of production and exchange.[40] Rather, the major emphasis was placed on improving the economic and political position of the English working class. Cipriani's political stance reflected much of this: the expansion of the franchise and improved economic conditions were core issues, although compromises with the opposition were often necessary, especially to maintain middle-sector support.

By the early 1930s, the link to London had become close since the British party relied upon the Trinidadian movement for its information on regional affairs so that questions could be raised in Parliament that would benefit the colony.[41] In August 1934 the TWA formally changed its name to the Trinidad Labour Party (TLP). This was done in response to the passing of a new law in 1932 that allowed the formation of trade unions. This law, however, was introduced by the conservatives and empowered the attorney general to register or refuse to register a trade union.[42] Moreover, the Trade Union Ordinance of 1932 did not legalize peaceful picketing nor protect unions from legal torts for damages occurring during a strike action. Although not directly affecting the middle sectors, the passage of this law and the internal repercussions of the change from union status to that of a political party, helped undermine Cipriani's position vis-à-vis a younger and more radical generation of leaders. This younger group chaffed under the captain's authoritarian leadership and rejected his view that it was better to work within the system.

THE TURBULENT 1930s AND THE DECLINE OF CIPRIANI

The 1930s marked both the zenith of Cipriani's career as a "man of the people" and his decline. While he was charismatic, supported by the middle sectors, and able to rejuvenate the TWA, forming the colony's first mass party, his political talents were limited. Due to a combination of words and action, he was unable to preside over the transformation of Trinidadian politics because of the growing complexity of party politics, which required organizational skills, a degree of financial acumen, and well-conceived campaign programs. As Max Farquhar of the *Trinidad Guardian* commented of Cipriani: "His leadership did not survive the evolution of the barefoot man . . . into the working class proletariat protected by trade unions. . . . His rugged individualism was soon overrun . . . and he was left stranded, a lonely monument of defiance, forgotten."[43]

The cleavages within the TWA/TLP began with the 1931 bill legalizing divorce. Initially the TWA's leadership had declared its neutrality over the issue, leaving the dispute to the Catholic Church and the government. Cipriani, however, broke policy when he gave his support to the Catholic Church, which was a highly conservative institution. Not only did the working class have apprehensions over this alignment; the issue created dissension within the middle-sector leadership. Bishop, through the publication, *Labour Leader*, criticized Cipriani, who in retaliation closed the paper in 1932. Cipriani's actions also alienated the East Indian membership: both Teelucksingh and Roodal had voted in favor of divorce.[44]

Disunity within the labor movement's leadership continued to worsen throughout 1932-34 over the issue of the 1932 Trade Union Ordinance. Although the decision was made to change into a party, it alienated the younger members. Cipriani, however, remained in command despite the discontent.

The most serious factor in Cipriani's decline was the TLP's failure to introduce practical improvements in the living and working conditions of the people.[45] This factor became increasingly apparent during the 1930s, a time of depression in which jobs were scarce and wages low. Disillusionment with the TLP and frustration over deteriorating economic conditions first erupted into demonstrations in Port of Spain in 1933. In the following year, as the situation worsened, demonstrations spread to the largely East Indian sugar districts where managers had reduced employment, lengthened hours, and lowered wages, all in an effort to retrench. A severe drought complicated matters as the planting of rice was delayed: many unemployed sugar workers often turned to rice cultivation as an alternative means of livelihood and economic survival. Refused credit by shopkeepers, out of work, and near starvation, the workers turned to mass demonstrations, which erupted in July 1934 in the island's sugar belt. A violent and spontaneous upheaval, claiming a considerable amount of property damages, the disturbances caught many by surprise, including the TLP.

When many of the demonstrators were arrested and imprisoned, the TLP, which had no role in the riots, lost considerable prestige. The demonstrators refused to consult the TWA and Cipriani, who had attempted to plead with the workers to cease their action, had largely been ignored. His siding with the forces of the status quo, the colonial authorities and the sugar companies, led many to regard the TLP leader as a "traitor" or "sellout" and helped radicalize the popular sectors, led by the workers, which were once again looking for a leader. Direct action and revolution began to have more appeal than Cipriani's gradualism.

By 1934 Cipriani appeared to have lost the will to fight on the behalf of the working class. The TLP leader, increasingly became representative of the urban Afro-Creole middle class as worker support slowly eroded. Disappointment over the 1935 wages bill, which in effect legalized low wages, and continuing bad economic conditions combined to spark new riots in March that year at the southern oil fields.[46]

Tubal Uriah Butler, a black Grenadian who had served in the West Indies Regiment, emerged as the leader of the predominantly Afro-Creole oil workers in the early 1930s.[47] Strongly influenced by Cipriani, he had gone to Trinidad in the early 1920s to work in the oil boom and joined the TWA. Since he was black and an excellent speaker, he could agitate his audience, which could easily identify with him, especially as he spoke to the Afro-Creoles in their own idiom, something that Cipriani, a white Creole, could not. Moreover, Butler, also a Moravian Baptist evangelist, had a strong sense of mission, firmly believing that God was on his side in leading the people of the West Indies from the wilderness of colonialism.[48] Eventually Butler concluded that Cipriani had lost the torch of political change and was thus jeopardizing the advancement of the workers.

When employees at the Apex Oilfields went on strike in 1935 over poor working conditions, Butler and John Rojas, the heads of the Fyzabad branch of the TLP, backed them. Cipriani, however, refused to sanction the strike, which led the two branch heads to disobey their party leader. The strike gradually ended due to poor organization with the workers accepting a minor pay increase. By 1935, therefore, Butler emerged as a serious challenge to Cipriani's hold over the Afro-Creole popular sectors. And, although the challenge was met in 1935, as Cipriani helped bring an end to the disturbances without violence, black workers had become impatient with his calls to use constitutional procedures to articulate grievances and increasingly looked to new younger and more radical leaders, such as Butler and Rojas, who advocated direct action and spoke of rapid changes.

Butler added the element of race back into Trinidadian politics since he provided himself as a black leader for black workers, discarding the bridging concept of having a neutral ethnic type as leader. Race also served to fragment the middle-class-worker alliance. This trend to fragmentation was evident by the foundation of a number of short-lived organizations, usually based upon racial identification; these groups included the National Unemployment Movement, the Negro Welfare, Cultural and Social Association, the Club L'Ouverture, and the Trinidad Citizens League. Most of these sought to draw attention to the problems of working-class conditions, maladministration, and corruption.[49] The leadership of at least two of the above organizations included Butler and Rienzi; both had represented the younger generation's discontent with Cipriani and had left the TLP.

As Cipriani's grasp over the labor movement weakened between 1932 and 1935, the stage was set for further confrontation in 1936 and 1937 as the colony headed toward its worst riots yet. An underlying current in Trinidad's politics leading to the 1936-37 riots was the spread of black nationalism and a furthering of racial consciousness. The invasion of Ethiopia in 1935, in particular, was an issue around which black awareness formed. The failure of Western democracies to stand against another white nation, Italy, which invaded a black African state, stimulated racial anger among Trinidad and Tobago's Afro-Creole population of all classes. Not only did the Negro Welfare, Culture and Social Association organize a massive demonstration; longshoremen refused to handle Italian cargo in Port of Spain and a "Friends of Ethiopia" organization was established. On another level, the original link established with the Pan-African Movement by Williams had been maintained by the Negro Welfare, Cultural and Social Association.

The East Indian community was not immune to changing times. The harsh living conditions in which many Indians toiled in the 1930s certainly were one factor in their growing awareness and attraction to the possibilities of change. As the largest class of landowners in the colony, in small plots and producing sugar, the East Indians were highly sensitive to the fluctuations in the international market.[50] By the mid-1930s prices for sugar continued to be low, and the sector had to be assisted by the preference granted by the Imperial Government and Canada.[51] Albert Gomes describes the situation of the East Indian community living in "the indescribable dilapidation and squalor of the barracks." Concerning the condition of the laborers, he writes, "most of them [are] prematurely aged and diseased because of the horrible conditions which they were forced to live."[52]

The emergence of black nationalism increased race consciousness amongst all groups in the colony, while the successes of the nationalist movement in India, as conveyed by visits of leaders from the Asian subcontinent, created a new interest in the traditional homeland and all things Indian. By the mid-1930s the East Indian community was confronted with the reality of politics in a colony of predominant Western cultural values. At the bottom of the political and social pyramid, with the exception of a growing, yet small middle class, considerable frustration existed, which needed an outlet. The emergence of a generation of younger radical Indian leaders who agreed with the principles of direct action would help give that frustration its outlet.

In June 1937 widespread riots erupted due to the terrible conditions confronting the working class on a day-to-day basis in the face of an expanding oil industry that was making a profit for overseas British investors.[53] The disturbances commenced in the southern oilfields, and the man responsible for organizing them was Butler. In July 1936 he formed the British Empire Workers and Citizens Home Rule Party (BEW & CHRP). Referred to as the "Butler Party," the BEW & CHRP was a highly personalistic organization that could not exist without the leader's charismatic presence.[54] The goals of the party were to pass proper trade union and health insurance laws, to establish the right of blacks to reach the highest position of thought and labor in the colony, to achieve security of tenure for all workers, to secure the passage of more liberal divorce laws, to provide facilities for the unemployed to get jobs, and to support social legislation for workers.[55]

What made the Butler Party a powerful organization in Trinidad was its membership. Butler was able to tap the most organized group of workers on the island, the oil workers. Not only were they the best paid in the colony and most closely linked to the industrialization of the economy; they were also the most politicalized. More than other groups, with the possible exception of the longshoremen, they were very much aware of the inequalities of the society around them. Furthermore, they also aspired to upward social mobility, something that was blocked by the difficulties facing the colony's economy in the 1930s. Added to these factors was that considerable frustration had been built up by laws that allowed unions, but did not allow union activities, due to the discrimination of the white ruling class and unfulfilled promises of change by Cipriani and the TLP. Butler offered direct action with the intent to right what were perceived as wrongs. His message of immediate change was far more persuasive than Cipriani's message of future change.

Although Butler lacked a cohesive organization, he was able to capture the imagination of the Afro-Creole industrial worker and channel the frustration of the oil belt's popular sectors against the inequalities of a system in which the oil companies' white managers from the United Kingdom, the United States, and especially South Africa had a "South African gold mining complex" about "niggers."[56] The high standard of living that these foreign managers enjoyed created a highly visible, hostile white class living in large homes surrounded by exceedingly poor blacks. All this, together with the oil industry's high profits and the depression of wages, resulted in an explosive situation, charged with racial overtones.

To protest these conditions, Butler organized widespread demonstrations in the southern oil belt. The local government, fearful of the large crowds, attempted to arrest Butler at a gathering. This action triggered massive riots that rapidly spread throughout the islands. In struggles with the police, more than a dozen people, including two policemen, were killed and over 50 were wounded. To restore order, the British government landed marines from Barbados, in effect, occupying the colony. Butler, along with a number of others, was arrested, put on trial, and imprisoned for a brief period. Despite the riots, their suppression, and his internment, Butler continued to have faith in the British Empire, perceiving, as did many in the popular sectors, that the oil companies and the local white ruling class were the real villains. Without Butler, however, the island's most radical force was headless, leaving the scene open to more moderate middle-class politicians to assert themselves.

MODERATING THE LABOR MOVEMENT

The TLP, which had progressively moved to the center and become more middle class in outlook, condemned the 1937 riots, especially the use of "mob rule" tactics. Cipriani even implied that groups with communist tendencies were involved. In fact, at the hearing that followed, TLP spokesmen said that it had placed its resources at the governor's disposal "in an endeavor to help put down the trouble."[57] The Trinidad Labour Party advocated gradual constitutional and legislative change, and the upheaval in 1937 was regarded with disdain.

Moreover, by 1937 Cipriani was nearly 70 and lacked much of the dynamism that had characterized his earlier actions. Simply stated, the TLP and its leader failed to come to the worker's aid, and the party's popularity, already in decline, plummeted nationwide after 1937, except in Port of Spain where a moderate Afro-Creole middle class preferred him to more radical and conservative figures. Cipriani's strict adherence to constitutionalism and accommodation with the colonial government had given way, with the rise of Butler, to confrontation.

The British government, concerned about the instability in the West Indies and, in particular, Trinidad, sought to restore order in the region. The apprehension of a new war in Europe made London sensitive to what occurred in its major oil producer. The outbreak of further disturbances in Jamaica during May-June 1938 reflected that a quick and easy remedy was not at hand and that the British government had not yet formulated a response to the "surprising" popularly based revolt in the West Indies.[58] A royal commission headed by Lord Moyne visited the Caribbean during 1938-39, listened to evidence, and submitted memoranda.

One important issue that emerged in the Moyne Commission was the dispute over the definition of the Crown Colony system between those seeking democratic change in Trinidad and Tobago and the British Colonial Office.[59] The latter felt that the Crown Colony concept had little to do with politics; rather it was "a system of administration which aimed at the reconciliation of interests and the creation of consensus out of disparate groups."[60] For those seeking the democratization of their colony, political reform, rather than administrative and economic change, was the primary consideration. The British disagreed, arguing that important prerequisites were necessary to aid the very gradual process of devolution of power from limited elected government to the enlargement of the elected bloc to a quasi-ministerial system through internal self-government to eventual independence. These necessary prerequisites were the establishment of adequate infrastructure, a stable and sizable middle class, and the required elites to run a civil service.[61] While education was important in the emergence of a self-governing political unit, stability was needed to attract British and North American investment that would help strengthen the infrastructure. These factors, in turn, were necessary in the expansion of a middle class that was to be democratic and capitalistic in orientation. Ultimately, it would be from this class that the colony's economic managers, administrators, and political leaders would emerge. Key to these developments was the gradualist approach, aimed at shunting aside those with radical tendencies who would jeopardize the eventual middle class rise to power.

Although the British government did not enact sweeping political reforms that would bring the franchise to a larger bloc of the population, important concessions were made. In taking notice of the growing political consciousness in Trinidad and Tobago, the Moyne Commission recommended a reduction in the number of nominated members and an increase in elected members in the Legislative Council. It also recommended a widening of voter qualifications. These constitutional changes were delayed by the lengthy deliberations of the colony's conservative leadership and the interruption of World War II. Although the pace of change must have appeared agonizingly slow to democratic forces in the middle sectors and in the working class, the state's structure had changed considerably since the beginning of the century. At least part of the population could vote and hold office, and the pressure could be exerted to open the franchise further. The British, great gradualists, were difficult to move quickly, and the democratic groups in the colony would have to wait until after the war to claim a substantial victory. In a Johnsonian sense, however, they had taken one major step forward as they had begun experimenting with political parties.

The emergence of strong, yet moderate trade unions was enacted before the outbreak of hostilities. Rienzi became the rising star of the labor movement, a development aided by the TLP's eclipse and by the support of Walter Citrine and the British Trade Unions Congress.[62] Under Rienzi's guidance, the Oilfield Workers Trade Union (OWTU), the All Trinidad Sugar Estates and Factory Workers Trade Union (ATSE/FWTU), the Federated Workers Trade Union (FWTU), and the Trinidad and Tobago Union of Shop Assistants and Clerks (T & TUSAC) were formed with the assistance of Albert Gomes, Quitin O'Connor, Rupert Gittens, MacDonald Moses, John Rojas, Earl Blades, and Ralph Mentor. The movement was split geographically as well as functionally between Port of Spain (with the FWTU and the T & TUSAC under Gomes, O'Connor, and Gittens) and the south, which was the base of the others. Furthermore, the labor movement remained predominantly Afro-Creole, although Rienzi was president of the OWTU and ATSE/FWTU. There was considerable East Indian representation only in the predominantly Indian sugar belt. Most Indo-Trinidadians, however, remained outside of the trade unions' activities. The importance of these groups to the democratization process was that they would eventually become political bases of support for middle-class politicians when the franchise was widened in the post-World War II era. Furthermore, many of the union leaders, who were of middle-class backgrounds, would also be the leading politicians of the late 1940s and the 1950s.

The moderating British influence was well accepted by most labor leaders, and by 1940 the labor movement was established along lines favored by London. The radicalization of the Afro-Creole working class had gradually lost impetus as the colonial government and metropolitan labor organizations helped form politically moderate trade unions that would not use the revolutionary and disruptive tactics of direct action. In return, the Trinidadian labor groups were given the right of peaceful picketing and immunity from actions for damages arising out of strikes. Moreover, they were able to form, with British union help, the Trinidad and Tobago Trade Union Congress, an umbrella organization that sought to unite the northern and southern movements. Rienzi was the Trade Union Congress's first president.

The British government, hastily rearming in 1937-39, found it in its national interest to keep peace in Trinidad, which meant allowing the development of the trade union movement. It was tolerated as a necessary evil to keep the workers satisfied, especially when considering that both the Royal Navy and Air Force relied on the colony's oil industry for more than half of its fuel.[63] To be tolerated, Trinidadian unions, as in other parts of the British Caribbean, had to become responsible, which meant that they were given certain rights in exchange for constructive responses to labor-industrial problems and an appreciation for some of the core needs of the British Empire. The latter understanding was reflected in a "no-strike" agreement that was in effect for the duration of World War II.

THE WAR YEARS: THE INFLUENCE OF THE U.S. OCCUPATION

Trinidad was an important colonial possession during World War II. Not only was the island the source of fuel for the Allied war effort; it also was the convoy-assembly point for the dispatch of tankers from Caribbean oil ports and the stopping point for all ships and aircraft in transit to Europe and North America. Furthermore, the Gulf of Paria was used by U.S. carriers and planes for their final exercises before going to the Pacific Ocean via the Panama Canal.

Through the Destroyers-for-Bases Deal, the Churchill government received 50 mothballed U.S. destroyers in return for the granting of

U.S. bases throughout the British West Indies. The United States established two bases in Trinidad, a naval station at Chaguaramas on the northwest peninsula and an army base in central Trinidad at Waller Field. The agreement was concluded in March 1941; although the bases were leased for 99 years, they were later returned to Trinidad and Tobago in the 1960s.

Large numbers of white U.S. soldiers arrived in the colony in 1941 as construction crews and were followed by army personnel. Although there was a tremendous amount of activity in the oilfields in the early 1940s, the structure of the economy moved further away from agriculture since labor was attracted to the new construction sites where, as one Trinidadian noted, "anyone who could lay his hands on a hammer or saw was considered a skilled craftsman."[64]

Those employed in the sugar industry plummeted from 13,042 in 1940 to 9,299 in 1944.[65] Thousands were employed at the highest wages ever witnessed in the colony; consequently, the cost of living rose, and a great deal of money was circulated among many sectors of the population. In the "boomtime" atmosphere, prostitution and organized crime increased, and a cruder and less subtle discrimination was practiced by many U.S. personnel. At the same time, Trinidadian workers were brought into the highly efficient personnel system of their U.S. employers, which provided benefits previously unavailable in the colony. Organized labor, although harassed at times by the colony's authorities, also received some positive encouragement from the U.S. occupation, especially in the expectation of better employee-employer relationships.[66]

Another offshoot of the U.S. occupation was that it helped dispel the myth of white supremacy: the sight of whites doing hard manual labor and the antics of drunken soldiers and sailors certainly contributed to the decline of the deference to whites.[67] At the same time, Trinidadians were impressed by the efficiency of the high-level technology that the U.S. personnel brought to the colony.[68] The use of this technology helped bring tremendous changes in Trinidad, which would later help expand the size of the middle sectors and raise the level of the population's expectations of a better life in the postwar era. Most significant of these transformations were the improvements in the colony's infrastructure: thousands of acres in the Waller Field area were cleared, the first substantial islandwide network of roads was constructed, and Port of Spain's docking facilities were improved.[69]

Perhaps the most enduring dimension of the U.S. occupation was the change in expectations among the working class. While the occupation brought a tremendous acceleration in the exposure of the Trinidadians to the outside world, the free-spending habits of the U.S. soldiers were not missed by the colony's population, and the hope of having a similar lifestyle was thus generated.[70] North American consumer ideas were also disseminated by the radio and newspapers. Moreover, the influence of the cinema could not be ignored as most films shown in the 1930s and 1940s were made in the United States, such as *Casablanca, Till the Clouds Roll By, Dodge City,* and *The Spoilers.* Serials like *Spysmasher* and *The Shadow* were also favorites that conveyed a Hollywood B-movie image of reality in which money was freely spent, men were tough and virile, and women were either seductive or pure, but all were attractive. As Naipaul notes, "In the immigrant colonial society, with no standards of its own, subjected for years to the second-rate in newspapers, radio and cinema, minds are rigidly closed; and Trinidadians of all races and classes are remaking themselves in the image of the Hollywood B-man."[71] In essence, improved communications in the 1930s and 1940s and the U.S. occupation helped implant North American middle-class ideas, which were founded, in part, on the influence of Hollywood. The war period, therefore, witnessed the commencement of the "revolution of rising expectations," as Trinidadians experienced firsthand better living conditions and pay and were made aware that superior lifestyles existed.

World War II and the U.S. occupation did not completely disrupt Trinidad and Tobago's political life. In 1941 certain political reforms were enacted as the Legislative Council was reorganized. Nine officials were dropped, and the number of elected officials was increased from seven to nine. Further changes were introduced in 1944 that gave greater significance to the elective element, although the governor remained the most powerful force in the colony's political structure. From 1941 to 1944 the expansion of the franchise was deliberated, with three union-based leaders, Rienzi, Gomes, and Mentor, sitting in the franchise committee.

Support for universal franchise was mobilized by the trade unions, the Trinidad and Tobago Socialist Party (founded by Rienzi), and the Port of Spain city council under the left wing mayor, Tito Achong, a Chinese Creole.[72] Conservative white elements, however, dominated the franchise committee, and, despite the passage of a universal adult suffrage law, a rider was attached adding property and income qualifications. An attempt had been made to pass a law that claimed voters had to be literate in English. Upon pressure from the East Indian representatives, the Colonial Office rescinded that stipulation before the passage of the enactment of the Order in Council of 1945, which granted adult franchise to 46 percent of the population.[73] Under the new constitutional changes, elections were set for 1946, which were to be an important turning point in Trinidad and Tobago's political development.

CONCLUSION

By 1945 Trinidad and Tobago's politics witnessed considerable structural change in the colonial state, moving from an almost entirely nonrepresentative government to adult franchise with elections set for 1946. These changes were, in part, due to the actions of the bourgeois-worker alliance and the politicalization of the latter class. Moreover, the labor movement, at the forefront of the mobilization of the "masses," has gone through several stages, finally reaching a more moderate, but far from conservative approach to achieving political power and economic betterment. Although eclipsed by younger and more radical leaders, in the 1930s, the contribution of Cipriani, who died in 1945, cannot be forgotten, especially considering that he was one of the first to instill a sense of national consciousness among many Trinidadians, a crucial step in the nation-building process. Where Cipriani provided a temporary bridge between the Afro-Creoles and East Indians, Butler and other leaders took the labor movement down the road of radicalism tempered by racial identity, hence setting the stage for ethnic divisions in the political realm in the postwar era. Both Cipriani and Butler also reflected that, although experimentation with party politics had begun, it was still dominated by strong individual leaders.

Another factor to be considered during the 1919-45 period was why the middle sectors sought to aid the working class. Since this relationship continued to be a factor in the political and economic development of Trinidad and Tobago, it should be emphasized that middle-sector leadership, in both major ethnic groups, was aware that it would need an electoral base of support once the political system opened. Consequently, middle-sector leaders or those leaders of middle-class backgrounds who were actively involved in politics, played to the popular sectors for support, while maintaining their support with their bourgeois voters. As Johnson notes, "A sense of social obligation and the need to pay off political debts have combined to induce the middle sectors to support advanced labor and welfare legislation in favor of the industrial working groups."[74] In the increasingly complex realm of Trinidadian politics, the ethnic factor would grow to overshadow the class factor on a nationwide basis, leaving the stage open to middle-class politicians of neutral ethnic backgrounds who were capable of bridging the gap between Afro-Creoles and East Indians. The dimension of rising expectations, stimulated by the U.S. occupation, and the individualistic nature of politics of the 1946-55 period were clearly founded on the period that preceded it.

NOTES

1. Eric Williams, *History of the People of Trinidad and Tobago* (London: André Deutsch, 1964), pp. 215-16.

2. The price of sugar on the world market declined from 5.45 cents (U.S.) per pound in 1890 to 3.51 cents per pound in 1913. *1939 Commodity Yearbook* (New York: Commodity Research Bureau, 1940), p. 294.

3. Noel Deerr, *The History of Sugar*, vol. 1 (London: Chapman and Hall, 1949-50), p. 202.

4. *Commodity Yearbook 1941* (New York: Commodity Research Bureau, 1941), p. 145.

5. Trevor M. A. Farrell, "The Multinational Corporations, the Petroleum Industry and Economic Underdevelopment in Trinidad and Tobago" (Ann Arbor: University of Michigan Microfilms International, 1974), pp. 89-90. Also see Vernon C. Mulchansingh, "The Oil Industry in Trinidad," *Caribbean Studies* 11 (April 1971): 73-76.

6. Farrell, "Multinational Corporations," p. 90.

7. Ibid.

8. Ibid.

9. Williams, *People of Trinidad and Tobago*, p. 215.

10. Sahadeo Basdeo, *Labour Organization and Labour Reform in Trinidad 1919-1939* (St. Augustine, Trinidad: Institute of Social and Economic Research, 1983), p. 7.

11. Ibid., pp. 7-8.

12. B. Samaroo, "Constitutional and Political Development in Trinidad, 1898-1925," Ph.D. dissertation, 1969, pp. 21-22.

13. Selwyn Ryan, *Race and Nationalism in Trinidad and Tobago: A Study of Decolonization in a Multiracial Society* (Toronto: University of Toronto Press, 1972), p. 28.

14. Bridget Brereton, *A History of Modern Trinidad* (London: Heineman Educational Books, 1981), p. 160.

15. These riots happened in Cardiff and Liverpool, and the dead Trinidad sailor's name was Charles Wotten. See *Liverpool Daily Post* and *Mercury*, June 11 and 14, 1919; *South Wales News*, June 14, 1919; and *The Times* (London), June 14 and 19, 1919.

16. For a history of Hercules and his movement, see W. F. Elkins, "Hercules and the Society of Peoples of African Origin," *Caribbean Studies* 11 (January 1972): 47-59.

17. See W. F. Elkins, "Black Power in the West Indies: The Trinidad Longshoremen's Strike of 1919," *Science and Society* 33 (1969). Also see T. Martin, "Revolutionary Upheaval in Trinidad, 1919," *Journal of Negro History* 58 (1973).

18. Brinsley Samaroo, "Politics and Afro-Indian Relations in Trinidad," in John La Guerre, ed., *East Indians in Trinidad* (Trinidad and Jamaica: Longman Caribbean, 1974), p. 86.

19. Gordon K. Lewis, *The Growth of the Modern West Indies* (New York: Monthly Review Press, 1968), p. 203. For Cipriani's early life, see C. L. R. James, *The Life of Captain Cipriani* (London, André Deutsch, 1932).

20. For a study of the British West Indies Regiment, see C. L. Joseph, "The British West Indies Regiment, 1914-1918," *Journal of Caribbean History* 2 (May 1971): 94-124.

21. Samaroo, "Constitutional and Political Development," p. 15.

22. Ryan, *Race and Nationalism*, p. 38.

23. Brereton, *History of Modern Trinidad*, p. 165.

24. *Report by the Hon. E. F. L. Wood, MP, on His Visit to the West Indies and British Guiana, December 1921 to February 1922* (London: Colonial Office, 1922), p. 25.

25. Ibid., p. 5.

26. Ibid.

27. Ryan, *Race and Nationalism*, p. 33.

28. Brereton, *History of Modern Trinidad*, p. 165.

29. Ibid.

30. Ibid., p. 166.

31. Williams, *People of Trinidad and Tobago*, p. 219.

32. Ibid.

33. Ryan, *Race and Nationalism*, p. 35.

34. Lewis, *Modern West Indies*, p. 205.

35. Brereton, *History of Modern Trinidad*, p. 167.

36. Ryan, *Race and Nationalism*, p. 168.

37. Brereton, *History of Modern Trinidad*, p. 167.

38. Cipriani also traveled to regional conferences. See *Report of the First British Guiana and West Indies Labour Conference* (Georgetown, British Guiana: Caribbean Trade Union Congress Association, 1926).

39. The British Labour Party was founded as the political arm of the Trade Union Congress, which was a moderate socialist organization founded in the

1800s. See Henry Peeling, *A History of British Trade Unionism* (Harmondsworth, England: Penguin Books, 1977), pp. 113-20.

40. T. O. Lloyd, *Empire to Welfare State: English History, 1906-1967* (London: Oxford University Press, 1976), p. 130.

41. Brinsley Samaroo, "The Trinidad Labour Party and the Moyne Commission, 1938," paper presented at the Fourteenth Conference of the Association of Caribbean Historians, San Juan, Puerto Rico, April 16-21, 1982, p. 6.

42. Ibid., p. 7.

43. *Trinidad Guardian*, February 9, 1956, p. 2.

44. Brereton, *History of Modern Trinidad*, p. 170.

45. Ibid., p. 171.

46. Ryan, *Race and Nationalism*, p. 41.

47. For his life see W. Richard Jacobs, *The Trial of Uriah Butler: A Study of Colonial Injustice* (Trinidad: Inprint Caribbean, 1975).

48. Ryan, *Race and Nationalism*, p. 45.

49. Brereton, *History of Modern Trinidad*, p. 174.

50. Colonial Office, *Report of the West Indian Sugar Commission, Part IV* (London: Her Majesty's Stationery Office, 1930), p. 20.

51. *Colonial Reports—Annual Report on the Social and Economic Progress of the People of Trinidad and Tobago* (London: Her Majesty's Stationery Office, 1936), p. 14.

52. Albert Gomes, *Through the Maze of Colour* (Port of Spain: Longman Caribbean, 1974), p. 20. Also see *Colonial Reports—Annual Report*, pp. 10-11.

53. For the rising value of exports of crude oil and byproducts, see *Colonial Reports—Trinidad and Tobago 1935* (London: Her Majesty's Stationery Office, 1936), p. 20.

54. W. Richard Jacobs, "The Politics of Protest in Trinidad: The Strikes and Disturbances of 1937," *Caribbean Studies* 17 (April-July 1977): 20.

55. Condensed from the *Trinidad Guardian*, December 10, 1937, p. 3.

56. See Public Records Office (P.R.O.) Files, London, C.O. 295/599/70 308/8A note by secretary of state after an interview on October 8, 1937.

57. *TLP Memo*, p. 19, quoted in Samaroo, "Trinidad Labour Party," p. 18.

58. Samaroo, "Trinidad Labour Party," p. 3.

59. Ibid., p. 4.

60. John La Guerre, "The Moyne Commission and the Jamaican Left," *Social and Economic Studies* 6 (1982): 9.

61. Samaroo, "Trinidad Labour Party," p. 22.

62. See Saadeo Basdeo, "Walter Citrine and the British Caribbean Workers Movement during the Moyne Commission Hearing, 1938-1939," paper presented at the Fourteenth Conference of the Association of Caribbean Historians, San Juan, Puerto Rico, April 16-21, 1982.

63. Howard Johnson, "Oil, Imperial Policy and the Trinidad Disturbances, 1937," *Journal of Imperial and Commonwealth History* 4 (October 1975): 48-54.

64. P. E. T. O'Connor, *Some Trinidad Yesterdays* (Trinidad: Inprint Caribbean, 1975), p. 96. Also see Ivar Oxaal, *Black Intellectuals Come to Power: The Rise of Creole Nationalism in Trinidad and Tobago* (Cambridge: Schenkman, 1968).

65. *The West Indies Year Book, 1941* (Montreal: Thomas Skinner of Canada, 1941), p. 245.

66. Brereton, *History of Modern Trinidad*, p. 189.

67. Lloyd Braithwaite, "Social Stratification in Trinidad," *Social and Economic Studies* 2 (October 1953): 133.

68. Brereton, *History of Modern Trinidad*, p. 192.

69. O'Connor, *Some Trinidad Yesterdays*, p. 98.

70. Oxaal, *Black Intellectuals*, p. 81.

71. V. S. Naipaul, *The Middle Passages: Impressions of Five Societies—British, French and Dutch in the West Indies and South America* (New York: Vintage Books, 1962, 1981), p. 61.

72. Brereton, *History of Modern Trinidad*, p. 193.

73. Ibid., p. 194.

74. John J. Johnson, *Political Change in Latin America: The Emergence of the Middle Sectors* (Stanford: University of Stanford Press), p. 184.

4

The Maze of Color, 1946-56

The period of 1946-56 in Trinidad and Tobago can be regarded as a decade of quasi-bourgeois rule. In many respects, it was a transitory time with the white upper class relinquishing its power before the advance of the middle sectors. As the drama unfolded, the political arena was inherited by the colony's two major ethnic groups, the Afro-Creoles and the East Indians. Both communities, however, had become increasingly suspicious of the other, making electoral alliances difficult. As ethnic tensions developed, a group of multiracial power brokers emerged, referred to as the "middle minorities" by Ivar Oxaal. Composed of Chinese, Portuguese, Syrian-Lebanese, and mixed (people of mixed Afro-Creole and Indian descent), this new group became an important bridge between the colony's rival forces "by virtue of the fact that they were mainly middle class and belonged to neither of the two major racial groups."[1] In essence, they occupied strategic positions in the social structure, being ideal brokers and emissaries between the Afro-Creoles and East Indians, while also being able to interact with the white upper class.[2]

Throughout the 1946-56 period, six major trends dominated Trinidad and Tobago's political and economic development. First and foremost, political power was passed on to the middle class, especially in the 1950-56 period when the Colonial Office allowed a quasi-ministerial system, headed by a chief minister. Although given limited self-rule, the government led by Albert Gomes, a Portuguese Creole, operated within a narrow framework, dependent upon the governor and the Colonial Office for policy implementation. Moreover, this experimental government marked a second trend, the emergence of the middle-class political right. There was a distinct difference between the new middle-class right and the traditional white upper-class conservatism. The former sought to implement progressive, yet gradual, changes in the state's structure along democratic lines, while the latter fundamentally opposed change in almost any form, regarding it as a threat to its privileged political and economic status. The bourgeois right was also perceived by the British as a more viable force to deal with the transferal of power when compared to the conservative white upper class and the colony's labor-based leftist movements.

During the 1950-56 experimental government, three trends were observable: a rejection of communism; an acceptance of capitalism as the correct doctrine for development; and an emphasis on economic diversification with industrialization. The diversification also provided for a sizable state sector in the economy. The final trend was further experimentation with political parties, a process complicated by ethnic divisions. The 1946-56 period, therefore, was a time of bourgeois experimentation with governing the nation, providing a solid foundation for the parliamentary system as the colony moved to independence in the late 1950s and early 1960s.

THE 1946 GENERAL ELECTIONS: THE LEFT'S FAILURE TO CAPTURE POWER

By the 1946 general elections, Trinidad and Tobago's political arena was characterized by an increasingly complex mixture of groups based on race, class, ideology, region, and personality. On the far right were the white upper-class conservatives, representative of the traditional planter and merchant elites. Because of the government structure that allowed the governor an appointed bloc of seats in the Legislative Council, they continued to exert an influence on the colony's political affairs. Seemingly unable to create a viable party, the white conservatives remained dependent on the goodwill of the colonial authorities.

Right of center was a number of middle-class politicians who, in 1946, lacked both dynamic leadership and official support. The Trinidad Labour Party, which had become representative of the urban middle-sector vote, had declined considerably and by the postwar era was an ineffective shell.[3] The more dynamic TLP members left with Gerald Wight to form the Progressive Democratic Party (PDP). This party, a revised version of the Ratepayers Association, was probusiness and competed with the defection-ridden TLP in Port of Spain. By the 1946 general elections, the colony's political right wing offered two weak parties that had little mass appeal.

On the surface the Trinidadian left appeared to be a powerful force, founded upon the strength of the islands' labor unions. There were, however, serious divisions, largely along personal and regional lines. In 1942 the West Indian National Party (WINP) was founded in Port of Spain. Socialist in outlook, the WINP advocated immediate self-rule for Trinidad and Tobago, self-government for a federated West Indies, and nationalization of the oil and asphalt industries. Almost upon inception, the new party's leadership did not trust the southern-based Oil Workers Trade Union (OWTU) and its political ally, the Socialist Party of Trinidad and Tobago, both of which were headed by Adrian Rienzi. WINP leaders, such as David Pitt, an Afro-Creole, Roy Joseph, a Syrian Creole, Albert Gomes, and Quinton O'Connor, a white Creole, found the East Indian leader a threat to their power. Rienzi was an effective spokesman for the working class, and his views were not tainted by racial and ethnic prejudice. As the racial animosity increased in the colony, however, Rienzi left active politics in 1944 due to his wish to avoid ugly incidents between East Indians and Afro-Creoles.[4]

Rienzi's withdrawal from politics left the labor movement without any clear-cut leader, and the newly formed WINP was unable to fill the gap, especially as it was labeled as a "black" party by the East Indians. The loss of the East Indian leader meant that not one, but several, new leaders and rival unions would emerge, fragmenting the labor movement and the colony's left wing.

The Socialist Party of Trinidad and Tobago, without Rienzi, continued to have the support of the OWTU and the Trinidad and Tobago Union Council. Eventually, the executive members of the OWTU, MacDonald Moses, Ralph Mentor, and John Rojas, became the party's leadership. Although radical, the socialist-OWTU alliance was against the nationalization of the sugar and oil industries, which was a departure from the northern-based WINP. Moreover, the southern group felt that change should proceed along gradualistic lines that would guarantee the worker an improved standard of living.

The plethora of political groupings of the left clearly underscored the movement's disunity, especially since other groups existed such as the Butler party. Looking to the general elections of 1946, many union and party leaders felt that the movement should attempt a joint platform. Under the guidance of Jack Kelshall, a white lawyer and leading member of the WINP, the United Front (UF) was formed. The organizations that initially agreed to stand together were the WINP, the Federated Workers Trade Union, the Negro Welfare, Cultural and Social Association, the Southern Workers Society Trade Union, the Oil Workers Trade Union, and the East Indian National Council. Moreover, a number of independent politicians joined the UF, including Norman Tang, Lawrence Edwards, and B. Mithra Nathai. The alliance, however, was plagued by many problems, and the OWTU quickly parted ranks, running its own candidates under the socialist-OWTU alliance banner.

Albert Gomes, Dr. P. J. Solomon, and Roy Joseph successively ran for office on the UF platform. The strongest rival to this leftist coalition was another leftist coalition, the Butler party, which received three seats, followed by the socialist-OWTU alliance, with two seats in the Legislative Council. Both the TLP and the PDP received no votes, and only one independent, Ranjit Kumar, was successful.

While it could be argued that the left won the 1946 elections, the disunity of the movement put three groups in the Legislative Council: the Butlerites, the UF, and the socialist-OWTU alliance. Within those groups were further divisions, as exemplified by Alfonso James. Officially allied to Butler, he originally had agreed to be a UF candidate and was more concerned with the needs of Tobago, which he represented, than any "nationwide" plans.

The 1946 elections meant that, although universal suffrage made the popular sectors the bulk of the electorate, labor failed to capture political power due to the fragmentation of the vote. Moreover, the governor was able to "divide and rule" in the aftermath of the elections as certain members of the left joined ranks with the more moderate and conservative elements in the Legislative Council in order to obtain seats in the Executive Council, which was given greater administrative power. Within a year of the elections, the UF was a spent force, and the opposition in the Legislative Council was divided and in a weak position vis-à-vis the conservatives and moderates.

The 1946 elections signified other important developments in Trinidad and Tobago's political evolution. It was recognized, at least in the UF manifesto, that the outgoing Legislative Council had been ineffective due to the large number of independents. Although slow to leave the political landscape, the independent candidate was gradually being eclipsed by political alliances and parties. Only one independent, Kumar, had captured a seat in 1946. It was becoming clear that the old-fashioned regional political machine was fading in significance in the developing electoral system, which placed an increasing emphasis on unified action to pass legislation.

On a more somber note, ethnic tensions were visible during the campaign. One observer commented that it was "a bitter and confused campaign in which party labels and purposes were inextricably tangled with racial animosities and personal ambitions."[5] Race and bribes were a strong part of a candidate's appeal to his voters and vote getters. Despite efforts to create multiracial parties, the UF was plagued by desertions of its East Indian allies since the Indo-Trinidadian population perceived it as an Afro-Creole party. Even the Butler party had its problems of unity since the East Indian membership appeared ready to part company on many issues.

The campaign of Ranjit Kumar in the County of Victoria, in particular, raised the race issue since the East Indian community, which outnumbered the Afro-Creoles three-to-one, voted solidly for their fellow Hindu over David Pitt, a black UF candidate and president of the WINP. The significance of this event was not missed by Solomon, who stated, "The ugly spectre of race which reared its ghastly head during the 1946 elections in the County of Victoria left a country which, until then, had no more than its normal share of prejudices of all kinds which exist in a Colonial Society."[6]

There were several reasons for the upsurge of racial tension in 1946. In the late 1930s an increased black awareness, stimulated by pan-Africanism and Garveyism, generated a certain militancy in the Afro-Creole community and a defensive mentality in the East Indian community. Despite earlier attempts at racial solidarity and emphasizing class struggle of workers against capitalists, the gap between the two ethnic groups widened in the 1940s. Rienzi's withdrawal from active politics was a devastating blow to Afro-Indian solidarity, at a time when the presence of such leaders was needed. It is probable that the racial question was one reason the East Indian leader retired from the scene, wishing to avoid ugly incidents that would pit Afro-Creoles against his people.

By 1946 racial slurs had become part of the campaign rhetoric. Moreover, the East Indian community, like the Afro-Creoles before them, began looking outside for inspiration and strength. Visits by Indian missionaries and high commissioners, especially after 1947 when India gained independence, emphasized ethnic differences. While the growing racial barriers hurt the left, they helped set the stage for a group of ambitious politicians who were of neither major ethnic group and were capitalist in orientation.

THE DOCKER'S STRIKE, BUTLER'S SOUR
GRAPES, AND CONSTITUTIONAL REFORM

In the new Legislative Council, sides were quickly taken to form "the government bloc" and "the opposition bloc." The former consisted of the three Crown Colony officials, six nominated members, and, after negotiations, four elected members who would be seated on the Executive Council. The latter was composed of the five remaining elected members. The opposition, a fragile coalition, was weakened by the lack of commitment of its "members," many of whom would side with the government on particular issues. Although the opposite was also true, with members of the government siding with the opposition bloc, most issues ran in favor of the government.

The opposition was further weakened by the placement of Gomes and Joseph on the Executive Council as it immediately created a division between them and Solomon, the other UF member who remained outside of the decision-making core. The other members of the Executive Council were Timothy Roodal, C. C. Abidh, and L. C. Hannays. Of these only the last mentioned officially represented the white conservatives since he was appointed by the governor. The appointment of the two East Indians indicated the weakness of the Butlerites as both men had run under his banner. Although four members of the Executive Council were elected on the strength of the left, they were more moderate than the others and were conducive to working within the governmental framework. The Executive Council, therefore, remained a conservative organ of government, aimed at gradual change beneficial to the competing interests of first, the white merchant and planter elites and, second, the Afro-Creole and middle minority middle sectors. Moreover, the governor increasingly had to take into consideration the growing strength of the colony's middle class.

The colony's politics were dominated by the docker's strike, the disruptive activities of Butler, and the question of constitutional reform. Each of these served to undermine the position of the left and help the moderate right gain momentum. Furthermore, it provided the middle minority politicians, such as Gomes and Joseph, an opportunity to experiment with the exercise of power, while obtaining nationwide exposure.

The failure of the Seaman and Waterfront Workers' Trade Union (SWWTU) strike of December 1946 was one of the first setbacks for the left after the elections. The SWWTU had sought a new contract with the Shipping Association, which refused to meet union representatives. Consequently, the workers declared a strike, and shipping operations in Port of Spain temporarily came to a standstill. The company brought in scab labor, and, after several weeks of tensions, clashes occurred between strikers and strikebreakers. This eventually culminated in a police raid on the union's headquarters and the arrest of the SWWTU president.

Despite the loss of its leader, the longshoremen's strike dragged into 1947. Finally, when it became a government issue open for discussion in the Legislative Council, the opposition bloc recommended that settlement be found through immediate negotiations and that the government refrain from harassing union leaders.[7] Gomes, however, defended the government's actions, and Joseph, acting in accordance with the governor, Sir Bede Clifford, motioned that the government would seek to bring the two parties together to settle the dispute while remaining impartial.[8] Beyond that motion, with no set date or binding commitment, little else was done on this matter in the Legislative Council. The strike was eventually broken as the dockers were confronted with starvation. Much weakened, the Seaman and Waterfront Workers' Trade Union capitulated.[9] Not only did the labor movement suffer a defeat, but the leftist opposition was proven largely ineffectual. Furthermore, the entire episode signaled the demise of the United Front since Gomes and Joseph had sided with the government and the traditional vested interests, leaving Solomon the odd man out.

Other events weakened the left. During the 1946 elections, Butler had challenged Gomes in Port of Spain North and was decisively beaten. With a sour grapes attitude, the labor leader retired to the south, his traditional stronghold where he challenged the OWTU leadership. Butler's bid to recapture the loyalty of the oil workers failed, and he next turned to provoking strikes. When this also failed, he had his followers turn to acts of violence, damaging pipelines, starting fires, emptying water reservoirs, and sabotaging installations.

The violence increased to the point that the government, with the opposition concurring, intervened. As Solomon, one of the leading figures of the latter, wrote, "I was supporting the bill in the interests of the community and for the maintenance of law and order."[10] The opposition, therefore, favored and supported the government's use of force to restore order, a position that they had strongly opposed with the docker's strike. The importance of this was that the opposition had remained a loyal opposition, siding against what was a radical attempt to disrupt the southern part of Trinidad, which, in a distinctive manner, jeopardized national interests since oil revenues were important to the colony's budget. Moreover, the majority of oil workers rejected Butler's calls to disrupt the island, and it could not be said that the workers were being repressed as in the case of the longshoremen. At the same time, Butler's activities further undermined the left and put his own political career in question.

While the Docker's Strike and the Butler-inspired disturbances were important factors in the 1946-50 period, the major issue of those years was constitutional reform. In 1946 half the Legislative Council was elected and half nominated with the governor having the deciding vote. There was considerable discontent with that situation, especially within the ranks of the middle sectors. Gomes summarized the feelings of many when he stated, "It is impossible to produce truly representative legislation within a body which is not truly democratic."[11] Consequently, a constitutional reform committee, chaired by Sir Lennox O'Reilly, was established, and once again it was dominated by white upper-class conservatives selected by the governor who were strongly opposed to the dismantlement of the Crown Colony system since it protected their economic interests.

After considerable deliberation and debates involving the governor, the Colonial Office, and the Legislative Council, a majority and two minority reports were presented. The majority report favored a Legislative Council of 27 members (including the governor) of which 18 were to be elected, 6 nominated, and 3 ex officio. The Executive Council would consist of 3 ex officio and 9 nonofficials of which 6 were to be elected members of the legislature and 3 nominated. From the ranks of the nonofficials a "leader" or chief minister was to be appointed. Initially, the majority report mentioned the possible mixing of the Executive and Legislative Councils in order to "avoid friction and crises between the two."[12] This, however, was modified and the dual council system was maintained.

The minority report of Solomon argued for the adoption of the British parliamentary system with an entirely elective legislative body from which a prime minister would be selected from the ranks of the ruling party. The system of proportional representation would meet the wishes of the people, which Solomon noted "is the standard in nearly every country where there is a pretense at popular representation."[13] He also took exception to the fact that the Constitutional Reform Committee was not the mouthpiece of the people; rather it represented the colonial society's traditional vested interests. Solomon also maintained that the majority report's proposed constitution would create a new government that was not radically different from the old, leaving the governor as the chief executive.

In the Legislative Council the strongest attack on Solomon's minority report came from Gomes, who favored gradual political change. To the Portuguese Creole, the institution of proportional representation and self-rule was a revolutionary act since it would mean "an almost complete transference of power from the hands of the Governor whose role and position are pivotal in the Crown Colony system, to the people through their elected representatives."[14]

Gomes was joined in his attack against the radical progressives by "conservative elements of the coloured middle class, who feared that responsible government on a fully elective basis would rob them of the legacy of political power which they felt it was their turn to enjoy."[15] Their justification for such a position was that people of caliber and education were eminently more qualified to run a government than the labor leaders and irresponsible radical middle-class intellectuals. There was also a fear that proportional representation would greatly enhance the left's standing, perhaps not in terms of bringing one party to power, but in terms of sheer numbers, in which case coalitions could occur. The continuance of nominated members helped guarantee that the conservative and moderate middle sectors would not be swept from the political system.

The second minority report, that of Ranjit Kumar, reflected the status of race relations in Trinidad and Tobago. Kumar was against immediate self-rule, maintaining that, since the colony's economy was not yet viable, a Crown Colony presence was still required in the political sphere. His main point, however, was the race issue: Kumar felt that the Crown Colony system was the only safeguard for minorities. Like many East Indians, he argued that an Afro-Trinidadian-dominated majority party would not consider his community's needs fairly. Kumar states:

> In Trinidad we have a minority problem, and it is the duty of the majority to gain the confidence of the minorities by showing them that in any proposal for self-government, the minorities would have equal rights. I am afraid that in this colony, the majority community has not yet done that. It has made no effort to try and instill confidence in the hearts of the minorities. In fact, there have been leaders whose actions and utterances have given minorities suspicion.[16]

Kumar's perceptions of the "race problem," as it was now being called, led him to suggest that nominated members hold the balance of power between the ethnic communities. If this were not done, he warned, "We have to make provision to see that Government is not controlled by a dictator and his party."[17] As an alternative, Kumar offered communal representation in which the East Indians would be given half the seats in the Legislative Council and a third of all positions in the civil service.[18] Kumar, who was also the president of the East Indian National Congress, was aided by the actions of the traditional power brokers in the Hindu community who preached in the temples against the movement to self-government as a machination of ambitious Afro-Creole politicians. The communal idea, however, was strongly rejected by most groups, including the more radical East Indians who felt that their community had to decide between Trinidad and India. It was feared that a communal political system would even more sharply divide the colony's society and ultimately lead to a race war.

Although the issue was debated until 1949, the majority report, with minor changes, was accepted by the Colonial Office. Its acceptance was another blow to the radicals. Moreover, due to political tensions and growing discontent with his performance, Joseph, who had supported the majority report, was expelled from the now almost defunct West Indian National Party. Combined with the left's problems in Trinidad and Tobago was the frustration caused by the nature of the metropole-colony relationship in which the Labour Government of Clement Atlee quietly abided by the recommendations of the majority report. The government did not wish to argue with the Colonial Office, especially when the needs of reconstruction, the cold war, and problems in the international economic system were more pressing. The majority report went into effect as the April 1950 Law, creating a transitional, quasi-ministerial government, which for the first time gave elected members a clear majority in both councils. The governor, however, retained reserve powers and continued as the de facto prime minister.

THE 1950 GENERAL ELECTIONS

Between 1946 and 1950 the major foundation of the left's strength, the labor movement, continued to fragment. The failure of the longshoremen's strike, the activities of Butler, and the "defections" of Gomes and Joseph to the government did not help left wing groups in the 1950 general elections. Not only was the United Front dead; the WINP had collapsed, its president, David Pitt, having gone to London. Solomon, frustrated by the situation, founded the Caribbean

Socialist Party (CSP). However, it was a weak organization held together by personal ties and was never an effective party machine. Although competing for 14 of the 18 possible seats, many of its most prominent members deserted its platform during and after the elections. One member, Simbhoonath Capildeo, even left for England upon realizing that his chances for victory were slim.[19] Solomon, the CSP's leader, was himself defeated in the election by a Chinese Creole, Norman Tang.

Other parties of the left were the Trinidad Labour Party, revitalized by new leadership, and the Trinidad and Tobago Union Council. The former organization was led by Raymond Hamel-Smith, a white Creole, who sought to make the old party a new force. With a more radical program, favoring the nationalization of the economy, the TLP attempted to capture the support of the urban working class. The working class, however, was not attracted to an organization tainted by the logo "old wine in a new bottle." Like the CSP, the TLP was unable to field the full number of candidates for the seats offered and suffered some of the same structural problems of personality over organization.

The most successful electoral alliance from the left was that formed between Butler and a group of young East Indian politicians. Unlike other groups, Butler was able to create a multiracial alliance between factions of the black oil workers and East Indian sugar workers, in a sense, forming a popular sector following. Butler's objectives were to forge a sugar-oil alliance, capture political power through electoral means, create a "people's" government, and restructure the distribution of political and economic power in the colony. Somewhat radical, the "plan" was not well conceived, lacking a clear-cut program.

Butler's major appeal was his charismatic personality, while his East Indian colleagues benefited from Indian discontent with traditional ethnic organizations and leaders advocating isolation and nonparticipation. Pro-Butler Indian politicians were also attracted to his banner as it attacked the orthodox trade union movement and threatened to destroy the influence of their rivals who controlled trade union "vote banks" in the sugar belt.[20] An exemplification of this was C. C. Abidh, the president of the Sugar Workers Union in central Trinidad, who was regarded as a conservative figure who had "sold out" workers after he had come to power in 1946. Due to changes in the electoral structure, Abidh's old constituency of Caroni, a core East Indian area and heartland of Trinidad's sugar industry, was divided into two new voting districts, Caroni South and Caroni North. Abidh was not reelected since a Butlerite, M. G. Sinanan, won in Caroni South and Kumar, an independent, won in Caroni North.

At the close of the election, the Butler alliance had won six seats, making it the largest bloc in the Legislative Council. Four of those successful candidates were East Indians, one was Butler, and one was A. P. T. James from Tobago. Of the other parties, the CSP, the TLP, and the rightist Political Progress Group (PPG), each captured two seats, while six independents were successful. Of those six, two soon joined the Butler bloc, giving that group eight seats, clearly the most numerous political formation in the incoming Legislative Council.

Although the parties of the left had a total of 12 seats, more than half of the 18 elective positions, they were 4 short of having half of the 26 seats in the Legislative Council, which included five nominated and three ex-officio members. This combination allowed the governor, Sir Hubert Rance, to outmaneuver the left and exclude the Butlerites from the Executive Council. With control over eight positions and support from moderate and conservative members, such as Gomes and Joseph, the governor was able to impose his will and maintain a conservative element in the government. Aided by the left's inability to present a strong coalition and by the structure of the government that maintained nominated members, conservative and moderate forces won a substantial victory that was earlier denied them at the polls.[21]

The left in Trinidad and Tobago failed to take power in 1950 for two major reasons. First, the official colonial government was hostile to populist-radical leaders like Butler and, when possible, sought to exclude them from positions of authority. Second, Trinidad's "maze of color" helped create a situation in which non-Afro-Creoles and non-Indo-Trinidadians were able to become power brokers between the major racial groups, while also dealing with the white political and economic elite. These two factors were the fundamental reasons for the left's inability to capture power and to form lasting political parties on a nationwide basis in 1950. In essence, the lack of any strong nationalistic party, in a time of growing racial awareness and communal tensions, made it necessary to deal with individuals who could easily traverse racial barriers and create multiracial alliances. Later, in 1956, the Peoples National Movement, fundamentally a middle-class Afro-Creole organization, would fill the gap. Before then, however, the middle minority politicians, such as Gomes, Tang, and Joseph, filled the vacuum and, by working with traditional conservative forces, kept the left, which was an alliance of radical bourgeois politicians and the many-headed labor movement, from power.

Another factor contributing to the left's failure in 1950 was the personality of Butler, who was regarded by many in the colonial administration as unsuitable to exercise power in the Executive Council due to a lack of education and general sophistication. It is important to note, however, that Butler's party was one of the first attempts at a truly multiracial working-class organization. As a leader Butler was, as Ryan notes, "a mesmerizer par excellence."²² A galvanizing orator, he stirred the black oil workers to vote and made the southern oil belt his personal stronghold even after the failures of the 1946-47 disturbances. His major shortcoming was a disdain for organization and inability to institutionalize a lasting party. Without its leader, the Butler party was nonexistant. Furthermore, Butler's radicalism and simplistic approach to politics alienated the majority of the Trinidadian middle sectors, who voted for more moderate political figures. Excluded from the Executive Council, Butler traveled to London on a political mission, and, without his presence, the party fragmented. By the 1956 elections it had ceased to be an important force.

THE MAZE OF COLOR AND THE MIDDLE SECTORS

During the period of 1946 to 1950, race and ethnicity emerged as important factors in Trinidad and Tobago's politics. The gradual retreat of the white elites from their positions of political dominance signaled that with representative government the field was increasingly open to other groups in society. The realization of this trend pushed many Afro-Creoles and East Indians to call for racial solidarity to defend their communal rights. From this situation the middle minorities arose, forming alliances and cooperating with both the Afro-Creole and East Indian middle sectors. On a wider basis the Trinidadian middle sectors found the maze of color, as Gomes called the colony's racial mixture, perplexing, and, like other societal elements, it was a source of disunity: there was a black, mixed, middle minority and an East Indian middle class. Each felt the pull of the other ethnic groups, while, at the same time, the capitalistic system pulled them together as a class sharing the same economic interests.

For the Trinidadian middle sectors, the 1950 general elections were significant in two ways. First and foremost, the government that emerged was led by a clique of men, predominantly from the middle minorities, who pursued a strong capitalist program to development, hence, strengthening the middle sectors vis-à-vis not only labor, but also the traditional vested interests.

Secondly, the success of the Political Progress Group (PPG) at capturing two seats in the Legislative Council indicated a change in the thinking of moderates in the middle sectors who realized that, if "they were to maintain some influence on the society, they had to be prepared to take part in its political life on an equal basis with other political formations."[23] A party composed of moderate members of the middle class, the PPG was a spinoff of the TLP, having a white Creole and mixed following. One of the leading figures affiliated with the PPG was Gomes, who had by 1950 moved to center-right in the political spectrum. Although Gomes and the PPG would not survive the elections of 1956, both were significant in the political and economic development of Trinidad and Tobago and the ascendancy of the middle class from 1950 to 1956.

THE KNOX STREET QUINTET

Changes in the world, ranging from the cold war to liberation struggles in Africa and Asia, had an influence on the formation of the government in Trinidad and Tobago in 1950. Sir Hubert Rance, the governor, sought to form a "responsible" government that would not seek rapid political change without consideration of developing an economic infrastructure capable of expanding the middle class, which was regarded by the British as an essential element in the emergence and maintenance of a democracy. It was crucial, therefore, to select members of the middle class who were conservative or moderate in political outlook and favored capitalistic economic development. Simultaneously, the question of race could be skirted if the new Executive Council was led by men who were from the middle minorities. Consequently, Rance turned to Albert Gomes to be de facto chief minister in his capacity as the minister of labor, industry and commerce. Also appointed were Norman Tang as minister of health and local government; V. Byran, the only Afro-Trinidadian, became minister of agriculture and lands; Roy Joseph was appointed minister of education and social services; and Ajodhasingh, the only East Indian, was minister of communications and works. The most visible members of the new administration were of Portuguese, Syrian, and Chinese descent, with the balance being held by a member from the Afro-Creole and East Indian communities. The one nominated member of the Executive Council, L. C. Hannays, was a white Creole and represented the conservative white upper class, although his role was minor.

The quasi-ministerial system worked for Trinidad and Tobago despite certain difficulties. Important to the usual smooth running of government was the "consistent adherence of the ministers to the principle of collective responsibility, despite the absence of any form of party system to command or sustain their allegiance."[24] This was an important development considering that some of the ministers had been political rivals in the past. It could almost be said that each individual minister ran his departments as he would his own government, and the unified front was no more than a thin veneer.

The driving power behind what became known as the "Knox Street Quintet" (the government was located on Knox Street) was Albert Gomes. While all ministers shared a common anticommunist ideology, the Portuguese Creole had the most dominating personality and was the main figure in Trinidad and Tobago's development from 1950 to 1955. As a contemporary notes of the Gomes period, "Albert Gomes was at the height of his power, bestriding the little world of Trinidad and Tobago like a colossus."[25]

The Portuguese Creole began his political career as a radical in the 1930s, gradually moving to the right. In the early 1940s he served on the Port of Spain Town Council, and in 1944 he was made deputy mayor. Voted into the Legislative Council in 1946 by the Afro-Creole working class, which had perceived him as a new Cipriani, his base of support changed as he became a leading member of the PPG (formed in 1947). He was reelected to the Legislative Council and the Executive Council in 1950.

At the time of his reelection, Gomes commented favorably upon the new constitution that maintained nominated members that allowed the governor to exclude the Butler alliance from the Executive Council. In his own words, he states, "I am glad that some of us insisted in the face of opposition that without the nominated system, this country would have been consigned to persons lacking in experience, balance and perspective; and indeed our plight might have been extremely desperate at this moment."[26] This attitude, his move to the right, and his appointment as labor, industry and commerce minister led many to call him a traitor to the working class and a servant of the white upper class. Despite his dectractors, of which there were many, Gomes and his fellow ministers did bring certain important advancements to the colony in both the political and economic sectors.[27]

THE CAPITALIST PATH

In early 1950 the British government reduced the West Indies sugar quota. To most British Caribbean colonies, the situation was worrisome due to the high dependence on that commodity.[28] Trinidad and Tobago, however, were not as dependent on sugar, having oil to stave off the spector of economic collapse. The Trinidadian political elite decided, in view of the plight of those islands highly dependent on sugar, to adopt a policy of import substitution, the domestic production of many goods usually imported, a trend followed by many tropical countries after World War II.[29]

Two ideas were behind the adoption of the import substitution policy: one, dependency on the metropole would be reduced and, two, capitalist economic development, along domestic lines, would help expand the size of the middle sectors. To make the entire program successful, responsible government was needed to guarantee political stability conducive to creating a climate attractive to foreign investment. Large injections of foreign capital, it was perceived, were required to improve the colony's infrastructure and, eventually, through trickle-down economics, improve the "average" Trinidadian's living standard. To this end Gomes, as minister of labor, industry and commerce, sought to provide the responsible government needed, and he mediated usually in favor of management, though not always, in labor-industrial disputes. From 1950 to 1956 few strikes disrupted the colony's affairs in sharp contrast to the turmoil in neighboring British Guiana.

The "Red Scare" in the Caribbean, caused in part by the leftward movement of the Guatemalan government under Jacabo Arbebz (1950-54) and the Marxist leanings of the People's Progressive Party (PPP) in British Guiana, allowed Gomes to bring pressure against the more radical union leaders.[30] Trinidad and Tobago's trade unions were forced to withdraw from the Soviet-dominated International Workers Union, and the colony's small number of Marxists were harassed by the police and forced to curtail their activities. Other leftist leaders, such as Rojas, had to emphasize that they were not communists and did not favor revolutionary tactics. To Gomes communism was an evil that threatened to disrupt not only capitalist development, but also Westernization of Trinidad and Tobago, a process already jeopardized by "extraterritorial nostalgia" held by the various ethnic groups for their respective "homelands." Gomes strongly felt that Westernization or the continuation of the assimilation process was a "sine qua non of national survival to the islands" and communism cast a shadow over this.[31]

Under the Gomes administration, Trinidad and Tobago's economy enjoyed a moderate boom.[32] Although manufacturing was an auxiliary sector of much less quantitative significance than petroleum and agriculture, it began to grow. Considering the few light industries that existed in the 1940s, by 1952 asphalt, beer, bricks, cigarettes, cotton textiles, glass bottles, matches, rum, and wooden boxes were in production, and asbestos cement products, cement, industrial chemicals, and paints were planned to begin production.[33] A considerable number of smaller firms also existed dealing with a plethora of products ranging from aerated waters and artificial teeth to stockfeeds and toys.

One of the first actions undertaken by the Gomes administration to develop the colony's economic life was the creation of a five-year economic program for the years 1951-55. With a budget of $36 million, its purpose was to improve water supply, education, electricity, agricultural supplies, roads and communications, public buildings, housing, and medical services.[34] The costs for the five-year program were met by the colony's surplus balances ($6 million), the Colonial Development and Welfare Fund ($4.8 million), and a $28 million loan under the Economic Program Ordinance. The government also worked with the Barclays Overseas Development Corporation Limited, a financial organization formed by Barclays Bank in 1946 to assist economic development in territories in which the bank operated by providing medium-term finance for sound development projects of all kinds.[35]

The government's most effective measure was the passage of the Pioneer Industries Ordinance of 1952, which endeavored "to smooth the path of the would-be investor by special privileges such as the duty-free import of construction materials and plant" and a five-year income tax holiday.[36] In addition, the government offered facilities for the remission of capital and profits abroad, reserved certain areas of Crown Land for industrial purposes at moderate rentals, and took steps to establish an Industrial Loan Fund to assist the financing of approved industries.

The Pioneer Industries Ordinance was also passed in British Guiana, Barbados, and Jamaica and was a significant piece of legislation in that it marked a definite move away from, though not an abandonment of, the agricultural sector. Trinidad, like its Caribbean Commonwealth neighbors, was attempting "by all means . . . to encourage the expansion of industrial activity."[37] Paradoxically, the policy to encourage industrial growth brought new competition among the territories that had earlier competed in the production and exportation of primary commodities. Unlike its neighbors, Trinidad, with cheap and available oil and a stable and capitalist-oriented government, "led the way for British colonies in offering inducements such as tax holidays to pioneer industry."³⁸ The successful growth of the industrial sector, though not massive, and the continued wealth of the petroleum industry still led to Trinidad's being regarded as the island that was by "far the richest of the British Caribbean Territories."³⁹

Since over 80 percent of Trinidad's exports in 1953 were petroleum and asphalt products, the importance of these industries, especially the former, was not lost on the government, which was careful not to neglect this sector.⁴⁰ By 1953 annual production, at 22.3 million barrels, up from 21.3 million in 1952, was clearly on the upswing. This was influenced, in part, by increased refinery capacity caused by the opening by Trinidad Leaseholds Ltd. of a modern fluid catalytic cracking plant, which was an important step in keeping the island's oil industry competitive on the world market. It also reflected that the oil firms, like the British-owned Trinidad Leaseholds, had confidence in the colony's stability and in the administration of Gomes and his associates.

Another factor contributing to the prosperity of Trinidad's petroleum industry was the importation of Colombian and Venezuelan crude, which supplemented local production. In 1952 alone, 17 million barrels of this foreign crude passed through the colony's refineries. The combination of political stability, strategic location for the importation of Colombian and Venezuelan crude, and the modernization and expansion of refinery capacity caused the total value of output created by the industry to rise from $100 million (British West Indian dollars) in 1952 to $180,961,800 in 1955-56.⁴¹

While the industrial and petroleum sectors of the Trinidadian economy expanded under the quasi-ministerial government, agriculture, with few exceptions, like citrus fruit and coffee, continued to have difficulties. Sugar, the colony's second major export, and cocoa, the third, declined in exports in the early 1950s. Although total sugar production declined from 146,508 tons in 1950 to 137,358 in 1952, a recovery briefly set in and, by 1955, 192,793 tons were produced. The fortunes of the cocoa industry, however, continued to decline as prices on the world market often fluctuated considerably, and the cocoa plant itself in Trinidad and Tobago was afflicted by a persistent disease.

The cocoa farmers' plight did not go unheeded by the government. Under Victor Byran, minister of agriculture, public expenditure for the agricultural sector rose from $1,259,636 (British West Indian dollars in 1951) to $2,016,060 (1955), part of which funded the "cocoa pool," a mechanism to help cushion the small farmer against seasonal price changes.[42]   Although the minister of agriculture was often accused of being partial to the planters and the merchant shippers of the colony's agricultural goods, he clearly had not forgotten the "little man" as exemplified by the cocoa pool and assistance provided small growers in the rehabilitation of abandoned and semi-abandoned plantations.[43]

POVERTY, RACE, POPULATION, AND UNEMPLOYMENT

The period of 1950-56 was one of overall economic growth for Trinidad and Tobago. This growth, however, was not balanced since the bulk of profits flowed out of the colony to the metropole where the shareholders of large companies, especially in the oil industry, reaped the benefits. Alongside the wealth of the white upper class and the improving standard of living of the middle sectors, the largest part of the population, the Afro-Creole and East Indian popular sectors remained on the margins of economic growth. Moreover, unemployment at 6.6 percent in 1951 was growing.[44]

Significantly, the sector that employed the most people was agriculture. Real wages, though increased, were often not high enough to adjust to rising prices for food and other items due to inflation. Furthermore, the declining fortunes of agriculture cast long shadows over the futures of those it employed. Of a working population of 216,186 in 1952, 66,950, mainly East Indians, were employed in the agricultural sector, while the most lucrative industries, petroleum and asphalt, combined with those of electricity, water supply, and sanitary services, numbered 13,065, a substantial difference. The latter industries employed mainly Afro-Creoles, hence, in effect, dividing the colony's major sources of employment along racial lines. The second and third largest employers respectively were in government, community, and personal services (the civil service) with 52,514 and in manufacturing with 31,610.[45] Like the construction industry (12,344), the workers were predominantly Afro-Creole. Outside of agriculture, the East Indians had penetrated the transport and storage businesses and were gradually moving into the commercial sector alongside the Syrian, Portuguese, mixed, Afro-Creole, and Chinese middle sectors. The bulk of East Indians, however, remained in rural areas, tied to the production of sugar, cocoa, and coffee.

The East Indians, on the lowest societal rung for many years, began pushing for a higher place in society and competing with other races in all professions. Their push for equal status alarmed not only the Afro-Creole middle class, but also the black working class, both of which hoped to gain political power before the East Indians. Therefore, the continued self-imposed insularity of many East Indians, the rapid increase in their numbers as large families was their societal norm, and the gradual assimilation brought on by state funds for Hindu schools to teach English made race, birth control, economic policy, and constitutional reforms difficult and related issues.

The problems of political and socioeconomic development, emerging as increasingly important forces in the 1950s, were reflected in W. A. Arthur Lewis's report, *Industrialisation and the Gold Coast* (1954) and the Colonial Office's *Industrial Development in Jamaica, Trinidad, Barbados, and British Guiana* (1954). While both reports varied in their approach, Lewis was careful to underscore, "If agriculture is stagnant, industry cannot grow."[46] He further argues that "industrial development . . . must depend upon an increase *pari passu* with internal consumption," which "must come in the main from an expansion of agricultural production."[47] Both reports sought to dissuade colonial governments from rushing into industrial enterprises, except for public utilities. Industrialization was regarded as an important stage of development, but not as a panacea; it was something that had to be approached on a gradualistic basis with proper agricultural foundations.

To attract foreign investors, Lewis outlined a number of "relevant actions" that included conducting research, gaining the interest of industrialists, advising the initiators of new industries, devising the right forms of assistance, providing and administrating credit, organizing industrial estates, and occasionally operating state-owned enterprises. In following this line of thought, the Colonial Office mission stated: "Overseas investors cannot be forced to invest in the West Indies [and] can afford to be selective." They "will wish to be satisfied . . . that any facilities granted are not likely to be capriciously removed as soon as their money is committed, and that the general political atmosphere is not hostile to private enterprise."[48]

The Colonial Office was against company managers having any legal objection "to employ local personnel in senior posts against his better judgement." Lewis's opinion differed somewhat and foreshadowed what was eventually to occur in both the Caribbean and Africa: "foreign business men should not be allowed in the country unless they play their part in training Africans to do their job." Gomes and his associates had followed what the two reports outlined, although concurring with the Colonial Office on the last point concerning the role of foreign nationals and employment procedures. It was clearly not in their interests to antagonize the foreign firms at a time when their investment was wanted.

While industrialization had been initiated, it was not a massive affair. It did, however, have the effect of reinforcing the pattern of relegating the agricultural sector to the economic periphery. Moreover, Trinidad traditionally imported many of its foodstuffs, such as vegetables and meats, from Venezuela, Canada, and the United States. Although fishing was done, most of the colony's fish came from North America, mainly Canada. The export orientation of the economy, founded upon the profits of the oil industry and supplemented by sugar, therefore, made Trinidad a comparatively wealthy colony, able to afford the importation of food, with the exception of citrus fruit locally grown and canned. Even citrus had limited growth by the mid-1950s as overseas competition and freight charges undercut West Indian produce on the British market.[49]

Like other nations emerging in the developing world that were dependent on the petroleum industry, Trinidad and Tobago's agricultural sector would decline, and, from the 1950s onward, food imports would continue to rise. The decline of domestic agriculture created problems of unemployment and underemployment, factors that had occurred in the 1930s. What was now different was the rapidly expanding size of the population. In 1940 the population was estimated at 484,900.[50] By 1955 the population had risen to an estimated 720,450, a substantial increase of 48.6 percent.[51] The Colonial Office had also warned that industrialization would not solve the West Indian problem of a rapidly growing labor force.

The West Indies, with the exception of British Guiana and British Honduras (Belize), were island-states with limited space. No vast hinterlands existed as possible escape valves for surplus people. Even the larger islands of Jamaica, Trinidad, and Barbados were affected as overpopulation became a cloud on the horizon. The answer was family planning, which Barbados, with its highly homogeneous population of Protestant Afro-Creoles, quickly adopted.

Trinidad and Tobago's population was very different than its sister colony's. These differences, Afro-Creoles, East Indians, and middle minorities, greatly complicated the issue. Birth control soon became a major political issue in Trinidad, especially when considering the high birthrate of the East Indians. Black Trinidad's trade union mouthpiece, *Clarion*, criticized Barbados: "If ever there was a time when the coloured people of Trinidad could ill afford to reduce their numbers by the practice of artificial birth control, it is now. Yet we are being advised to commit race suicide."[52] Resistance to birth control remained a major issue as the rapidly growing population threatened to far outstrip the limited resources of the two islands. Overpopulation meant more unemployed, more mouths to feed, and less economic advancement. For groups like the East Indians, however, it meant more help on the farms, more voters, and, hopefully, more say in governing the colony, something the Afro-Creoles feared. Furthermore, Gomes, as a conservative Catholic, had considerable influence in the obstruction of any introduction of family planning. This would continue to be a major issue in the nation's politics, which would ultimately help to undermine Gomes's position in government.

FEDERATION AND CONSTITUTIONAL REFORM

Although earlier attempts at federation of the British Caribbean islands had been attempted, the United Kingdom in 1947, at the Montego Bay Conference in Jamaica, initiated a new effort, clearly aimed at creating a federal state that one day would become an independent member of the British Commonwealth. In 1950 the Standing Closer Association Committee, which had come out of the 1947 meeting, recommended federation along Australian lines as "the shortest path towards a real political independence for the British peoples in the region."[53] Moreover, according to *The Economist*, "A federal West Indian Government should be able to aim at a better balanced economy for the whole area whereas there is always the danger of overlapping and competition between the islands if each tries to diversify its economy at its own sweet will."[54]

The British envisioned a state composed of Barbados, British Guiana, British Honduras, Jamaica, Antigua and Barbuda, St. Kitts-Nevis, Montserrat, Trinidad and Tobago, Grenada, St. Vincent, St. Lucia, and Dominica. The federation would have a governor general, senate, and house of assembly, the last of which would handle defense, external affairs, exchange control, and the raising of external loans. The house of assembly would have 23 seats with each territory represented according to the size of its population: Montserrat, the smallest, was to have 1 seat; Jamaica, the largest, 16; and Trinidad and Tobago, the second largest, 9. A council of state, with 14 members, would be the executive arm, elected from the house of assembly, the latter being the "policy forming instrument in the Constitution."[55] The governor general, before independence was to be granted, was to act on the council's advice, although he would have reserve powers to override its decisions in matters of defense, foreign affairs, and financial stability.

The proposal of creating a federal state caused a negative reaction in the Eastern Caribbean where the East Indian communities of British Guiana and Trinidad feared Afro-Creole preponderance. The East Indian community of British Guiana even suggested its own "federation" with Trinidad.[56] With the background of ethnic and religious rioting in India, to which many Indo-Trinidadians were sensitive, the government of Trinidad was "cautious in comment," saying only that the federation idea "provides a workable basis for the attainment of ultimate Dominion status."[57] Although the government of Trinidad and Tobago sent representatives to the federal discussions, such as the London meeting in early 1956, little was done to promote the issue except when it was used as a political tool in the constitutional debate of 1955-56, which dominated the closing days of the Gomes's administration.

The major issue of the constitutional debate, which reopened in 1955, was whether the ministerial system has "worked satisfactorily enough to allow removal of the restraints with which it was hedged, or was there need for a further transitional period?"[58] The federal issue obviously had an impact on the findings of the Sinanan Committee, which argued that the colony's political development had not advanced to the point that extensive changes were needed in the constitution. One underlying reason for the committee's conclusion was the failure of any strong party to emerge that was multiethnic and had "nationwide" appeal as did the political parties of Jamaica. Moreover:

> The imminence of a West Indian Federation also influenced some members to advocate the continuance of the unicameral system as they considered that the existence of the Federal Parliament would make a more complicated system undesirable on grounds both of the extra expense involved and the reduction in legislative jurisdiction of the island legislature.[59]

After lengthy debates, the governor, Sir Edward Beetham, accepted a majority report with certain recommendations. While agreeing to have an elected minister of finance replace the appointed financial secretary, he suggested that the size of the Executive Council should be 10, rather than the suggested 12, since anything over 8 elected ministers and 2 officials would be "top heavy."[60] Beetham also felt that the Executive Council could govern with the support of 5 nominated members.

Crucial to this system was the need of having an elected head of state from the majority party who would function as a spokesman for Trinidad and Tobago in the federal negotiations and, in effect, be a team leader at home. Responding to the governor's criticism that such a structure would inhibit the development of political parties as "the pluralism of the society and the absence of an undisputed popular leader made such a majority difficult to mobilize," an agreement was made that a leader could be selected by a government coalition.[61]

The Trinidad and Tobago (Constitution) Order in Council of 1956 was the end-product of the majority report and the governor's recommendations: the number of elected seats in the Legislative Council was increased from 18 to 24, a chief minister was to be appointed, and the number of ministers rose from five to eight, including a minister of finance for the first time. Two ex officio and five nominated members would be maintained in the Legislative Council, and the former group would also be in the Executive Council with the governor.

The new constitution, in general, was well received, although members of the East Indian community had doubts that were related to the entire question of West Indian federalism. Like their counterparts in British Guiana, the majority of Indo-Trinidadians opposed federation, fearing that the immigration of blacks from the smaller islands would "come and mix with the Indian race and pollute it."[62] While being accused of being antifederation, East Indian legislators argued that what they opposed was not the concept of federation; rather, it was the idea of unrestricted immigration.[63] Despite protestations by East Indian politicians, non-Indian leaders regarded their obstruction as planned and dangerous. The fear also existed that the People's Democratic Party (PDP), founded in 1953 by Bhadose Maraj, could bring a Hindu-dominated government to Trinidad and Tobago. In an effort to stave off that possibility, Gomes and his associates postponed elections from September 1955 to September 1956 during which time the old ministerial clique advocated federation and sought to organize political machines to help their reelection bids. The postponement, however, allowed the Afro-Creole middle class to mobilize behind Eric Williams and the People's National Movement. By 1956 the decade of the middle minorities had come to an end as the federation issue helped stimulate the Afro-Creole middle sectors to action.

NOTES

1. Ivar Oxaal, *Black Intellectuals Come to Power: The Rise of Creole Nationalism in Trinidad and Tobago* (Cambrdige, Mass.: Schenkman, 1968), p. 89.
2. Ibid.
3. John La Guerre, "The General Elections of 1946 in Trinidad and Tobago," *Social and Economic Studies* 21 (June 1972): 187.
4. Patrick Solomon, *Solomon, An Autobiography* (Trinidad: Inprint Caribbean, 1975), p. 87.
5. Paul Blanshard, *Democracy and Empire in the Caribbean: A Contemporary Review* (New York: MacMillan, 1947), p. 115.
6. Solomon, *Autobiography*, p. 87.
7. Ibid., pp. 82-83.
8. Ibid., p. 84.
9. It should be noted that a number of workers were not taken back since the Shipping Association sought to make an example of those who went on strike.
10. Solomon, *Autobiography*, p. 86.
11. Quoted in Ann Spackman, "Constitutional Development in Trinidad and Tobago," *Social and Economic Studies* 14 (December 1965): 285.
12. Selwyn Ryan, *Race and Nationalism in Trinidad and Tobago: A Study of Decolonization in a Multiracial Society* (Toronto: University of Toronto Press, 1972), p. 107.
13. Solomon, *Autobiography*, p. 107.
14. "Debate on the Constitutional Reform Proposals," *Hansard*, November 22, 1946, pp. 41-43.
15. Ryan, *Race and Nationalism*, p. 83.
16. *Hansard*, December 6, 1946, p. 178.
17. Ibid.
18. Ryan, *Race and Nationalism*, p. 83.
19. According to the July 29, 1950, issue of *The Clarion*, "CSP Rats Desert Sinking Ship," the rats were Capildeo, Jack Kelshall, A. P. T. James, and C. P. Alexander.
20. Ryan, *Race and Nationalism*, p. 89.
21. The problems of unity on the left were well known as exemplified by the September 23, 1950, issue of *The Clarion*, which stated, "There is little likelihood of a coalition of elected members in an effort to decide the composition of the Executive Council. Such a coalition will have to include Butler. It is doubtful whether other members would agree to that."
22. Ryan, *Race and Nationalism*, p. 92.
23. Ibid., p. 87.
24. *Colonial Reports: Trinidad and Tobago 1952* (London: Her Majesty's Stationery Office, 1954), p. 4.

25. Winston Mahabir, *In and Out of Politics: Tales of the Government of Dr. Eric Williams from the Notebooks of a Former Minister* (Trinidad: Inprint Caribbean, 1978), p. 21.

26. "The PPG and the Political Future," *Trinidad Guardian*, October 19, 1950, p. 1.

27. One of his most bitter detractors was Solomon, who wrote, "I do not see, even now [1975], how I could have possibly have cooperated in any administration with people like Gomes, Roy Joseph and Norman Tang." See Solomon, *Autobiography*, p. 130. Solomon's feelings against Gomes and his associates were founded on that group's Machiavellian political tactics, which included bribery and other acts of corruption, as well as the use of name calling.

28. "West Indian Sugar Negotiations," *The Times*, May 2, 1950, p. 3; "West Indies Sugar, Criticism of the British Offer," *The Times*, June 7, 1950, p. 5; and "Empire Sugar Policy, Ministers' Reply to West Indies, No Revised Offer," *The Times*, June 8, 1950, p. 6.

29. W. Arthur Lewis, *The Evolution of the International Economic Order* (Princeton: Princeton University Press, 1978), p. 31.

30. In both Guatemala and British Guiana, the United States and the United Kingdom intervened in domestic affairs to crush Marxist-Leninist or leftist-leaning forces. See Stephen Schlesinger and Stephen Kinzer, *Bitter Fruit: The Untold Story of the American Coup in Guatemala* (Garden City, N.Y.: Doubleday, 1982); Cole Blasier, *The Hovering Giant: U.S. Responses to Revolutionary Change in Latin America* (Pittsburgh: University of Pittsburgh Press, 1979); Thomas J. Spinner, Jr., *A Political and Social History of Guyana, 1945-1983* (Boulder: Westview Press, 1984); and "Causes of the Crisis in British Guiana, Why the Troops Were Sent," *The Times*, October 16, 1953, p. 9.

31. Albert Gomes, *Through the Maze of Colour* (Port of Spain: Longman Caribbean, 1974), p. 83.

32. *Report on the Colony of Trinidad and Tobago for the Year 1953* (Trinidad: Government Printing Office, 1955), p. 2.

33. *Colonial Reports: Trinidad and Tobago, 1952* (Trinidad: Government Printing Office, 1952), p. 80.

34. Ibid., p. 10.

35. Ibid., p. 4.

36. "Industrial Report on West Indies," *The Times*, October 8, 1953, p. 8. Also see *The West Indies and Caribbean Year Book, 1953-1954* (Montreal: Thomas Skinner of Canada, 1954), p. 154.

37. "Industrial Report on West Indies."

38. "Land of Calypso, Oil and Sugar, the Secret of Trinidad's Wealth," *The Times*, January 28, 1955, p. 9.

39. Ibid.

40. *West Indies and Caribbean Year Book, 1953-54*, p. 159.

41. *Colonial Reports, 1952* (see note 33, above), p. 2; and *West Indies and Caribbean Year Book, 1955-56* (Montreal: Thomas Skinner of Canada, 1956), p. 307.

42. *The West Indies and Caribbean Year Book, 1952* (Montreal: Thomas Skinner of Canada, 1952), p. 152; and *West Indies and Caribbean Year Book, 1955-56*, p. 299.

43. Ryan, *Race and Nationalism*, p. 96.

44. *Colonial Reports, 1952* (see note 33, above), p. 13.

45. Ibid., p. 16.

46. *Report on Industrialization and the Gold Coast* (Accra, Ghana: Gold Coast Government, 1954) as quoted in "Rules for Developers" *The Economist*, January 2, 1954, p. 6.

47. *Industrial Development in Jamaica, Trinidad, Barbados and British Guiana* (London: Colonial Paper No. 294, Her Majesty's Stationery Office, 1954) as quoted in *The Economist*, January 2, 1954, p. 6.

48. Ibid.

49. "Jamaica's Claims," *The Economist*, July 9, 1955, p. 116.

50. *The West Indies Year Book, 1941-42* (Montreal: Thomas Skinner of Canada, 1942), p. 265.

51. *The West Indies and Caribbean Year Book, 1956-57* (Montreal: Thomas Skinner of Canada, 1957), p. 265.

52. Quoted in *The Times*, January 6, 1955, p. 9.

53. "A West Indies Federation, Proposals for the Colonies," *The Times*, March 10, 1950, p. 5.

54. "Standing Closer," *The Economist*, July 8, 1950, p. 66.

55. Ibid.

56. "British Guiana and Federation, Guarantees Required," *The Times*, March 11, 1950, p. 5.

57. "West Indies Report," *The Times*, March 13, 1950, p. 3.

58. Ryan, *Race and Nationalism*, p. 97.

59. *Report of the Constitutional Committee, Council Paper No. 16* (Port of Spain: Government Printery, 1956), p. 5.

60. Ryan, *Race and Nationalism*, p. 98.

61. Ibid., p. 99.

62. Albert Gomes in Parliament, *Hansard*, December 10, 1954, p. 690.

63. Ryan, *Race and Nationalism*, p. 100.

5

Eric Williams and the Birth of the PNM, 1955-56

The People's National Movement (PNM) was officially launched on January 19, 1956. Its undisputed leader, Dr. Eric Williams, an Afro-Creole, soon caught the attention of not only the Afro-Trinidadians, but also the black popular sectors. Although the PNM became a colonywide organization and won the general elections of 1956, Williams was the figure with whom the majority of voters identified. Beyond the strongly worded speeches about decolonization of Trinidad and Tobago, the need for sweeping political changes and calls for racial unity, Williams turned the PNM into an effective and enduring political organization, founded upon the support of mainly the Afro-Creole middle sectors. Added to this elite were elements of the white Creole community and, significantly, a number of Muslim and Christian East Indians. This racial and political combination would undermine the position of the middle minority politicians by dividing society between the Afro-Creoles and their allies and the Hindu East Indians, in effect, terminating the need for racial and ethnic go-betweens. To comprehend fully the post-1956 period of Trinidadian political development, the maintenance of the capitalist system with moderate changes and emergent Afro-Creole dominance, an understanding of Eric Williams and the founding of the PNM are, therefore, essential.

WILLIAMS AND THE INFLUENCE OF CHILDHOOD

Eric Eustace Williams was born in 1911, the son of a minor postal official. The future prime minister was the first of 12 children in a family that was lower middle class and struggling to maintain its position in society. It is probable that the Williams family feared "falling back" into the ranks of the working class and, despite financial difficulties, sought to maintain the veneer of being bourgeois. An exemplification of this is observable in Williams's comments on the family diet:

> The Christmas table was incomplete without its imported delicacies. Our Sunday table was also good, its variety of meats and vegetables again proving us good Trinidadians. But for the rest of the week the meat supply was supplemented by beef bones for soup, salt fish, corned beef, and, not infrequently, our meat was bought in the afternoons when it was cheaper.[1]

While the family diet was usually constant, the Williams's housing changed several times since "descending family fortunes were reflected in the descent from the water closet to the cesspit and in one bad case the bailiff appeared."[2]

To Eric Williams the reasons for his family's position were the structure of colonial society, which discriminated against those of darker skin, and "the steady and inexorable disproportion between population and resources."[3] His father was dark brown, lacked money, and had no more than a primary school training. By the time of his retirement in 1935, his salary had risen from $56 a month in 1910 to $180.[4] Considering the rising cost of living and the needs of a large family, the salary of a minor postal official did not go far. The larger and more fundamental problem, however, was that his parents, who were devout Catholics, did not practice any kind of birth control; hence, the failure "to control births meant an increasing inability to provide for the children after birth."[5] His parent's dilemma was "to be faithful children of the Church or not be poor parents." Consequently, life was difficult and, of the 12 children born between 1911 and 1931, one died at the age of nine months, and medical attention for the family was almost nonexistent. Even after Williams's serious fall in a game of football, which eventually resulted in the loss of hearing, a doctor was not called. Williams himself admits that he did not see a dentist until he was 16. The only exception was his mother, whose health deteriorated due to repeated births. As Williams comments, "She became prematurely old, fat, and querulous, a constant victim of headaches. She called more and more for dental care and protective foods . . . each birth bringing her closer and closer to the edge."[6]

While the two factors of racial discrimination and overpopulation shaped Williams's perception of the world, his father's understanding that education was the vehicle of upward social mobility was deeply ingrained in his son. Encouraged by his parents, Eric Williams became a highly successful student, attending Queen's Royal College, the state school. Winning a coveted island scholarship, Williams left Trinidad to attend Oxford.

From his childhood in Trinidad, Williams developed three perceptions that were later evident in his politics. First and foremost, the discrimination suffered by his father due to skin color made him sensitive to the inequalities of the colonial world, something that was reinforced and turned into "a chip on his shoulder" during his time with the Anglo-American Caribbean Commission. Second, Williams, from personal experience, saw the need for birth control in a society of limited resources, a view that later brought him to clash with the conservative and rigid Catholic Church. Third, the importance of education was never forgotten. Some of the major reforms during Williams's long tenure of office were made in this area.

FROM OXFORD TO THE ANGLO-AMERICAN COMMISSION

In the heart of the British Empire and close to the events leading to World War II in Europe, Williams's Oxford years in the 1930s were important in how he regarded England and race relations in predominantly white societies. While his dissertation, "The Economic Aspects of the Abolition of the West Indian Slave Trade and Slavery," brought him his doctorate in December 1938, he felt that its research had been handicapped by a lack of funding due to racial discrimination. Leaving Oxford, Williams went to Howard University in Washington, D.C., where he became an assistant professor of social and political science (1939-48). At the "Negro Oxford," as he called it, Williams published some of his major works including *The Negro in the Caribbean* (1942) and *Capitalism and Slavery* (1944) in which the fall of slavery was "proven" to be a part of the movement of mature British capitalism. Both books, influenced by Marxist dialectic, dealt with the history of slavery, the sugar industry, the Negro wage earner, the structure of Caribbean society, the racial problem, education, the political system, and U.S. intervention and trade.

In researching his books, Williams traveled extensively throughout the Caribbean, meeting many of the leading intellectuals in the non-Anglo regions. In particular, a trip in 1940 made a lasting impression as it occurred during the time when Churchill gave Roosevelt the right to have bases in Trinidad. After visiting Haiti, with its history of poverty and U.S. intervention, Williams pondered what U.S. involvement in Trinidadian affairs would bring. As he comments of Haiti, "It sufficed to see the Presidential Palace and the well-to-do middle class houses against the background of the peasantry who seemed to be everywhere, tattered, barefooted, eternal *marchands* selling their vegetables and fruit and their astonishingly good handicraft for a pittance. Other things stood out—the intellectual poverty reflected in the bookshops (such a contrast with Havana) and the ubiquity of the army."[7] In comparing Haiti and the Trujillo dictatorship in the Dominican Republic to the Germany of Hitler and in depicting the desolation of Puerto Rico, Williams regarded U.S. intervention with serious misgivings. He comments, "Was this, I asked myself, the manifest destiny of Trinidad and Tobago? If Haiti's isolation, poverty and tyranny after independence represented one lesson to West Indian colonials, did the land of Toussaint L'Ouverture pose yet another lesson—that West Indian colonials were destined to graduate from European colonialism to American?"[8] By asking such questions, Williams had recognized, at an early stage, the emerging structure of international relations in the Eastern Caribbean. His sense of West Indian nationalism, already fueled by various episodes of racial discrimination, was further developed by his travels in the Caribbean and his period of teaching at Howard.

What gave Williams his "sense of mission" and the need to "strive after power" in a Laswellian fashion was his work with the Anglo-American Caribbean Commission. Formed in March 1942 with the purpose of encouraging and strengthening socioeconomic cooperation in the Caribbean, the Anglo-U.S. organization became a battleground between Williams and British colonial officials. Even his appointment to the commission as a researcher was done against the wishes of the British and at the urging of Charles W. Taussig, one of President Roosevelt's close associates. The critical views of the Trinidadian, as expressed in his books, on the structure of colonial society, with its prejudices, and privileged positions of the vested interests in the region, had made him many enemies both within the Anglo-American Caribbean Commission and without. U.S. support continued until Williams pointed to race relations problems in Puerto Rico and the Virgin Islands in a report. As the U.S. government did not want to acknowledge that a racial problem existed, the report caused some irritation. In June 1948 Williams returned to Trinidad as the deputy chairman of the Caribbean Research Council of the Caribbean Commission, but by that time both U.S. and British officials were locked in a battle of words with him. Part of the problem lay in different interpretations of events in the Caribbean, since Williams was strongly anti-imperialist and his colleagues were conservative. However, personality differences were also a factor. Finally, on May 26, 1955, after several years of bickering, the commission informed Williams that his service contract, due to expire on June 21, 1955, would not be renewed. It was a bitter pill to swallow, but an essential factor in pushing him into the political arena.[9]

By 1955 Williams, fired by self-righteousness over constant discrimination, had moved left of the political center, his ideas bordering on socialism. The core of his thinking, however, had shifted from the academic to the need for action, and that action was to be the push to independence and the decolonization of Trinidad and Tobago. In a sense his strategy had already been outlined in *The Negro in the Caribbean*, where he "praised the rise of working-class leaders in the West Indies and exhorted the traditionally aloof coloured middle class to join the struggle."[10] He would continue to praise the working class while bringing the middle sectors into the struggle for independence.

FORERUNNERS OF THE PEOPLE'S NATIONAL MOVEMENT

Significantly, Williams's dismissal from the Caribbean Commission coincided with the emergence of a new middle-class political movement in Trinidad, the People's National Movement. The year of 1955 was crucial not only to the future prime minister, but also for the middle classes. Prior to 1955 the Afro-Trinidadian middle sectors had failed to produce a responsible, educated, and polished leadership as had their counterparts in Jamaica and Barbados.[11] Simply stated, the bulk of the middle sectors had long been alienated from the political system due, in large part, to a "crisis of confidence."[12] It was felt that the West Indies would never be able to "stand alone nationally, economically, culturally or otherwise without the protection of a great power."[13] The dependence on an outside power was coupled with a reluctance to become involved in the gritty game of politics, which had, since the 1930s, been dominated by leftist demagogues such as Butler, who a large majority of the Afro-Creole middle class avoided being associated with. This reluctance was strengthened by a fear that a political system without the guiding hand of the governor and appointees would result in the victory by the left as occurred in British Guiana. The "rum and rotti" political campaigning of Trinidad and Tobago had no appeal to a group that was more concerned with improving its material well-being and was apprehensive of falling back into the ranks of the lower classes.

Not all members of the middle sectors avoided politics. Three groups were evident: the radicals, including such individuals as Solomon, who were very active in government but were usually in the opposition; the progressives such as those who were members of the Teachers Economic and Cultural Association (TECA) and the Political Education Group (PEG); and the moderate-conservative clique, which was dominated by the mixed minorities and had enjoyed power from 1950 to 1956. Of these three, the second group was the one destined to produce the first nationwide political party, which would dominate Trinidad and Tobago's government well into the 1980s.

The Teachers Economic and Cultural Association was founded in 1935 by a group of radical urban Afro-Creoles who were frustrated by the discriminatory practices of religious and state schools, which were largely staffed by whites. These practices included low salaries, slow advancement, and limited possibilities of upward mobility. The established Teachers Union was regarded as weak and ineffectual, and TECA sought to remedy the situation. While the TECA was concerned with financial and professional dimensions, it had another important objective—uplifting the people.[14] To help the formation of a mass culture, a subcommittee, referred to as the People's Education Movement, was established in 1950. Its members included A. A. Alexander, J. Sheldon Donaldson, and F. G. Maynard, all of whom were to be important early figures in the PNM. Interestingly, the majority of the subcommittee were "renegade" Catholics who had, like Williams, come to disagree with their church over a number of issues including education and birth control.

Predominantly an Afro-Creole organization, the Political Education Group was composed of urban professionals and had developed from a number of private discussions inspired, in part, by a series of public lectures given in Woodford Square in 1955 by Eric Williams. As Ryan notes of the PEG, "Every aspect of the country's political, economic, and social life was systematically discussed at their meetings. By the middle of 1955 the group agreed that there was need for a new party which would emphasize mass political education and not the mere pursuit of power."[15] The natural choice for political leader was Eric Williams, who had become the group's informal head. Williams, involved in the battle of words with the Caribbean Commission, did not immediately become fully active and hesitated in accepting any commitments. However, with his dismissal he changed his mind.

CASTING DOWN THE BUCKET

Shortly after receiving notice of his dismissal by the Anglo-American Caribbean Commission, Williams was involved in discussions about the formation of a new political party in Trinidad and Tobago. As Williams noted, the basic strategy "was to reach the public."[16] Sponsored by the People's Education Movement, he made a public lecture of his relations with the Caribbean Commission in Woodford Square, which sits before the Red House, the colony's legislative building. Significantly, the evening on which he spoke was the same date, June 21, 1955, that he left the commission.

Speaking before a large crowd of an estimated 40,000, Williams made clear that his struggle was the audience's struggle, that the discriminations and attacks on him were attacks on all West Indians. As he stated:

> I stand before you tonight, and therefore, before the people of the British West Indies, the representative of a principle, a cause, and a defeat. The principle is the principle of intellectual freedom. The cause is the cause of the West Indian people. The defeat is the defeat of the policy of appointing local men to high office.[17]

The argument that a qualified Afro-Creole from the West Indies had been so poorly treated by lesser-trained white colleagues, that the local man had been discriminated against because of color, hit a responsive cord. Williams made the predominantly Afro-Trinidadian crowd identify with him. Furthermore, he clearly laid down his challenge to the forces of colonialism when he stated: "What was I, a blasted football of the Commission? Who the bloody hell were the Commission anyway? I let them have it."[18] Finally, Williams let his audience know that a new era of politics was at hand, as he was "going to let down my bucket where I am, right here with you in the British West Indies."[19] The crowd's response was enthusiastic as the Afro-Creole population had a new hero who was of international academic renown and a fiery speaker who did not mind twisting the British lion's tail in emphasizing Trinidadian nationalism. In effect, Eric Williams and Trinidad and Tobago had crossed a Rubicon, and the political structure of the two island state would never be the same.

Throughout the rest of 1955 and into 1956, Williams and members of the Political Education Group and the People's Education Movement worked to organize a party and create a comprehensive program that would bridge the gap between the educated, Westernized, and sophisticated Afro-Creole middle sectors and the black popular sectors.[20] As the new "hero" who was to lead his people to the "Promised Land," Williams was the pivotal figure, and much of the new party's ideology was a reflection of his views. His strong personality, authoritarian in many aspects, also helped keep the organization unified in sharp contrast to the many-headed animal that the leftist dominated labor movement had become.

In a series of lectures ranging from Trinidad and Tobago's economic problems to race relations in the Caribbean and constitutional reform, Williams outlined what the People's National Movement, officially founded on January 24, 1956, represented. In many aspects the charter of the PNM was a summation of Williams's speeches: the People's Charter called for immediate self-government in internal affairs; a West Indian Federation with dominion status within five years of establishment; improved working conditions for the worker; provision of more and improved housing; schools and social services for the public; and reorganization of the economy to make the fullest use of all of Trinidad and Tobago's human and physical resources.[21] Concerning the constitution, the PNM favored the substitution of the one-chamber crown colony legislature with its elected official and nominated members, for a completely elected lower chamber and an entirely nominated upper chamber, which would include representatives of the major religious and economic groups.[22] To charges that the PNM was a radical organization along the lines of Cheddi Jagan's People's Progressive Party (PPP), Williams emphasized, "The PNM states categorically that it is neither communist, Fascist, Poujadist nor Messianic or Jaganist."[23] Rather, the PNM was a "national Party, deriving its inspiration from the best in democratic practice, applying to the affairs of Trinidad and Tobago the intelligence, the democratic party discipline and public morality which in the opinion of the PNM are lacking from the political life of the community."[24] As for safeguards on religion and ownership of private property, Williams argued that there was nothing subversive in the People's Charter and that the economic model most favorably looked upon was the Puerto Rican, which was, at the time, being given high priority by the U.S. government with "Operation Bootstrap."

THE 1956 ELECTIONS: THE ISSUES AND THE OPPOSITION

With elections set for September 1956, the People's National Movement entered the campaign with a well-publicized and easily understood program. Williams and his fellow PNM candidates, like Winston Mahabir and Patrick Solomon, served notice that under

Gomes the colony had suffered "six years of corruption, mismanagement, maladministration and party acrobatics, in public affairs" and that they, as a new party, were offering a change for the better.[25]

The PNM, which declared itself a multiracial party, was careful in presenting its image, not wishing to alienate the Afro-Creole middle class from which it had sprung. The PNM leaders also made certain that their organization would not become dominated by the trade union bloc vote by creating party groups in each voting district that were separate from any other organizations and responsible to the PNM's General Council, headed by 12 officers, including a chairman.

While the support of labor was sought and welcomed, the PNM did not want to become a party of labor since they were apprehensive over the factionalism that had plagued leftist political organizations. Union members were allowed to join the party as individuals, but not as a unit. This, in effect, kept leadership in middle-class hands and made the PNM attractive to unions that were predominantly Afro-Creole in membership. The support of labor was a crucial bloc of votes for any party in the colony. Williams, with his charisma and appeals to the Afro-Trinidadians, as well as his concern for the worker, brought this group to the PNM fold.

The PNM's electoral catchwords were "nationalism and democracy," and it was the interpretations of these words with which opposition groups took issue. To the PNM, the need to develop a sense of nationalism, founded upon West Indian history and culture, was essential to the political advancement of the two islands. For the creation of such a mass culture, which would insure democratic development, it was necessary to restructure the educational system as it was badly fragmented with state, Catholic, Protestant, and Hindu schools, each teaching a different perception of West Indian reality. Therefore, the educational system, a major factor in the socialization process, became the principal battleground in what the PNM perceived as a nationalist struggle. The school was highly important since the "national" culture had to be passed on to its citizens, especially the future generations. To these ends, the PNM proposed the standardization of textbooks and teaching methods and a new curriculum suited to the needs of the expanding economy that the PNM would furnish.

While the Presbyterian Church quickly reached an accord with the PNM, the Catholic Church quickly sought allies to help crush what it regarded as a "godless" party. The politicalization of the Catholic Church brought it into a strange coalition of anti-PNM forces, adding a religious element to a situation already confused by racial and ethnic tensions.

Although the PNM had repeatedly emphasized that it was a multiracial organization, it was largely Afro-Creole with small numbers of Christian and Muslim East Indians and a few white Creoles. To the majority of the Hindu East Indians, the PNM represented nationalism, but Afro-Trinidadian nationalism. The situation was not improved by Williams who, Oxaal notes, "On one hand would always denounce racial prejudices and affirm the multi-racial convictions of the PNM but on at least a few occasions at the University [Woodford Square] he insinuated a racial undertone into his oratory."[26] In response, the Hindu community turned to the People's Democratic Party (PDP), which soon became the second largest party in the colony.

The PDP had been founded in 1953 by Bhadase Sagan Maraj, who was born in 1919 in Caroni, the heart of the East Indian community. Maraj was the son of the village headman, a traditional authoritarian figure who was a self-appointed judge, solving all disputes. At an early age Bhadase became involved in politics since his father was shot and killed at home and his brother-in-law was strangled by another village faction. Saving his money from work in the cane fields, he soon bought a boat and established himself as a small-scale contractor for construction on the U.S. bases. At the close of World War II, Maraj bought a considerable amount of equipment from U.S. personnel, which made him somewhat wealthy. Financially established, he turned to politics and was elected in 1950 as an Independent on the Legislative Council.

Maraj's major political base was the *Sanatan Dharma Maha Sabha* (SDMS), a Hindu religious organization formed in 1952 from two older organizations, the *Sanatan Dharma* and the *Maha Sabha*. Aimed at reviving and maintaining the Hindu religion and culture from the inroads of Christian missionary activities, the organization became a powerful political force during the 1950s in areas where East Indians were the most numerous ethnic group. Its leadership was composed largely of Brahmins seeking to continue their caste's traditional hold over the leadership and guidance of the Hindu community.

Maraj was the first president of the *Sanatan Dharma Maha Sabha*, and under his forceful personality it became, according to Malik, "one of the most powerful religious and political forces among the Hindus of Trinidad. . . . A candidate seeking election in the Hindu majority areas of Trinidad would be running the risk of losing by openly criticizing the *Sanatan Dharma Maha Sabha*."[27] Since Maraj was the president of this religious and cultural organization, it was only natural that the SDMS strongly supported the PDP, which was founded the following year by the same individual. The relationship between the cultural organization and political party, however, came under attack during the 1956 campaign since Eric Williams and the PNM linked the SDMS to the similarly named Hindu *Maha Sabha* of India, which had been responsible for Gandhi's assassination. Although the SDMS denied any linkages, pointing out that their's was not a political organization and had been incorporated several years after the mahatma's demise, its political influence had been made public.

Another area in which the PNM attacked the PDP-SDMS bloc was educational reform. Like the Catholic Church, the SDMS had opened schools largely staffed and attended by "their own kind," East Indians of Hindu background. Hindu religious classes were held daily, and children were acquainted with the Mahabharata and Ramayana stories.[28] The fact that few non-Hindu and non-East Indian students attended these schools guaranteed an exclusive Indian cultural and religious education, seconding the Hellenic-Christian-dominated West Indian culture and sense of nationalism favored by the Afro-Creole community. For the Hindus the school system provided employment for young Hindu teachers and functioned as a bulwark against Christian conversion.[29] For the PNM it was a dangerous factor in continuing and exacerbating the divisions in Trinidad and Tobago's society. In a sense Afro-Trinidadian nationalism was colliding with Indo-Trinidadian nationalism, and the PNM's programs for educational reforms alarmed the Hindu community as much as it did the Catholic Church and the Franco-Creole community.

The PNM's emergence, with its well-publicized People's Charter, eliminated many independent candidates and caused the PDP to seek an alliance with non-Hindu East Indians. Two independents to join the PDP were the Sinanan brothers, Mitra and Ashford, both Brahmins who had served in the Legislative Council. Moreover, these men were well educated and assimilated, being Presbyterians who had gone to England for university degrees. In the 1950 elections, they had worked with Butler. Realizing that the political leadership in the East Indian community had shifted to the Hindu-dominated PDP, they joined in 1956. Their move reflected an important change in Indo-Trinidadian politics. As Malik notes, "Since Hindus constitute 64% of the East Indian population, it became difficult for non-Hindu East Indians to assume political leadership. Therefore, like the Sinanan brothers, both of whom are Presbyterians, other politically ambitious East Indians started rallying around Bhadase."[30] Furthermore, Hindu domination of the PDP led to the alienation of Christian and Muslim Indo-Trinidadians who feared being overwhelmed and left out of the political system, hence their turn to the PNM.

The Democratic Party, under attack from the PNM for being a racist organization, moved to rectify the situation. In attempting to modify its East Indian character, it publicly advocated the need for multiracialism and secular reforms. At the same time, PDP leaders moved to gain some support from other groups that felt threatened by the PNM. Consequently, two Catholic nuns and a Baptist minister were brought in to speak in favor of the People's Democratic Party, testifying to its secular and multiracial nature.

In a more significant action, the PDP made several alliances: support was given to Albert Gomes, the leader of the Party of Political Progress Group (POPPG); Roy Joseph, T. U. Butler; and A. P. T. James, leader of the Trinidad Labour Party. Support was even given to other independent candidates. One unifying factor between these forces was their "attack" on the PNM's "godlessness."

By 1956 the Political Progress Group was known as the party of the Chamber of Commerce. Now largely white and limited to the major urban areas, it was comprised primarily of orthodox Catholics and was alarmed by the PNM's call for secular reforms. Led by Gomes the party lacked any other "big names" and was forced to ally itself with the PDP, hoping to split the vote in so many ways that the strong political figure of Gomes would have to be turned to in order to form a coalition government.

The September 1956 elections were one of the most important turning points in the political development of Trinidad and Tobago, and the significance of the stakes for all sides was recognized. There was a high level of suspense due to the tension generated by the core issues of education and religion.[31] Sporadic incidents involving threats and minor violence occurred, culminating in the burning down of a Hindu school in the district of Caroni.[32]

Racial, religious, and ethnic differences, as emphasized by the various political groups, helped clarify the divisions in Trinidadian society and the election results reflected this. The PNM, the only party to contest all the seats, won 13, capturing 39 percent of the vote. The total would eventually be 14 when an independent joined the party. The PDP, which contested 14 seats, won 5 and received 20 percent of the vote, all in the predominantly East Indian sugar belt. Butler's party, with 11 percent of the vote, captured only 2 seats, an absolutely dismal showing considering that it had contested a total of 18. Of the other parties participating, only the Trinidad Labour Party was able to win 3 seats.

All POPPG candidates, including Gomes, were defeated. Significantly, of the five ministers of the outgoing government, only two were reelected, Victor Byran and Ajodhasingh. As *The Economist* notes of Gomes's demise and those close to him, "Mr. Gomes stood, on the whole, for stability and businesslike administration; in the eyes of Trinidadians he was, if anything, rather too close to business interests."[33] Gomes and other defeated middle minority politicians had been caught by the ethnic polarization caused by the creation of two ethnically based parties. With such organizations, the need for minority middlemen and power brokers had been diminished considerably.

The PNM won mainly in the urban areas where the Afro-Creole population was a majority. One factor that gave the PNM an edge was that Hindu dominance of the PDP alienated Christian and Muslim East Indians who functioned as an important swing vote.[34] This was noticeable in districts that were close or evenly divided between Afro-Creoles and East Indians. The PNM, which was better organized than its opponents, got the vote and carried the day.

Williams's victory created somewhat of a crisis in the colony. Although the PNM had received 39 percent of the popular vote and held 14 of the 24 seats, 61 percent of all votes cast were non-PNM, which, in effect, would, if the governor consented, make a PNM government a minority government. The British government realized that, while Gomes had proven himself efficient and a strong federalist, he had been drawn from a small marginal ethnic group and had eventually lost his rapport with his former radical and trade union supporters.[35] Furthermore, with a Portuguese Creole in office from 1950 to 1956, it had been possible to maneuver around the racial issue of appointing either an East Indian or Afro-Creole as chief minister. This had been helped by the factionalization of the legislature into small blocs and highly individualistic personalities.

The absence of a strong nationalistic party had made the 1950 election decision easier. With the emergence of the PNM and the PDP, the situation had changed. The Afro-Creole, part of the white and the non-Hindu East Indian communities, which were largely urban-based, had an alternative to the rural-based PDP led by Maraj, who many, including the Colonial Office, felt had a shady reputation. For the British, Maraj posed another problem, in that he, like many East Indians, opposed federation. Butler was also regarded as a poor candidate for chief minister, being too radical and simplistic.

Eric Williams and the PNM offered what the Colonial Office needed, a "cohesive, middle-class-led party" that enjoyed substantial trade union and lower-middle-class support.[36] This was what had developed in Barbados and Jamaica in the aftermath of the 1930s. It was not until 1955-56 that Trinidad and Tobago's political development matched that of Britain's other major Caribbean colonies. Significantly, when Williams was asked to form a government, Afro-Trinidadian nationalism had come of age in a society divided between the two largest ethnic groups. Both communal groupings had their allies in a divided white upper class, while the East Indian community was divided. The middle class, like the society around it, was also divided, but with an important difference. The PNM's victory symbolized, in large part, the victory of progressive elements in the Afro-Creole middle class, which would lead the nation to independence and continue to follow capitalistic development programs conducive to the growth of the native middle class.

NOTES

1. Eric Williams, *Inward Hunger: The Education of a Prime Minister* (Chicago: University of Chicago Press, 1969, 1971), p. 28.
2. Ibid., p. 27.
3. Ibid.
4. Ibid., p. 26.
5. Ibid., p. 27.
6. Ibid., p. 28.
7. Ibid., p. 65.
8. Ibid., pp. 65-66.
9. Ramesh Deosaran, *Eric Williams, The Man, His Ideas, and His Politics: A Study of Political Power* (Port of Spain: Superservice Printing Company, 1981), p. 8.
10. Ivar Oxaal, *Black Intellectuals Come to Power: The Rise of Creole Nationalism in Trinidad and Tobago* (Cambridge, Mass.: Schenkman, 1968), p. 137.
11. Yogenda Malik, *East Indians in Trinidad: A Study in Minority Politics* (London: Oxford University Press, 1971), p. 89.
12. Selwyn Ryan, *Race and Nationalism in Trinidad and Tobago: A Study of Decolonization in a Multiracial Society* (Toronto: University of Toronto Press, 1972), p. 106.
13. "Henry Hudson-Philips, QC," *Port of Spain Gazette*, August 8, 1948, quoted in Ryan, *Race and Nationalism*, p. 106.
14. Ibid.
15. Ibid., p. 107.

16. Williams, *Inward Hunger*, p. 132.
17. Ibid., p. 131.
18. Ibid., p. 132.
19. Ibid.
20. Malik, *East Indians in Trinidad*, p. 90.
21. Williams, *Inward Hunger*, p. 144.
22. Ibid., p. 134.
23. Ibid., p. 150.
24. Ibid.
25. *Peoples National Movement Election Manifesto 1956* (Port of Spain: College Press, 1956), p. 1.
26. Oxaal, *Black Intellectuals*, p. 184.
27. Malik, *East Indians in Trinidad*, p. 33.
28. Ibid., p. 34.
29. Ibid.
30. Ibid., p. 87.
31. As *The Times* of London predicted, "The indications are that no party is likely to win a clear majority in tomorrow's general election." *The Times*, September 24, 1956, p. 6.
32. Ibid.
33. "Turnover in Trinidad," *The Economist*, September 29, 1956, p. 1034.
34. Kelvin Singh, "East Indians and the Larger Society," in John La Guerre, ed., *Calcutta to Caroni* (London: Longman Caribbean, 1974), p. 64.
35. Oxaal, *Black Intellectuals*, p. 93.
36. Ibid., p. 94.

6

Consolidation of Power, 1956-61

The PNM's 1956 victory was a stunning achievement as it brought into office a party dominated by the Afro-Creole middle sectors. That success and the victory at the subsequent municipal elections (1956), however, did not guarantee an easy term of office for the new party. The Democratic Labour Party (DLP) soon emerged as the official opposition and won the 1958 federal elections, the PNM's "radical" phase (1958-60) strained relations with the United States, and the racial issue threatened not only to further divide society, but also the ruling party. In many respects, it would appear that the Afro-Creole middle sectors, motivated by fear of their East Indian counterparts, operated with the intention of excluding the Indo-Trinidadians from as much of the political process as possible. At the same time, Williams and the PNM elite were Machiavellian enough to criticize the opposition for its lack of "nationalism" on the major and interrelated issues of the 1956-61 period: constitutional reform leading to independence, the West Indies Federation, and the U.S. military base at Chaguaramas. Therefore, from 1956 to 1961 Eric Williams sought to consolidate the PNM's hold over the nation while also consolidating his hold over the party. In this scenario the 1961 general elections were a crucial turning point as it was the first time that one party had not dissolved between elections. Furthermore, with the continued existence of the DLP, it appeared that the colony had made the transition from independent candidates and weak electoral coalitions to a two-party system. All factors considered, it would appear that many of the important foundations for an independent democractic political system were planted during this period.

THE FEDERAL ISSUE AND THE CHANGING CARIBBEAN

As the British Empire presided over the transformation of an empire of colonies into a commonwealth of nations, it was recognized that the West Indies would eventually achieve independence. Concern over the economic and political viability of the smaller islands in the Windwards and Leewards led many in the region and in London to conclude that a West Indies federation would be the most appropriate approach to independence. While federations had been attempted at earlier periods, geographical, political, and economic obstacles had proven difficult to overcome, and such efforts as the Leewards Islands Act of 1871 were demonstratively ineffective.[1]

In the aftermath of World War II, when a number of Britain's possessions in Africa and Asia were moving toward independence, the prospects of a new Caribbean federation were discussed. Following the Montego Bay Conference of 1947, the Standing Closer Committee was established with the purpose of examining the viability of such an organizational model. The 1949 Rance Report, in which the committee ratified federation as the way to independence, was accepted by all British possessions with the exception of British Guiana and British Honduras, which indicated their preference for individual independence.

The last conference before the PNM's coming to power was held in London in February 1956 and was attended by Albert Gomes, who favored the federal approach.[2] At this conference a constitution was discussed, and a tentative date was set for federal elections in 1958. Serious differences, however, were emerging over the questions of a customs union and the site of a federal capital. The resolving of both issues was deferred to later dates.

Despite the change in government in 1956, Trinidad and Tobago's commitment to a West Indies Federation remained firm as most of the PNM elite initially favored that approach. The emerging dispute with the United States over its base at Chaguaramas, however, gradually helped drive a wedge between the PNM's commitment to federation and the desire to reach independence without a new foreign military presence on the island. At the 1957 Standing Closer Committee meeting, it was decided that Trinidad was the most suitable location for a federal capital because of its better communications and essential services. Williams, upon learning that the British governor in 1941 had opposed U.S. bases on the island, declared that the site of the federal capital in Trinidad had to be Chaguaramas, the peninsula north of Port of Spain. The U.S. government, however, was reluctant to surrender the peninsula even though it was to be the federal capital.

Williams regarded the issue as "a case . . . of Trinidad against the United States."[3] At the same time, he was aware that U.S. capital and goodwill underpinned the islands' economy. The sale of the British company, Trinidad Oil, to the Texas Company in 1956, in particular, made the PNM leader conscious of the decline of London's ability to maintain adequate rates of investment in the United Kingdom's overseas dependencies.[4] Simply stated, the traditional imperial policy of protecting the empire for solely metropolitan investment had broken down as U.S. capital, supported by superior political and military strength, penetrated the region.[5] With its string of military bases throughout the Caribbean, its tradition of intervention, and its extensive financial resources, the United States emerged from World War II as the unchallenged master of the Caribbean's political economy. After the intervention in Guatemala in 1954, the British Caribbean increasingly came under U.S. scrutiny, especially as the push to independence brought with it questions of ideological alliances and the possibilities of expanding trade. Although North American trade had been carried on with Trinidad, substantial direct foreign investment commenced only in the 1950s as exemplified by the Texas Company's purchase of Trinidad Oil.

Following his victory at the polls in September 1956, one of Eric Williams's first statements was that the PNM was not socialist nor did it believe in nationalization.[6] He further remarked that the new government would invite outside and local investors to participate in the colony's development. While Williams's statements were aimed at quelling local apprehension over the nature of the PNM, it is probable that they were also intended for British and U.S. audiences, especially considering the leftist orientation of politics in British Guiana, where Cheddi Jagan's party was seeking to introduce Third World socialism. The new chief minister was, no doubt, aware that his party had come to power only two years after the U.S. intervention in Guatemala. Since that time, U.S. interest in the Caribbean Basin had not diminished as the economic penetration of Central America and the West Indies continued.

In an article entitled "Aspects of the Caribbean Economy," published in the *P.N.M. Weekly* (July 23, 1956), Williams publicly recognized the transformations in the international economic system and welcomed the turn of U.S. investors to Trinidad since it would bring a new and badly needed infusion of capital, help expand certain sectors, such as energy and manufacturing, and, most of all, provide employment. U.S. investment in offshore drilling and in the modernization and expansion of the refineries brought considerable growth in that sector during the 1956-60 period despite the increases in government taxation. The acceptance of investment by invitation, the so-called Puerto Rican model, was designed to attract U.S. investors by the appeal of tax holidays and other financial incentives. In many respects, the economic policies pursued by the first PNM government were continuations and improvements of those undertaken during the Gomes period. Despite this approach, elements of the conservative business community remained apprehensive over the ideological stance of the PNM. After 1956 they found natural allies in the Hindu East Indian community.

THE DEMOCRATIC LABOUR PARTY

The exclusion of non-PNM elements in the formation of the government meant that there was little representation of the East Indian community, and this heightened racial tensions. In this atmosphere the scheduling of the 1958 federal elections became a focal point for the opposition. Norman Manley, leader of the People's National Party in Jamaica, had managed to form an alliance at the federal level with the PNM. In response, Sir Alexander Butamante, leader of Jamaica's Democratic Labour Party, came to Trinidad in May 1957 and met with members of the opposition. The end result was the official launching of the Democratic Labour Party of Trinidad and Tobago.

The DLP was a merger of the Trinidad Labour Party, the Political Progress Group, and the People's Democratic Party. Its leadership included Bhadose Maraj, Victor Byran, A. P. T. James, Albert Gomes, and Carlton Achong, making it, as Ryan calls it, "a party of outs." The new party was launched as a multiracial and prolabor organization with Ashford Sinanan as provisional chairman, James, first vice-president, and Achong, provisional treasurer. DLP spokesmen carefully emphasized that their organization was not socialist and indicated that the PNM was.

Formally inaugurated on September 1, 1957, the DLP maintained its multiracial leadership. Ashford Sinanan, chairman of a special six-man steering committee, stated in the inaugural address that "the

DLP was going to play a much more constructive role and its sole purpose was not just to oppose."[7] In subsequent addresses, he attempted to clarify the differences between the DLP and the PNM. Accordingly, the Williams government was regarded as "the dictatorship of one man and the tyranny of a clique," while the PNM represented "state socialism or the regimentation of the life activities of the citizens."[8] The DLP, in contrast, stood for "the democratic rights of the people" and held a "rigid and inflexible stand against any type of socialism."[9] The danger to Trinidad and Tobago, as perceived by the DLP, was the "disrupting evils which socialism brings into the lives of people everywhere."[10] The correct path to national development was the private enterprise system, which was to be given encouragement. The antisocialist slant was very understandable considering the composition of the DLP's leadership, which was overwhelmingly from the business community or from well-to-do middle-class families, especially among the East Indians.[11]

The DLP had become, in a short period of time, the focal point of unity for societal forces that were apprehensive of the PNM. The formal merger of the three parties had been attractive to all groups involved since it had been recognized that a unified party at all levels was needed to compete with the highly organized PNM. The merger gave the new party a mass base, the East Indians, and the non-East Indians gave the DLP some credibility for its claims to being multiracial. Moreover, the DLP appealed to the East Indian popular sectors, who, as a peasantry, firmly believed in the sacredness of property ownership and feared that the PNM, regarded as socialists, were bent on nationalization policies.

On January 8, 1956, B. S. Maraj, the president general of the *Maha Sabha* and former president of the People's Democratic Party, was elected parliamentary leader of the DLP. The non-Indian factions of the DLP apparently had accepted playing a secondary role in the organization in consideration of their need for the East Indian vote.[12] The advance of the East Indian group within the new party was given further impetus when Bustamante agreed to let Sinanan become the prime minister of the West Indies Federation if the DLP won the 1958 elections on a regional basis.

By 1958 Trinidad and Tobago's society had become sharply divided along political and ethnic lines, and the emergence of two parties functioned to sharpen the divisions. On one side was the government in power, the PNM, led by the charismatic Eric Williams and the Afro-Creole middle sectors. Its base of support was the Afro-Creole community, in particular, the popular sectors of the black-dominated trade unions and urban workers. Allied to the more numerous Afro-Creole elements were middle-class Muslim and Presbyterian East Indians and parts of the white community. These elements, however, were beginning to waver their support for the PNM as a result of the high-handedness of Williams, who they felt pandered to the black masses. The chief minister's demands for the return to Chaguaramas also alarmed those elements in the white community that had initially sided with the PNM.

On the other side was the DLP, led by Maraj. As Trinidadian society polarized, the DLP became representative of the Hindu East Indians and those in the white and middle minority communities who were associated with the conservative views of the Catholic Church. Whites and East Indians were also apprehensive over the PNM's efforts to "West Indianize" the civil service. In the colonial system prior to 1950, the governor had been aided by a group of powerful civil servants who were appointed by the Crown. Between 1950 and 1956, as the Gomes administration sought to deal with the gradual transferal of duties and authority, a number of disputes had arisen between the government of the day and the civil service, some of which were finally settled by the governor. Officials also had a tendency to appeal to the governor over the heads of the ministers.

The nationalists in the PNM felt that ultimate responsibility for policy making belonged with the ministers of government and not with civil servants, especially taking into account that many in the upper echelons were white and had family ties with the local white upper class. The PNM wanted an administrative system that was subservient to the government and its policies. This was achieved, in part, by the policy of West Indianization, which bypassed whites and promoted mainly Afro-Creoles. This trend was only another factor in a widening racial rift. It is also probable that a slight majority in the business sector backed the DLP.

THE FEDERAL ELECTIONS OF 1958

The main focus of the 1958 federal elections was the contest between the PNM and the DLP as the two major ethnic groups, led by their respective middle classes and allied to the other smaller societal elements, squared off. While the ten seats at stake were important on the federal level, the real significance of the election lay in whether the PNM could maintain its dominance of the nation's political system.

Along racial and ethnic lines, the question was whether the Afro-Creole middle sectors would eventually have to surrender their leadership of the nation to the East Indians or, at the very least, make some concessions. While the election was important, it would not directly determine the domestic political structure. It would, however, determine how the nation regarded PNM leadership for the two year period.

The election's results did little to calm a campaign marred by several stone-throwing incidents and general heckling of candidates.[13] The DLP, which had campaigned vigorously with well-known non-East Indian figures such as Gomes, Joseph, and Byran, won six of ten seats, a stunning and unexpected outcome.[14] With what has been described as a mediocre platform, which asserted opposition to socialism, faith in free enterprise and foreign investment, and an equitable policy toward labor, the DLP played on the fear of the federation falling into the hands of the socialists.[15]

A major reason for the ruling party's defeat was its approach: it nominated politically inexperienced and unknown candidates to compete against a well-known multiracial slant, and it depended on the party's reputation and vigorous ministerial campaigning to see it through.[16] Other reasons were the higher turnout of East Indian voters and the defection of some non-East Indian elements to the DLP.[17] The dissatisfaction of some blacks and middle minorities was based on what they perceived to be the increasingly authoritarian nature of the ruling party. In St. Patrick, a predominantly Afro-Creole district, the black vote was divided between the PNM candidate and an independent, Butler, allowing Mohamed Shah of the DLP to win with only 43 percent of the vote. Non-East Indian candidates like Gomes and Byran also attracted Afro-Creole, white, and middle minority votes away from the PNM. At the same time, the racial element could not be entirely discounted as a factor: despite the DLP's emphasis on ideology and its multiracial slate, most of its victories came in regions where East Indians made up an absolute majority (over 60 percent).[18]

For Williams and the PNM, the outcome was a shock. Having fought hard to make Trinidad the federal capital, Williams felt betrayed and feared that the nation's bargaining power at the federal level would be impaired by the DLP's victory. Consequently, he lashed out at the DLP and the East Indians at an address in Woodford Square. An East Indian founding member of the PNM, present at the speech, notes that the speech:

> contained generous ingredients of abuse of the Indian community which was deemed to be a "hostile and recalcitrant minority." The Indian

community represented the greatest danger facing the country. It was an impediment to West Indian progress. It had caused the PNM to lose the federal elections.[19]

Other comments were made about "Indian illiterates of the country areas who were threatening to submerge the masses whom Williams had enlightened" and that the DLP had "brought to the polls the lame and the halt, the blind and the deaf."[20] This invective-filled speech not only threatened to drive away East Indian PNM members, it also helped to further aggravate racial tensions, especially since these utterances came from the colony's chief minister.

THE ROAD TO INDEPENDENCE AND CONSTITUTIONAL REFORM

On the road to independence, Trinidad and Tobago's middle-class elites had to contend with the issue of constitutional reform and the nation's relations with the federal, U.S., and British governments. To Williams it was necessary to update the colony's political institutions to a level comparable to those of Barbados and Jamaica in order to put Trinidad on an even basis of political evolution while diminishing the metropole's control over local affairs. Otherwise, Port of Spain would be at a disadvantage within the federal power structure. Furthermore, one of the campaign planks of 1956 had been a call for advancement to more autonomous government. Along these lines, the PNM, in September 1957, made recommendations for constitutional reform.

In moving closer to the Westminster model, three major changes were proposed: the governor would nominate the leader of the majority party as the prime minister (instead of chief minister) of a cabinet that would replace the Executive Council; the prime minister would decide the distribution of ministerial portfolios; and the prime minister, not the governor, would preside over cabinet meetings.[21] In effect, the PNM was asking for self-government by asking for a considerable curtailment of the authority and functions of the metropole's representative. Solomon, an ardent supporter of these changes, commented that such reforms would give "the people's elected representatives unfettered authority."[22]

DLP apprehensions were influenced by two perceptions. As a mainly East Indian party and, in a sense, the party of a minority, the DLP felt that it had to act defensively on the question of constitutional reform. The PNM had not made any offers of interparty cooperation, and the DLP was clearly excluded from the running of the government.

Any new PNM motions, it was perceived, would naturally lead to further exclusion. The DLP, therefore, argued that Trinidad and Tobago was not ready for the full-scale introduction of the Westminster system since the nation lacked the conditions necessary to make parliamentary democracy function as it did in the United Kingdom.[23] DLP members of Parliament advocated instead that the legislature should be transformed into a more representative body after which the Executive Council could be restructured.

The second perception held by the DLP was that it could win a general election. Hence, the longer the British stayed in Trinidad and Tobago, the greater the opportunity that the Colonial Office could be pressured into forcing the PNM to call new elections. Confidence in the DLP's strength came from the federal elections and from the 1958 county council elections in which the two major parties almost tied in numbers of seats. Accordingly, DLP strategy from 1958 was to put pressure on the Colonial Office to call general elections, which would, in effect, bring down the PNM government.

In June 1959 the PNM government formed the Select Committee on Constitutional Reform to which the public was invited to submit memoranda on the question of constitutional reform. The DLP, in a spat with the governor over procedure, boycotted the discussions, depriving the public of the opportunity to hear its views on the matter while leaving the field open to the PNM. The government's new proposals called for a bicameral system, the redrawing of electoral boundaries aimed at adding six new seats to the Legislative Council, the appointment of a West Indian governor on the advice of the cabinet, and a law that would make two-thirds of the Legislative Chamber the necessary majority to pass amendments on the constitution.

The DLP's reaction to these new proposals was swift, as it accused the PNM of attempting to restructure Trinidad's political system in such a fashion as to exclude the East Indians from power. In particular, the recommendation to change electoral boundaries stirred considerable discontent. The DLP argued that such changes would be aimed at minimizing or confining the East Indian majorities or dividing them in such a way as to make them a minority. The DLP would accept boundary restructuring only if conducted by an independent commission from Britain or the United Nations. Furthermore, the DLP opposed the local appointment of a governor since the governor, Sir Edward Beetham, had had good relations with the PNM.

Both parties sent delegates to London to express their views and awaited the Colonial Office's decisions. In most matters the PNM was granted its demands with the exception of its request of the bicameral system. This was rejected to placate the DLP. The constitutional issue, which was not resolved from the PNM viewpoint, dragged on through the closing months of 1959 and into 1960. One matter not immediately settled in this period was the question of police control, and this became enmeshed with the Chaguaramas issue.

LEFTWARD BOUND

The PNM's push to regain Chaguaramas, the question of constitutional reform, and the movement of the West Indies Federation toward independence occurred at a time of tremendous political change in the Caribbean. As of December 1956 Fidel Castro's insurrection had developed, and by January 1959 the dictator, Fulgencio Batista, had fled Cuba. The radical nature of the Cuban Revolution, the increasingly difficult relationship with the Dominican Republic's dictator, General Rafael Leonidas Trujillo Molina, and the general unrest in Central America made U.S. policymakers apprehensive about the possibility of further revolutions and the ability of leftist forces to penetrate the Caribbean. While North American influence had been felt in British Guiana in the early 1950s, that colony's political development continued to be unstable and leftist. Furthermore, across the Gulf of Paria from Trinidad, Venezuela had undergone tremendous political transformations since the downfall of the dictator Perez Jimenez in early 1958. On December 7, 1958, Romulo Betancourt, the Acción Democratica candidate, had been elected president, ushering in an unbroken return to democratic government. A controversial leader, Betancourt was initially regarded as a moderate leftist, and his action vis-à-vis the multinational oil companies generated some apprehension in Washington. It was in this atmosphere that Williams demanded the return of the whole of the Chaguaramas Peninsula from the United States.

In 1957 the United States met with West Indian leaders in London to discuss the matter of the bases. To investigate the matter, the Chaguaramas Joint Commission was formed, and in 1958 it reported its findings: the United States was entitled to a naval base on Trinidad, and, although there were other suitable locations, Chaguaramas was the best. It also stated that the matter might be reopened in ten years. At the same time, the British government hinted to the PNM that under no circumstances would the United Kingdom ask the United States to abandon the base. Added irritants to the PNM were the North

American decision to expand facilities at Chaguaramas and the federal government's quick acceptance of the commission's decision.

In April 1958 C. L. R. James, a noted international Marxist and friend of Eric Williams, arrived in Trinidad. In December of that year, he became the editor of the PNM's weekly newspaper, *The Nation*.[24] The installation of James coincided with the increasing use of anti-imperialist jargon in PNM publications and speeches. In this fashion Williams let it be known that "independence lay through Chaguaramas."

In the spring of 1959, when autonomous cabinet government was about to be granted, the matter of control of the police became a major issue. The secretary of state for the colonies, Ian McLeod, had decided not to relinquish control of the police because of strong appeals by the opposition. In such a racially charged atmosphere, this issue became a national dispute, with the Afro-Trinidadian middle sectors demanding control and the East Indian bourgeois opposing local control. Because of the DLP's stance, it became a target as the PNM argued that the predominantly East Indian party was also against federation and independence.

Williams made the dispute public in an address in Woodford Square. While making the customary jabs at the British "raj," the chief minister turned to the issue of the base, charging that U.S. personnel were using "radiation" at Chaguaramas, which was a threat to the safety of Trinidadians.[25] To add an air of mystery, two ministers, O'Halloran and Solomon, were dispatched on a "secret mission" to London where they pushed the Colonial Office on the police matter, arguing that since the Trinidadian government had no control over the local police it could not benefit from that department's information services to gauge the "threat" of radiation from the U.S. base. Solomon, in his own words, "made it plain to the officials at the Colonial Office that such a state of affairs could not continue and that on the introduction of Cabinet Government we must insist on control of the Police passing to an elected minister."[26] Without an answer the mission returned to Port of Spain where the radiation matter was quickly shunted to the background of events as the question of police control now dominated.

The date for the formal inauguration of cabinet government had been set for June 20, 1959, when Parliament was to reconvene. The PNM, the Colonial Office, and the DLP had reached an accord on most issues with the exception of the police. Williams, however, was determined that police control should pass to local hands and spoke on the radio on the night of June 16, announcing that the formal opening of Parliament was canceled. The British, who had not answered since the O'Halloran and Solomon mission, quickly capitulated, and Cabinet Day took place later that month with the administration of the police department coming under a PNM minister. While this brought Trinidad and Tobago closer to complete self-rule, Williams had made good use of Chaguaramas to achieve a political victory over the DLP, which he referred to as "enemies of the public."[27]

It is highly probable that the British government had given in on the police matter in the hope that the PNM would not push the Chaguaramas issue.[28] Williams, however, had other intentions: "I was not going to sacrifice my fundamental principles for a little power."[29] To the Trinidadian prime minister, the base issue was particularly irksome because, while the United States maintained bases in Iceland, Morocco, the Philippines, and a number of other places, rent was paid, economic assistance was provided, and base agreements could be renegotiated. In Trinidad the bases had been surrendered for 99 years, no rent was charged, nor was any economic aid given. The key issue that the PNM leader pressed, however, was whether Trinidad and Tobago had the right to negotiate with the United States over the matter. As long as Washington did not recognize this right, Trinidad would continue to be "anti-imperialist" and perhaps, it was hinted, neutral in the cold war, a stance that the United States regarded with suspicion.

In the August 8, 1959, issue of *The Nation*, James comments, "What hangs in the balance is whether this territory must submit to a new colonialism just at the time when it is making every effort to free itself from the old." Williams's strategy closely echoed James's statement. It was two-pronged, aimed at removing metropolitan influence from the daily running of the government by constitutional reform and ousting U.S. personnel from Chaguaramas before the achievement of independence.

The PNM's approach was a blatant challenge to the DLP, stating that it should stand either for "treasonable colonialism" or "independence with dignity."[30] With a pointed reference to the DLP and its predominantly East Indian support, Williams was quoted in the July 22, 1959, *Trinidad Guardian*: "The only alternative to the road to Independence is the road back to colonialism. . . . the issue has nothing to do with race at all, though race might complicate the objective, social, political and economic issues are involved." The base issue had become a point around which Williams and the Afro-Creole middle sectors sought to rally "Trinidadian" nationalism, while also strengthening their political position vis-à-vis the East Indian middle class.

The unfortunate casualty of the Chaguaramas affair, with its many twists and turns, was the West Indies Federation, as it was one factor of many leading to that organization's demise. Trinidad's relationship with the federal government became more strained as the PNM increasingly pushed for the return of the base. While the PNM was further alienated by the reluctance of the federal government to set a date for independence, personal relations between Grantley Adams, the federal prime minister, and Williams deteriorated as the two went on the radio and insulted each other. Williams's stance, so clearly outlined in the March 11, 1960, issue of *The Nation* ("Chaguaramas and Independence Go Hand in Hand; The Road to Independence Leads through Chaguaramas"), sent his message to the federal government that if it would not move with Trinidad, then Trinidad would move without the West Indies Federation—which is precisely what happened.

On July 17, 1959, Williams spoke at a mass party meeting in Arima. His speech, often claimed to have been ghostwritten by James, emphasized that Trinidad and Tobago was not a colony as it was now governed by a prime minister rather than a colonial governor.[31] As times changed, so should the 1941 deal for the bases, especially since the two-island state was moving toward independence.

The Arima speech was followed by a meeting on August 12, 1959, between Williams and Edwin Moline, the U.S. consul general. The PNM leader offered a new proposal that would set the stage for a joint base in which the Trinidadians would share security duties and the United States would provide aid. The size of the base at Chaguaramas would also be reduced, parts of it being turned over to Port of Spain to become the capital of the federation. While elements in Washington approved the idea of a joint base, the decision-making process moved slowly. Williams decided not to wait, and after several months the PNM moved to mobilize popular sector support for independence by taking action in some fashion. At a party meeting in March 1960, the more radical and hawkish elements advocated marching on the base or landing a boat and planting a Trinidadian flag. The majority, including Williams, wished to avoid any incidents that could lead to violence and be misinterpreted as too revolutionary. Instead, it was decided to march on the U.S. Consulate, the local representative of the U.S. government in the colony.

Before the famous March in the Rain, Williams pressured the United States in another fashion. On April 22 the Trinidad government requested Washington to stop landing military aircraft at Picaro International Airport as it was disrupting air traffic, circumventing customs, and taking up space that could be used for commercial purposes.[32] Copies of the request were sent to the British and federal governments. Only days later this was followed by the March in the Rain. A turnout of several thousand met in Woodford Square to listen to Williams, who stated, "For two years and eight months we have beaten our heads in vain against the forces and agents of colonialism—against the unswerving and often discourteous hostility of the British and American governments on one hand, and on the other, against the servile mentality and inferiority complex bred among some West Indians by centuries of colonial rule."[33] The last barb, of course, was aimed at both the federal government and the Indo-Trinidadian community as represented by the DLP. In the course of the march, Williams took part in a symbolic ceremony in which West Indian and Trinidadian constitutions and other documents, including the U.S. Lend-Lease Base Agreement of 1941, were burnt.[34] Solomon, the home affairs minister, publicly demanded the return of Chaguaramas and other areas that had been leased to the United States "without our consent and will."[35]

The March in the Rain's large turnout demonstrated that there was considerable public support for a revision of the base treaty and that Trinidad's prime minister had not created an issue where one had not existed. Consequently, two changes occurred. In June 1960 the Colonial Office gave in to PNM demands on constitutional reforms.[36] The existing single chamber (the Legislative Council) was to be replaced by a Senate of 21 and a House of Representatives of 30 members. Of the senators, 12 were to be appointed by the governor on the advice of the prime minister, 2 on the advice of the leader of the opposition, and 7 by the governor to represent special groups.[37] The Senate would have no authority to delay money bills but would have authority to delay other bills for more than one year or two consecutive sessions.

The lower house was elective and was given six new members from which members of the Cabinet would be drawn. The Cabinet would have 11 ministers, headed by the prime minister, and the attorney general now became a position for an elected member of Parliament. An important factor in the new reforms was that the governor no longer had reserve powers. This new constitution, therefore, brought Trinidad and Tobago the same type of governmental structure as those of Jamaica and Barbados.[38] One last problem remained: there was still no agreement over the rearrangement of the electoral boundaries. Despite that, the passage of these reforms was a major victory for the PNM and a blow to the DLP.

During the same month Ian MacLeod, the secretary of state for the colonies, proposed a meeting in three stages to resolve the bases issue. The first stage was to be in London between the United Kingdom and the United States, with federal observers; the second stage in Trinidad, between the United States and Trinidad, with British and federal observers; and the final stage in Tobago for the formal signing of a new agreement between the United States and the West Indies Federation and Trinidad and Tobago.[39]

Each stage of the talks proceeded smoothly, since all parties involved wished to settle the matter. By February 1961 a new treaty was agreed upon, and the PNM had won another substantial political victory. Some 21,000 acres of land under the 1941 agreement, including unused parts of the Chaguaramas Naval Station, were returned to Trinidad, while Teteron Bay remained under U.S. lease to be developed for the joint use by the West Indies Federation, Trinidad, and the United States. Certain other facilities would be open to U.S. personnel in case war occurred. Outside of joint military projects, U.S. economic aid was to help improve national communications and Port of Spain's port facilities and also to help develop a college of arts and sciences.[40]

Although the United States had surrendered much, it still maintained a substantial presence. The new arrangement was to be reviewed in 1968 and was to last until 1977 when all U.S. forces, depending on the global situation, would be withdrawn. It was a gradual approach, which was not meant to generate ill-feelings on either side. The United States was allowed to maintain a presence, although reduced, in the Gulf of Paria, while Trinidad and Tobago could move to independence without the presence of a substantial foreign military force just north of Port of Spain.

THE TURN TO THE RIGHT

Once it became clear that the United States had recognized Port of Spain's right to negotiate the bases issue, the PNM began to move to the right. In September 1960 the Trinidad government presented a check for $25,790 to the U.S. consul general for the sale of citrus fruit by the U.S. naval base to the Citrus Growers Association of Trinidad and Tobago.[41] The payment had been stalled by Williams as a means of pressure, and, once the matter of the bases began to clear, the prime minister used that to create a friendly atmosphere at the talks. Moreover, the anti-imperialist rhetoric that had characterized PNM speeches and publications disappeared.

The swing away from the left immediately created tensions between Williams and James. As Williams notes, "It became fashionable in certain quarters—particularly by James, former editor of our party weekly—to criticise me and our delegation for agreeing to the continued tenure of Chaguaramas for seventeen years."[42] In return, James comments, "Williams is a fundamentally immoral person, and being the politician that he is he can do anything which he thinks will assist himself as a political leader."[43]

James had been editor of *The Nation* from December 1958 to October 1960. During that period he also became the recognized leader of the PNM's left wing. James's brief ascendancy to the upper echelons of the party caused considerable discontent and resulted in some of the more conservative elements leaving. His rise to power, with easy access to the prime minister, also created tensions between the government and the business community, especially the Chamber of Commerce, which felt that the positioning of a well-known Marxist as editor of *The Nation* would eventually scare away foreign capital.

In the fall of 1960, when Williams had gotten what he wanted from Washington and with general elections scheduled for 1961, James was becoming a political liability in both domestic and international politics. Williams recognized that the moderate and conservative elements and the swing vote of the middle-class non-Hindu East Indians would be needed to win the elections. The PNM's radical stance with James would not only alienate those groups; good relations with the United States would bring substantial aid projects. James, therefore, was shunted aside and denied easy access to the prime minister that he had once enjoyed. Moreover, a committee was formed to investigate the PNM Publishing Company, which had been under James's authority.[44] In October he was found guilty of mismanagement and eventually expelled from the party. While it is questionable that James mismanaged the paper, there can be no doubt that Williams was apprehensive that his former friend would attempt to take his faction with him, which, in effect, would divide the PNM. The fall of James, however, brought no such split, and the way was now open for the PNM to return to the more moderate mainstream of Trinidadian politics.

The issue of education had yet to be resolved. This was an exceedingly controversial and emotional issue. For Williams, however, it was necessary to "bury the axe" with the Catholic Church due to the oncoming elections.

After the 1956 election campaign, education had been dropped to make way for other more pressing issues that dominated the national agenda. The publication of the *Education Report of the Committee on General Education* brought the issue back to the public's attention in the summer of 1960. The wording of the report, which advocated a restructuring of the education system with the intent of "integrating the diverse elements which comprise our cosmopolitan population," created a new church-state crisis.[45] Although representatives of the various religious groups had been on the committee, it was dominated by PNM loyalists. Because of that, the representatives of the Anglican and Catholic churches refused to endorse the report.[46]

Resistance to the government's education plans also came from the Hindu community, which regarded the PNM's attempt to control national education as an assault on their cultural identity. While the PNM pushed to unify the educational system in order to create a single curriculum, which was aimed at fostering a sense of Trinidadian nationalism with a common history, sense of tradition, and culture, the counterargument was that people had the freedom to decide how they wanted their children educated. Moreover, the nation's religious institutions offered the particular religious-cultural framework that certain elements of society desired.

The PNM's aim to make education free also stirred discontent. The Catholic Church was especially adamant on this point since free education would undermine their institutions, which depended on donations and were not free.[47] Ideologically, it opposed free education because "Catholic social doctrine disapproves of the welfare state in which the Government provides all social services free of charge to its citizens indiscriminately."[48] There was also apprehension that the education of young Catholics might come under the charge of Muslims or Hindus. On the issue of ethnic and racial integration, the Catholic Church felt that it was a good idea but should not be left to the state; rather, the best approach was through "the acceptance of the supranational ideal given the Catholic Church by its founder, Jesus Christ."[49]

Within the PNM two groups emerged. The first, a vocal group of egalitarians, advocated a policy of confrontation with the churches and the implementation of a secularized educational system at all levels. The leadership elite, however, was well aware that an election was coming and wished to remove all issues that were controversial enough to unify anti-PNM forces.[50] Consequently, negotiations were undertaken between the churches and the government, which led to the concordat announced on Christmas Day 1960.

For the Catholic Church the concordat was a temporary victory as the churches were allowed: to maintain their proprietary rights; to veto the introduction of books, curriculum changes, and apparatus in their institutions; to have their religions taught by only one of their own faith; and to have access to state schools at specified times to give instruction to children of their denomination.[51] Moreover, although the authority over appointment, retention, transfer, promotion, and dismissal of teaching staff was given to the Public Service Commission, denominational boards were granted the power to refuse, accept, or retain a teacher whose moral or religious conduct did not meet with their approval. The major concession to the state was over the recruitment of students: 80 percent of those entering the first form of the secondary schools were to be determined by the state on the basis of a standardized entrance exam.[52] The remaining 20 percent were to be left to the discretion of the various schools, while church-run schools remained eligible for state economic assistance.

The concordat with the Protestant and Catholic churches and the Hindu organizations had been one of the most complicated political problems that Williams faced as he was forced to concede on an issue about which he had strong personal feelings while also overriding a substantial force within the party.[53] The benefit from such maneuvers, however, was that the PNM's movement back to the right had been given a substantial boost, and opinion within the Catholic and Anglican churches was gradually swinging in favor of Williams's party.

By the close of 1960, the PNM had zigzagged from the center right to the left and back to the center right. While the radical phase had been marked by a tough stance on most issues, the move to the right was accommodational in nature and disarming to a political opposition that claimed the PNM was rigid and held authoritarian tendencies. With the U.S. and British governments and Catholic and Anglican churches neutralized, the prime minister was able to concentrate on the matter of the electoral boundaries and getting reelected.

THE 1961 ELECTIONS: ACCOMMODATION

The major remaining constitutional issue was that of electoral boundaries. Along with the PNM's push to change the borders of constituencies came proposals for a new set of voter registration rules and the introduction of voting machines in place of ballot boxes. To the DLP these transformations were seemingly an effort to curtail their ability to get a large East Indian turnout as in 1958. The limiting of transportation for voters on the day of the election, which the PNM regarded as solicitation, was outlawed over DLP opposition, and voting machines replaced the ballot box. The latter, the DLP claimed, was intended to confuse the many illiterates in the rural Indo-Trinidadian communities. Furthermore, the redrawing of electoral boundaries raised a bitter controversy in Parliament and in the nation at large, which was laden with racial overtones. The result certainly verified DLP claims that the new boundaries favored the PNM as the next election would divide the nation along strictly racial and ethnic lines.[54]

The East Indian reaction to these changes came at two levels: one was an exceedingly emotional public demand for a radical solution, the other more constructive and limited to the Parliament. Stephen Maharaj, a DLP member of Parliament, argued that "the action of this Government has certainly given a different status to different citizens," implying that the electoral divisions created between the largely urban Afro-Creole population and the largely rural East Indian community were in favor of the former group.[55] In Parliament Maharaj introduced an amendment asking the Colonial Office to overturn the majority report responsible for the changes and called for the creation of an independent commission to redraw the boundaries. The amendment, which was presented to a PNM-dominated assembly, was quickly rejected. The lack of compromise and the high-handed nature of the PNM only served to make the East Indians more defensive and alienated from the government. It also contributed to the spread of a more radical and aggressive response from the East Indian leadership.

By 1961 the DLP was not a unified party, having undergone considerable infighting. Maharaj, who had popular appeal among the East Indian masses and was able to manipulate non-East Indian party elements, had become less active in politics in 1959 because of illness. With his decline a younger generation of Indo-Trinidadian professionals and civil servants emerged, claiming that the old leader was an uneducated liability when compared to the charismatic and well-educated Eric Williams. To compete with the PNM effectively, the "Young Turks" of the DLP argued that new leadership was required. Without Maraj at the helm, "the DLP became a travesty or a mockery of genuine parliamentary opposition"[56] as faction fought faction. Ultimately, Dr. R. N. Capildeo, a native-born scholar like Williams, who had a doctorate in mathematics and had been the principal of Trinidad Polytechnic, became the DLP's new leader. Although a Hindu and born of high caste, he was not associated with *Maha Sabha* and was regarded at the time of his ascent as the missing "hero" needed to lead the East Indian masses to power as had Williams with the black masses. Capildeo, however, was to fall short of most expectations.

The DLP, with its new leader, remained unified, but only on the surface. Capildeo was ill-suited for the "rough and tumble" world of Trinidadian politics and lacked the political sophistication to deal with Williams. As the party was not created by Capildeo and as he was not a founding member, the new leader came as an outsider. It was only the fear of a PNM victory in 1961 and the possibility of another five years of Afro-Creole rule that made the various factions stand behind the new party head.[57]

As the DLP lost momentum as an opposition party and the PNM pushed through its constitutional reforms, Capildeo reflected the frustration in the Indo-Trinidadian community. In September 1961, addressing the question of voting machines, the DLP leader told a large audience in San Fernando, "I appeal to 1000 of you to come forward on election day and smash 1000 voting machines."[58] Capildeo also advocated the mass burning of identity cards and hinted at the possible formation of a civil disobedience campaign. Moreover, after several violent speeches at meetings, he reacted to PNM hecklers, calling the East Indian community to arms to retaliate against Afro-Creole harassment.

One of the offshoots of Capildeo's aggressiveness was the alienation of non-Indo-Trinidadian elements in the DLP. In 1961 Victor Byran and a number of Afro-Creoles left the DLP to form the United Labour Party (ULP). At its inaugural meeting, Byran, the chairman, invoked the ideals of Captain Cipriani and proclaimed that the ULP was "purely and simply a working-class movement."[59] The loss of these elements underscored the political and racial divisions in Trinidad and Tobago.

A policy of accommodation and co-optation was beginning to emerge in the PNM before the November 1961 general election. This was most observable in the government's relationship with labor. While the PNM had enjoyed three years (1956-58) of relatively manageable labor relations, 1959 and 1960 were difficult years as 69 strikes occurred in the former and 31 in the latter periods.[60] Significantly, the number of workers involved in strikes rose from 400 in 1957 to 12,595 in 1959 and 20,898 in 1960.[61]

In 1960 strikes ranged from those of the telephone workers, oil workers, and civil servants. A dispute between the Oil Workers Trade Union, led by John Rojas, and the oil companies even paralyzed the island for 18 days. While a settlement was reached with Texaco and Shell, the major foreign companies, Williams estimated that the government lost $5.5 million in disbursements and payment by the companies during the strike.[62] The prime minister comments, "Both sides played fast and loose with the government's revenue without asking the government its opinion."[63] However, Williams could not, at that point, afford to alienate the unions since most of them, with the exception of the sugar workers, made up the basis of his popular sector support.

The government was frustrated by the strikes as they disrupted development plans, but had to move with caution. In essence, Williams felt that the nation's long-term economic objectives "would be better served if the unions became primarily engaged in advancing the economic interests of their members through working for improvement in wages and other conditions of their employment and were secondarily concerned with the broader programs of political and social reform."[64] Consequently, as the DLP and the PNM campaigns gained momentum in the summer of 1961, the importance of the labor vote was noted by Williams. In July a long-standing labor dispute between the government and three trade unions was ended with the government giving wage increases to its employees, backdated to January 1960.[65]

While Williams sought to woo labor, Capildeo did the same. The DLP's labor policy argued that something had to be done about the industrial strife afflicting the nation. In effect, the DLP advocated stronger governmental action in dealing with strikes.[66] Capildeo followed this by announcing that unstable conditions in the workplace would make foreign companies apprehensive over investment in Trinidad and that Williams was using the union movement for his own ends.[67]

The National Trade Union Council's leadership, predominantly Afro-Creole, declared the DLP antilabor and turned to the PNM. This was followed by a number of pro-PNM mass demonstrations that had a strong anti-DLP slant.[68] Within the union movement, the East Indian minority was completely alienated and soon disassociated itself from the National Trade Union Congress and the Oil Workers Trade Union. The Cane Farmers Association and the All-Trinidad Sugar Estate and Factory Workers Union, both largely Indo-Trinidadian, gravitated toward the DLP as the situation polarized along racial lines.

The division of the labor movement reflected the general division in Trinidad and Tobago's society. By 1961 the middle sectors, both Afro-Creole and East Indian, understood the necessity of a bourgeois-worker electoral alliance, although the parties were not extensions of trade unions, having distinctive middle-class orientations. In this respect, both major parties had one trade union each on their slate. Significantly, the majority of candidates were middle class: four company directors ran, two for each party, while a single industrialist was on the PNM ticket. As Malik notes, "Both parties had university teachers, professionals, druggists, land proprietors . . . , farmers, solicitors, school teachers, and journalists among their candidates."[69] The major difference was that the Afro-Creoles had adapted at a quicker pace due to the political acumen of Williams. The PNM also demonstrated more flexibility in accommodating key minority groups, while the DLP reflected a less flexible and insular perception of reality distinctly colored by its Hindu foundation.

The Afro-Creole middle sectors, entrenched in power, held a definite advantage, which they would not easily surrender. The Afro-Creole community, while not strongly unified, was not as badly divided as their East Indian counterparts. The PNM's ability to co-opt the minorities in the East Indian community, the Muslims and Christians, and its ability to accommodate the islands' religious institutions made it a superior organization dominating the political landscape by "divide and conquer" tactics. Furthermore, in its relations with labor, the PNM was aided by positive economic conditions. The boom that began in the mid-1950s still appeared to be advancing, and, in the political field, the PNM felt that the nation could accommodate the flurry of strikes, especially since the ruling party needed popular sector votes to remain in power.

In the campaign both parties presented multiracial slates with the DLP putting 20 non-East Indians and 9 Indo-Trinidadians on the ballot, and the PNM had 8 East Indian and 21 non-Indo-Trinidadian candidates. Significantly, 3 of the 8 PNM East Indian candidates were Muslim, while 2 of the DLP's nominees were also of the same faith. Both sides felt that the Muslim vote was important and efforts were made to gain the support of other minority ethnic groups such as the white Creoles, the Chinese, and Syrian-Lebanese.[70] For the DLP a particularly strong effort was made to recruit non-East Indian candidates to challenge the PNM in Afro-Creole areas.

The PNM and DLP sought to clarify differences between themselves and their opponents. Although snide remarks abounded over the ideological stance of the leading political parties, Albert Gomes's comment was most telling: "In the ideological sense this is a battle between Tweedledum and Tweedledee, both of whom are driving hard on the right."[71]

The campaign was one of Trinidad and Tobago's roughest and most tension-filled. Heckling by party stalwarts was highly disruptive due to the use of high-powered megaphones.[72] The brunt of this was borne by the DLP as pro-PNM supporters turned to violence in the San Juan area, looting shops and throwing stones at the DLP office and candidates' residences.[73] The rise of violence had the unfortunate effect of causing the DLP to suspend temporarily its public meetings and turn to house-to-house canvassing. A DLP request to use the state-run broadcasting system was denied, furthering the bad feelings between the two leading ethnic communities.

Due to the heckling and stonings, Capildeo accused the police, largely staffed by Afro-Creoles, of being partisan and failing to maintain law and order.[74] In light of the deteriorating situation and the vocal militance of the East Indian leadership, the government declared a state of emergency in the East Indian majority areas and had the police, heavily armed, conduct house-to-house searches for arms and ammunition. While Capildeo's rash statements, in part, can be blamed, the governments's response clearly was excessive. The situation was made even more acrimonious when Williams asked for the West Indies Regiment to help maintain order.[75] The Colonial Office and the federal government refused the request, feeling that the 3,000 policemen on location were sufficient.

On December 4, 1961, the election took place with a high voter turnout. The PNM won a resounding victory, capturing 20 of 30 seats, with the DLP winning the remaining 10. Of the popular vote, the PNM had gained 57 percent and the DLP 42 percent.[76] While there was a limited crossover of voters to each party, the ethnic pattern of voting dominated.[77] Simply stated, the vast majority of Afro-Creoles voted for the PNM, and the vast majority of East Indians voted for the DLP. The party was more important than the individual candidate as it reflected racial and ethnic affiliation. Other factors included trade union support for the PNM and the relative economic success of government policies at raising the standard of living.[78]

The importance of the racial issue in national politics was most evident in the composition of the government for both the opposition and the PNM. Of the 12 cabinet places, 8 went to Afro-Creoles, including 1 women, 2 to Muslims, and 2 to white Creoles. In the Senate

PNM appointees were 1 Hindu, 1 Syrian, 1 Chinese, and 9 Afro-Creoles. The DLP refused to make nominations, leaving the governor to redress the balance. He appointed 3 white Creole businessmen, 1 trade unionist, 1 solicitor, 1 musical director, and 1 Hindu businessman. At least two of his choices were Afro-Trinidadians.

In the Legislative Council the DLP's members were divided into eight East Indians and two Afro-Creoles or mixed. Of the East Indians, three were Hindus, four were Christians (three Presbyterians and one Catholic), and one Muslim. The remaining two were Anglican and Catholic. Overall, the new government was overwhelmingly middle class and Western oriented in terms of cultural and political outlook. Hindu representation was minimal as no Hindus sat on the cabinet, and only two, non-DLP members, sat in the Senate.

Trinidadian society was sharply divided along lines of race and politics in the aftermath of the 1961 general elections. Not only was there the division between Afro-Creole and East Indian; there was also an urban-rural discrepancy as the former group was largely urban based and the latter lived mainly in the countryside. The DLP's defeat furthered Indo-Trinidadian alienation, and the shadow of ethnic conflict along the lines of Ceylon loomed in Trinidad.

DEMISE OF THE FEDERATION AND INDEPENDENCE

In September 1961 a referendum was held in Jamaica, and the population voted against joining the West Indies Federation. In Trinidad Williams had earlier made it clear that his nation would not single-handedly assume the responsibility of a federation without Jamaica.[79] Trinidad and Tobago had major concerns over federation and what it would bring. One of the apprehensions in Port of Spain was over the movement of labor: the smaller islands favored free movement, while the Trinidadians opposed it since it would cause unemployment to rise and take jobs away from local people. Trinidadians were sensitive to this since their island was by far the most economically promising. Moreover, personal differences between Adams and Williams soured the concept of a federation. In October Williams went so far as to say, "There is no Federation today," an ominous indication of what the Trinidadian view on the matter was.[80] This was followed in November by another statement that the federation issue had already had "one referendum too many" and that Trinidad and Tobago might "go it alone."[81] At the same time, Williams indicated that a federation of the remaining nine states was not entirely ruled out.

The majority within the PNM favored separate independence along the lines of Jamaica and were fiercely opposed to any arrangement involving the Windward and Leeward islands and Barbados.[82] Shortly after the elections, the PNM executive formed a committee to study the issue. The committee was then to give its report to a special party convention in late January 1962. The British, alarmed at the situation, rushed the new secretary of state for the colonies, Reginald Maulding, to Port of Spain in the hope of convincing Trinidad not to abandon the West Indies Federation. He arrived too late as an extraordinary meeting of the General Council of the PNM met on Sunday, January 14, the day he arrived, and declared that, "Trinidad and Tobago reject unequivocally any participation in a Federation of the Eastern Caribbean, and proceed forthwith to National Independence."[83]

Trinidad had decided to follow Jamaica, although an offer was made to the smaller islands for association with Port of Spain as a capital. Only Grenada, under the flamboyant Eric Gairy, considered the unitary state offer. The smaller states feared becoming wards of Trinidad, like Tobago, and, by and large, preferred to maintain their political individualism.[84]

The DLP's leaders were outraged that they were not consulted on the matter of scrapping the federation. Capildeo regarded it as another example of PNM high-handedness and called for new elections without ballot boxes.[85] The issue of forming a unitary state with Grenada or any other island was equally irritating and perceived as an attempt to swamp the East Indian vote with additional black votes. Moreover, the government's announcement that it was going to form a national defense force provoked Ashford Sinanan, a DLP member of Parliament, to make the demand that the East Indian party be permitted to form its own national guard. This demand did little to placate anyone's apprehensions over the racial tensions confronting Trinidad, especially since British Guiana was undergoing similar problems, but in a much more confronting manner.

In May 1962 the Marlborough House Conference was held in London to discuss Trinidad and Tobago's independence. With a background of deteriorating racial relations, growing East Indian militancy and acts of violence, it became imperative that compromise be made by all sides involved. Even at the conference, East Indian extremists, feeling that the DLP was not entirely representative of their views, advocated parity or giving 50 percent of jobs, government positions, and control of the public utilities, the police, and the civil service to

Indo-Trinidadians, who made up only 37 percent of the total population. The paranoia of such organizations as the Indian National Association, which attended the conference, helped put the DLP in a more moderate light.

The DLP went to the London conference transfixed by a difficult dilemma. While apprehensive over what independence would bring, the party recognized that to oppose it would be political stupidity. At the same time, the DLP wanted safeguards for minorities built into the independence constitution. Capildeo went to the conference bearing these paradoxes in mind, while reiterating his demand for new elections before independence.

Though the conference commenced in an atmosphere of mutual distrust between the PNM and the DLP, it ended on a note of harmony and promise. Colonial Secretary Reginald Maulding presided over the difficult meeting, which more than once threatened to collapse.[86] Finally, when the situation appeared to fall apart entirely, Williams conceded to a number of DLP demands: there would be an independent boundaries commission to delineate new constituencies that would vary by a margin of no more than 20 percent; an elections commission would be responsible for the conduct of elections, the registration of voters, and the testing of voting machines; a proclamation of a state of emergency would last only six months unless extended by Parliament; the auditor general and the judiciary were to be strengthened as offices independent of political parties; and there would be consultations with the leader of the opposition on important appointments including chairmanships of electoral and boundary commissions.[87] Furthermore, the right of appeal to the Privy Council would be widened, while the form of Trinidad and Tobago's new government was announced to be a constitutional monarchy. The most significant concession was the special entrenchment of an increased number of provisions by a three-fourths majority in the upper house.[88] In other words, clauses relating to constitutional amendments, the conduct of parliamentary procedures, and a plethora of other items would have to be ratified by 75 percent of the House of Representatives. In effect, that meant a degree of entrenchment and a widening of responsibility to the DLP, which controlled more than 25 percent of the seats in that governmental organ. The PNM's accommodationist stance greatly reduced tensions in Trinidad and Tobago and allowed the conference to set August 31, 1962, as the date for independence.[89]

For the DLP the outcome of the conference was highly successful and a badly needed boost to morale after the 1961 elections. The concessions made by the PNM were enough for the DLP to drop the demand for new elections, while neutralizing the radical East Indian groups. The East Indian middle sectors could now look to independence with some degree of assurance that their interests would be represented and safeguarded, and their Afro-Creole counterparts were ensured that their political dominance would not be easily jeopardized.

CONCLUSION

The 1956-61 period witnessed the entrenchment of the party system as the PNM became the political representative of the Afro-Creole middle class and the DLP, the representative of the East Indian bourgeois. The former party, however, clearly dominated due, in large part, to the strong personality and acumen of its leader, Eric Williams. Moreover, the PNM carefully clarified what it stood for—a moderate, procapitalist, yet nationalistic organization. While the Afro-Creole party was able to translate its ideology into viable programs, to be carried through in parliament by democratic majorities, the DLP's message to the public was less clear and muted by internal power struggles. The PNM's accommodation policy also gave the party more flexibility when co-opting key minority groups. The DLP's inexperience was evident as it lost the support of some of the same groups after the 1958 elections. Despite the divisions in Trinidadian society, the middle class had come to power and led the nation to independence. Those divisions, between Afro-Creole and East Indian, however, would determine the course of the nation's politics in the next decade.

NOTES

1. For the difficult time of federal attempts see W. Andrew Axline, *Caribbean Integration: The Politics of Regionalism* (New York: Nichols, 1979); John Mordecai, *The West Indies: The Federal Negotiations* (Evanston: Northwestern University Press, 1968); and A. J. Payne, *The Politics of the Caribbean Community, 1961-1979* (New York: St. Martin's Press, 1980).

2. *The Times*, February 5, 1956, p. 9; February 24, 1956, p. 8; and February 29, 1956, p. 9.

3. "West Indies, Capital Issue," *The Economist*, July 20, 1957, p. 204; and "Trinidad on a Sticky Wicket," *The Economist*, October 5, 1957, pp. 53-54.

4. "Trinidad Oil Realities," *The Economist*, June 15, 1956, p. 1113. Also see Ivar Oxaal, *Black Intellectuals Come to Power: The Rise of Creole Nationalism in Trinidad and Tobago* (Cambridge, Mass.: Schenkman, 1971), p. 121.

5. For this development see Robert Gilpin, *US Power and the Multinational Corporations: The Political Economy of Foreign Direct Investment* (New York: Basic Books, 1975).

6. "Trinidad Ministers Defeated, Election Victory for Dr. Williams," *The Times*, September 26, 1956, p. 9.

7. Quoted in Yogenda Malik, *East Indians in Trinidad: A Study in Minority Politics* (London: Oxford University Press, 1971), p. 98; from *Trinidad Guardian*, September 2, 1957.

8. Malik, *East Indians in Trinidad*; *Trinidad Guardian*, April 10, 1958.

9. Pearl Cameron, "New Democracy Party Upholds Peoples Rights," *Trinidad Guardian*, June 5, 1957, p. 2.

10. Ibid.

11. Malik, *East Indians in Trinidad*, p. 99.

12. Ibid.

13. In Tobago, a predominantly Afro-Creole island, DLP speakers were greeted by eggs and rocks, while pro-PNM East Indians were called "traitors" and "lackeys" of the Afro-Creoles.

14. "Socialists Win in the West Indies," *The Times*, March 26, 1958, p. 10.

15. Malik, *East Indians in Trinidad*, p. 101.

16. "Trinidad Aims in Federal Poll, Parties Seek Prestige," *The Times*, March 25, 1958, p. 6.

17. Malik, *East Indians in Trinidad*, p. 102.

18. Ibid., p. 101.

19. Winston Mahabir, *In and Out of Politics: Tales of the Government of Dr. Eric Williams from the Notebooks of a Former Minister* (Trinidad: Inprint Caribbean, 1978), p. 78.

20. Ibid.

21. The governor was to be removed from the Executive Council cabinet, and the remaining official members, the attorney general and chief secretary, would have no vote.

22. Patrick Solomon, *Solomon: An Autobiography* (Port of Spain: Inprint Caribbean, 1981), p. 160.

23. Malik, *East Indians in Trinidad*, p. 129.

24. C. L. R. James was a well-known Marxist historian well before he returned to Trinidad in 1958, having spent considerable time in London and the United States. It was in England that he met Williams, who was then a student at Oxford.

25. Mahabir, *In and Out of Politics*, p. 83.

26. Solomon, *Autobiography*, p. 161.

27. Eric Williams, *Inward Hunger: The Education of a Prime Minister* (Chicago: University of Chicago Press, 1971), p. 216.

28. Selwyn Ryan, *Race and Nationalism in Trinidad and Tobago: A Study of Decolonization in a Multiracial Society* (Toronto: University of Toronto Press, 1972), p. 203.
29. Ibid.
30. Ibid.
31. Williams, *Inward Hunger*, p. 220.
32. "Trinidad Move to Ban American Aircraft," *The Times*, April 23, 1960, p. 5. Also see *Hispanic American Review* 13 (April 1960): 248.
33. Williams, *Inward Hunger*, p. 220.
34. "Trinidad Constitution Burnt, Self-Rule Demanded," *The Times*, April 25, 1960, p. 10.
35. Ibid.
36. "Self-Rule for Trinidad Under New Constitution," *The Times*, June 17, 1960, p. 10.
37. *Hispanic American Review* 13 (June 1960): 388.
38. Ibid.
39. Williams, *Inward Hunger*, p. 237. Also see "Revising West Indies Bases Treaty, Three Stages of Talks," *The Times*, September 21, 1960, p. 11 and "Foreign Bases in West Indies," *The Times*, October 3, 1960, p. 11.
40. Williams, *Inward Hunger*, pp. 239-41.
41. *Hispanic American Review* 13 (September 1960): 616.
42. Williams, *Inward Hunger*, p. 224.
43. *Interviews With Three Caribbean Writers in Texas* (Austin: Occasional Publication of the African and Afro-American Research Institute, University of Texas, 1972), p. 37.
44. Williams, *Inward Hunger*, p. 268.
45. *Education Report of the Committee on General Education* (Port of Spain: Government Printery, 1960), p. 32.
46. Ryan, *Race and Nationalism*, p. 232.
47. *Trinidad Guardian*, July 27, 1960, quoted in Ryan, *Race and Nationalism*, p. 234.
48. Count Finbar Ryan, *Pastoral on the Roman Catholic Education of Youth* (Port of Spain, 1960), p. 7.
49. Ryan, *Race and Nationalsim*, p. 236.
50. Ibid.
51. Ibid.
52. Ibid.
53. Oxaal, *Black Intellectuals*, p. 157.
54. As Ryan notes, "The PNM took no chances even in Port of Spain, where the boundaries were redrafted to make sure that all potential DLP areas, i.e., the upper-class and upper-middle-class residential areas, were attached to heavily working-class areas where the PNM had been consistently strong. The DLP was not given an outside chance to gain a seat in the capital city as they had done in the 1958 and 1959 muncipal elections. . . . In the countryside there was strong

evidence to substantiate the DLP's claim that the PNM had herded as many Indian voters as was possible into constituencies which they could not possibly win, and had extracted from such areas large blocks of Negro voters who were then recombined into new constituencies." *Race and Nationalism*, pp. 244-45.

55. *Hansard*, March 10, 1961, p. 1650.
56. Malik, *East Indians in Trinidad*, p. 106.
57. Ibid., p. 107.
58. *Trinidad Guardian*, September 11, 1961, p. 1.
59. *Hispanic American Review* 14 (September 1961): 803.
60. *Year Book of Labour Statistics 1966* (Geneva: International Labour Office, 1966), p. 712.
61. Ibid.
62. *Hispanic American Review* 13 (August 1960): 457.
63. Ibid.
64. Caswell L. Johnson, "Political Unionism and Autonomy in Economies of British Colonial Origin: The Cases of Jamaica and Trinidad," *American Journal of Economics and Sociology* 39 (July 1980): 244.
65. *Hispanic American Review* 14 (July 1961): 615.
66. *The Statesman*, April 15, 1961, p. 2.
67. Malik, *East Indians in Trinidad*, p. 118.
68. Malik comments, "the DLP like the PNM made particular efforts to recruit non-East Indian elements." *East Indians in Trinidad*, p. 1.
69. *Trinidad Guardian*, November 19, 1961, quoted in Malik, *East Indians in Trinidad*, p. 116.
70. *Hispanic American Review* 14 (November 1961): 1001.
71. *The Statesman*, August 3, 1961, p. 2.
72. *Hispanic American Review* 14 (November 1961): 1001.
73. *Hispanic American Review* 14 (December 1961): 1101.
74. *Trinidad and Tobago Report on the General Elections of 1961* (Port of Spain: Prepared by the Supervisor of Elections, 1965), p. 74; "Trinidad Goes to the Polls," *The Times*, December 5, 1961, p. 8; and "Trinidad Victory by Dr. Williams, Party Wins 20 Seats Out of 30," *The Times*, December 6, 1961, p. 12.
75. As Malik notes, "Although both parties made limited inroads into each other's areas, the primary determinant variable in the voting behavior appears to be ethnicity. For instance, the P.N.M. secured heavy majorities in four Port of Spain constituencies, where the East Indian population was only 9 per cent and 26 per cent respectively. On the other hand, in such heavily East Indian majority areas as Pointe-a-Pierre, Couva, Chaguanas, Caroni East, Naparima, Nariva, Princes Town, Siparia and St. Augustine, the D.L.P. won with heavy majorities, although in all these constituencies, except St. Augustine, the P.N.M. put up only East Indian candidates." *East Indians in Trinidad*, p. 120. Malik's view is also reflected

in Ryan, *Race and Nationalism*, and Krishna Bahadoorsingh, *Trinidad Electoral Politics: The Persistence of the Race Factor* (London: Institute of Race Relations, Special Series, 1968).

76. *The Times*, December 5, 1961, p. 8, and *Hispanic American Review* 14 (December 1961): 1101.

77. *Hispanic American Review* 14 (April 1961): 326.

78. *Hispanic American Review* 14 (October 1961): 902.

79. *Hispanic American Review* 14 (November 1961): 1001.

80. Payne, *Caribbean Community*, p. 28.

81. *The Nation*, January 15, 1962, quoted in Payne, *Caribbean Community*, p. 29.

82. As Payne notes, "the leaders of the other eastern Caribbean islands privately made it clear that they had no intention of bowing to the terms offered by Trinidad, terms which they took to be the portent of a new local imperialism which would require their small island units to abandon their individuality and become wards of Trinidad after the example of Tobago." *Caribbean Community*, p. 29.

83. *Hispanic American Review* 15 (January 1962): 43.

84. The leader of the All-Trinidad National Association comments, "It is not so much the welfare of these little islands that the PNM is interested in, but the votes they believe they will receive from them, and which they hope will abrogate the voting capacity of the Indians in Trinidad. . . . The concept of a unitary state, therefore, is founded on racialism." H. P. Singh, *That Unitary State* (Port of Spain, 1962), pp. 11-12.

85. In "Trinidad Enters Independence States," *The Times*, May 29, 1962, p. 10, Capildeo comments, "We want a judiciary which is independent. We want provisions which really guarantee effectively the rights and freedoms which ought to exist in a democratic society. We want Parliament democratically constituted. We want a procedure for the amendment of the constitution which effectively protects us from the arbitrary exercise of power to amend. We want the various commissions so constituted as to ensure that they function effectively and impartially. Further, we want, above all, provision made to ensure free and fair elections in the country."

86. "Disagreement at Trinidad Talks," *The Times*, May 31, 1962, p. 10; *The Times*, June 1, 1962, p. 13; June 2, 1962, p. 9; and June 5, 1962, p. 11. One major obstacle was Capildeo's insistence that a five-year freeze on making constitutional changes be accepted. His other comments were most irritating to Williams, such as the following: "The financial position bothers me. The country is ripe to be taken over by an extremist party." *The Times*, June 1, 1962, p. 13. Claims by the opposition that the PNM wanted to establish a police state also infuriated the PNM. "Trinidad Rift Over Maulding Plan, Opposition Fear Police State," *The Times*, June 7, 1962, p. 10.

87. Ryan, *Race and Nationalism*, p. 333. Also see *Hispanic American Review* 15 (June 1962): 519; and "Trinidad Independence Fixed for August 31," *The Times*, June 9, 1962, p. 8.

88. Ryan, *Race and Nationalism*, p. 333.

89. "Independence Day for Trinidad," *The Times*, August 31, 1962, p. 7. Also see "Trinidad Hails Independence with Music," *The Times*, September 1, 1962, p. 5.

7

The Challenge of Independence, 1962-69

By 1962 party politics were firmly established as a middle sector realm. Both the PNM and the DLP were nationalistic, largely procapitalist, and led by elites that were overwhelmingly middle class in composition. During a brief period of accommodation between the two parties, a tacit, yet uneasy class "alliance" emerged. This middle sector hegemony over the political system was initially coupled with increased upward mobility between the lower and middle levels of the stratification system.[1] There was also the emergence of a highly unionized urban and industrial working class, which had considerable bargaining power within the growing modern sector of the economy. One offshoot of better workers' wages was the expansion of the lower middle class as a new group, largely black, which began to enjoy social respectability and could aspire to further upward mobility. However, the moderate economic growth of the 1950s led to a slowdown in the mid-1960s, a situation characterized by rising unemployment, declining oil revenues, and an end of the middle-class accommodationist alliance. The government's adherence to procapitalist development plans and deteriorating financial conditions ultimately led to social tensions, which were reflected, in part, by the radicalization of the trade union movement and a general restlessness in the lowest and unemployed echelons of the popular sectors.

THE ACCOMMODATIONIST MIDDLE-CLASS ALLIANCE

As A. N. R. Robinson, one of the PNM's early leaders notes, "independence began in a climate of rising expectations."[2] Part of these rising expectations included the hope that there would be better relations between the new nation's major racial groups. By the 1960 census, the East Indians had expanded the size of their community to 301,946 or 36.5 percent of the total population as opposed to the Afro-Creole's 358,588 or 43.5 percent of the total population.[3] The mixed population, including whites (1.9 percent) and Chinese (1.2 percent), stood at 143,344 (13 percent). Considering the racial balance, Williams and the PNM could not entirely ignore 36.5 percent of the citizenry. Since the founding of the party, the political leader, surrounded by largely middle-class Afro-Creoles, had preached racial unity and the need for cross-cultural linkages. Despite what appeared to be a firm intellectual grasp of the problem, Williams never attempted to "bridge the emotional gap that lay between him and the Indians."[4]

The prime minister's method of dealing with the East Indian population was by indirect contact, that is, through an intermediary. Winston Mahabir, a cabinet member and party founder, functioned in this capacity, providing Williams with a "window" on the Christian Indo-Trinidadian world. Another cabinet member, Kamaluddin Mohammed, was the window on the Muslim East Indians. Contact with the Hindu majority, however, was lacking and continued to be a PNM shortcoming. The PNM's accommodationist stance, which had emerged at the close of the independence conference, was an unexpected and welcome turn for many. Consequently, the DLP felt that the PNM could be met halfway. Although no formal alliance was ever concluded between Eric Williams and Rudranath Capildeo, an understanding was reached, and a middle-class alliance controlled the political system of Trinidad and Tobago in 1962 and 1963.

The opposition leader, during the alliance period, provided Williams with "an occasional window on the Trinidad Indian Hindu World."[5] In return DLP members were sent abroad on government missions, and there was some inclusion of the opposition in the national decision-making process. For Capildeo, who had become convinced after the 1961 elections that it was impossible for the DLP to win elections with Indo-Trinidadian leadership, it was more opportune to bargain for concessions from the government.[6] A personal motivation for Capildeo was a special leave of absence from Parliament granted by the Speaker, something that would never have occurred if Williams had opposed it. This arrangement allowed the leader of the opposition to be out of the country most of the year as he had returned to the University of London to teach. Although he returned to Trinidad during his vacations, his absence left the opposition party without its leader, a situation that the PNM no doubt favored.

END OF THE ALLIANCE

Capildeo's high-handed rule over the DLP, by telephone from London, and his continued absence from the political stage helped undermine the unity of the party and, with that, came the weakening of the middle-class alliance. From 1963 onward, when the DLP leader left the islands, unity within the organization began to decline. The situation of a party without its leader eventually generated considerable dissent, and since early 1963 some objections were vocalized.

In March 1963 Capildeo returned to Port of Spain and sought to provide his party with a coherent ideology. Using a poorly defined "democratic socialism" as the basis of party political thought, he announced that this was a departure from ethnic politics and was aimed at preserving the nation from the evils of racialism and communism.[7] In moving the DLP from its rigid antisocialist position, Capildeo created further discontent among the non-East Indian conservatives who dominated the party executive. A group of businessmen and merchants, largely situated in the capital, this group had rallied behind the DLP as a conservative counterforce to what they regarded as PNM radicalism.

Throughout 1963 and into 1964, the DLP was rife with tensions, as the party executive resisted the party leader and the party's members of Parliament resented the rise of Stephen C. Maharaj, who was a compromise choice as the leader of the opposition since Capildeo relinquished the post to preserve unity. Capildeo's major headache, however, continued to be the party executive. Although this group was a major source of the DLP's financial support, the East Indian professor felt that it was not essential to the party's survival. When the executive pressed Maharaj to accept the leadership in and out of the House, Capildeo dismissed the body and threatened his appointee's tenure as opposition leader. Since the membership of the executive lacked popular sector support among the East Indians and could not challenge the party leader's action, it accepted its dismissal.

Capildeo's victory over the executive was a bad blunder and would serve to destroy what remained of party and opposition unity. Although the DLP leader had thwarted a challenge, he deprived his organization of its major financial backers and alienated any remaining non-East Indians who had been pro-DLP. Moreover, another mistake was that no effort was made to regain non-Indo-Trinidadian support. The DLP's attraction to other ethnic groups was further undermined when three parliamentarians, M. A. Forrester, chairman of the party, Peter Farquhar, and Tajmool Hosein, left the ranks, citing the major reason as Capildeo's long absences.[8] Other reasons were discontent over accommodation with the PNM, the belief that the DLP would never capture power, and Capildeo's insistence on democratic socialism as the party's ideology. In March 1964 the more pragmatic defectors founded the Liberal Party of Trinidad and Tobago, reducing the DLP's membership in the legislature from ten to seven, while also clarifying publicly that Capildeo's party was now almost Hindu East Indian in rank and file.

Fragmentation of the DLP also meant fragmentation of the middle sectors in the governing of the nation. As accommodation and cooperation gradually ended due to the disarray of the opposition, the PNM once again turned to ruling without consultation, in effect, ignoring the DLP and the Liberal Party. The PNM's secure margin in the House of Representatives meant that it did not have to make any concessions. Significantly, the opposition's inability to maintain a united front played into the hands of the PNM as it had with the colonial government before independence.

ECONOMIC DIFFICULTIES AND THE ALIENATION OF LABOR

The period from 1961 to 1966 was active for the PNM as the party constitution was revised, a party headquarters was established, and the tenth anniversary of the party was celebrated. Although there was some dissension in the ranks, the forceful personality of Williams overrode any challengers. The prime minister's profile continued to loom over Trinidad and Tobago's political geography, especially since he sought to maintain personal contact with the population through a much publicized "Meet the People Tour" from March 1963 through January 1964, which was followed in June 1964 by a "Meet the Party Tour." The former was a part of the PNM's philosophy of "direct democracy," which was intended to bring Williams into contact with village organizations, hence allowing community participation in discussions of community problems.[9] The government also created a program to distribute Crown Lands, which was aimed at curtailing rising unemployment.

Williams sought to gain further political advantage from the Better Village Program, which created community centers and introduced mobile health, library, and postal services. The program facilitated better water supplies and, in general, attempted to improve the rural standard of living. In this development effort, the government was provided financial assistance from two of the nation's largest multinational companies, Texaco, which was involved in the oil sector, and Tate and Lyle, involved in the agricultural sector. Both companies, the former, a U.S. multinational, and the latter, British, were concerned with the political future of the nation due to a growing economic crisis.

The tours and the Better Village Program were efforts to bolster the PNM's image with the popular sectors, especially the black workers. Following the general election of 1961, the PNM lost some of the support of black industrial workers since union leadership, especially in the oil fields, became highly critical of the government's economic policies. This was due to the high levels of unemployment and the retrenching of various companies that were also making profits. Simply stated, the government's commitment to investment by invitation was not proving to be highly successful. In 1962 and 1963 there were especially serious problems in the Trinidadian economy, a situation generally attributed to unsettled political conditions after the demise of the West Indies Federation and the achievement of independence, as well as unfavorable developments in the external trade sector, caused by falling prices for Trinidad's main exports, petroleum, sugar, cocoa, and citrus fruit.[10] Whereas the 1951-60 period had been favorable in terms of trade to the extent of TT $327 million, the 1961-64 period was an adverse balance of TT $324 million.[11]

Although the petroleum sector was the major dynamic element of the economy, its share in the gross domestic product declined continuously from 30.4 percent in 1960 to 27 percent in 1965, and its annual growth rate in the early 1960s averaged only 2.7 percent. The declining oil industry and the continued decline of the sugar industry severely affected the rest of the economy as unemployment shot over the 10 percent mark and the cost of living rose. To complicate the situation further, the government was hard-pressed and largely unsuccessful in its efforts to get foreign loans.

In the trade union movement it was felt that the PNM leadership had been "bought out" by big business.[12] Moreover, labor leaders, both Afro-Creole and East Indian, increasingly perceived the government as attempting to maintain industrial peace at the cost of workers and to the benefit of local and foreign capitalists. The establishment of the National Planning Commission in January 1963 was done so by Williams to formulate the Second Five-Year Development Plan, which was similar to the first plan. To labor it was clear that the government would continue investment by invitation, tax breaks for large corporations, and the construction of industrial parks to the detriment of the needs of the popular sectors. The middle sector political alliance in Parliament further fueled mistrust in the formal political system and the two major parties.

The unrest in the labor movement was reflected in the rise of industrial disputes. In 1962 there were 75 disputes, involving 15,962 workers, and 164,647 workdays were lost. In the following period of 1963-64, 92 disputes occurred, involving 25,896 workers, and 300,877 working days were lost.[13] These strikes were not limited to the oil fields, but included agriculture, manufacturing, construction, and transport.

In the early 1960s the leadership of the labor movement underwent changes as a new generation came to dominate. One of the most articulate and longlasting, in the tradition of Butler, was George Weekes, an anti-PNM black who had political ambitions. Assuming the leadership of the Oil Workers Trade Union, Weekes enjoyed considerable political clout in the southern part of Trinidad where the oil belt is located. In the sugar belt another young radical, Krishna Gowandan, organized the Freedom Fighters and challenged Bhadase Sagan Maraj's hold over the All-Trinidad Sugar Estate and Factory Workers Union. The growing unrest of labor and the radicalization of the workers affected the PNM and the DLP, making the middle sectors somewhat apprehensive over what was unfolding.

In September 1964 the PNM held a tripartite conference on unemployment, which was attended by representatives of the sugar and oil trade unions, the oil and sugar industries' managers, and government advisers in agriculture, petroleum, and economic planning.[14] One of the major discussions at this conference was the Second Five-Year Development Plan's objective of creating 44,000 new jobs. To achieve this, the government asked for active cooperation from all parties, which meant an end to labor strikes and the companies' unilateral retrenching. A result of the unemployment conference was the creation of a number of tripartite committees to investigate labor utilization and industrial and agricultural development. Labor, however, perceived this as a ploy to snarl negotiations and slow the momentum of the trade union movement, which was now linked to developments on the political front.

In March 1964 close to 15,000 workers went on strike in the sugar belt. Five large companies were forced to close, including Caroni Ltd., the largest manufacturer of sugar on the island. Williams's response was to declare a state of emergency in the area against the advice of the opposition leader, Maharaj. Meetings and demonstrations were banned, and the police conducted searches for weapons and "subversive literature."

As the events of March 1965 unfolded, some solidarity was shown in the black-dominated unions. George Weekes, president of the nationwide Trade Union Congress (TUC), passed a resolution in the TUC Executive that declared support for the East Indian sugar workers and demanded an end to the state of emergency. The show of solidarity was highly significant, and, as Malik notes, "for the first time since the late 1930s, a coalition between Negro oilfield workers and East Indian sugar workers became feasible."[15] The political situation was relatively fluid, and Trinidad's political forces scrambled to make new alliances.

While the two most significant bodies of workers moved closer, Afro-Creole labor unity began to fragment. Not all groups were convinced that an alliance with the East Indians was in their best interest. A nagging fear remained that any substantial weakening of the PNM government would result in the election of an Indo-Trinidadian prime minister. Hence, the issue of race continued to weaken the thrust of labor as exemplified by the powerful and largely black Seamen's Union, which withdrew from the TUC in protest. At the same time, the unions were further alienated from the government on March 18, 1965, when the Industrial Stabilization Act (ISA) was enacted after passing the House of Representatives and the Senate by substantial majorities, which included DLP votes.

Williams describes the ISA as "an attempt to deal with industrial disputes by judicial process and to minimise the disruption of the national economy and the losses to the workers of their wages which strike action inevitably entails."[16] In his memoirs, he provides another reason: "The subversive elements in the society . . . were at work; the background was an open attempt to link the trade unions in oil and sugar."[17] Although Williams sought to cast the blame for the islands' difficulties on leftists, such as C. L. R. James who had returned to Trinidad in 1963, the ISA was a sweeping bill that was not popular with labor. It prohibited strikes in public services, imposed strong curbs on the right to strike, and stated that lockouts could occur only with advance notice to the minister of labor. The ISA, however, was effective: in 1965 only four strikes occurred, involving only 7,160 workers.[18] The following year was officially strike free.

DLP DISUNITY AND THE 1966 ELECTIONS

The political events of 1964 had an impact in the DLP. At the party convention of July 12-13, 1964, Capildeo expounded the DLP's ideology: "The central idea of democratic socialism is the brotherhood of man and its purpose is to make this a reality everywhere. Accordingly, it rejects discrimination on the grounds of race, colour or creed, and holds that men should accord to one another equal consideration and status of the fundamental dignity of man."[19] Capitalism was rejected as it was based on acquisition and competition. For the DLP, according to Capildeo, the cooperative movement was the correct economic path, rather than state ownership. As Trinidad and Tobago had only a limited number of skilled people, nationalization was a poor alternative for the future while communal sharing had more to offer. Furthermore, the DLP, at least on the surface, sought to be a prolabor party as it favored a new labor code, the regulation of wages, and employment insurance.

Despite the prolabor announcements that were issued at the conference, most labor groups were not convinced of the party's change of heart. Instead of benefiting from the labor-government strife in 1965, the DLP fragmented further at a time when the PNM was closing ranks and looking toward the 1966 elections. The DLP was hampered by many factors, including poor leadership, undisciplined members, and rejection by many of democratic socialism or at least a lack of understanding of it. The majority of the leadership elite were from middle-class backgrounds, and they had no desire to seek an alliance with workers, especially black workers. By 1966 the DLP had split into three factions—the Maharaj-Capildeo clique, the centrists, led by Vernon Jamadar and S. N. Capildeo, and the right wing of L. F. Seukeran and Ashford Sinanan.

The vote for the Industrial Stabilization Act had set in motion the crisis in the DLP. Maharaj, who was prolabor, attempted to stay true to democratic socialism, instructing the party in Parliament not to vote for the bill. Against his instructions, two House members and all DLP Senate members voted in favor. What now ensued was a three-way battle for control of the party with Capildeo waiting on the sidelines in London. In doing so he abandoned Maharaj, who was now allied to forces that wanted to broaden the base of the party to accommodate the disgruntled Afro-Creole labor movement. Maharaj was joined by C. L. R. James, George Weekes, and Jack Kelshall in an attempt to take over the DLP from without and convert it into a multiracial labor party, which would then challenge the PNM in 1966 along class lines and on economic issues instead of playing the traditional game of ethnic politics.

The DLP executive, now in the hands of middle-class East Indians, discovered the forces behind Maharaj and, after various episodes, managed to oust him from his position as leader of the opposition.[20] The centrists, led by Jamadar, were supported by middle-class professionals who were cautious of any interethnic unity. The centrists' major worry was that an alliance of black and East Indian workers would fail; it was feared that the PNM would consciously stir up racial tensions and thereby seek to win elections through playing upon resultant anxieties. Also it was feared that Afro-Creole radicals would be unable to retain the support of the black popular sectors for the DLP.[21]

Capildeo returned to Trinidad in July 1965 to find a party controlled by the centrists to whom he gave his support. Maharaj had left the party to help found the Workers and Farmers Party with C. L. R. James and George Weekes, while S. N. Capildeo, already a member of Parliament, had become the acting opposition leader. Therefore, as the elections of 1966 approached, the DLP was largely a middle-class East Indian party, which was opposed to the ISA and any association with the Afro-Creole left. It presented a moderate platform, attempting to appeal to the electorate on a largely ethnic basis. It also attacked the PNM on the reorganization of the civil service and the educational administration. While warning that "the country is now racing down the steep path of one-party rule, and pretty soon from one-party it will become one-group rule, and thereafter, it will become one-man rule," DLP candidates argued that the mechanization of the sugar industry, a measure supported by the PNM, would put thousands out of work.[22]

Despite the nation's economic problems and labor's alienation, the opposition was unable to unify and take advantage of the situation in the months before the November 7, 1966, elections. A number of independents and three parties challenged the PNM—the DLP, the radical Workers and Farmers Party (WFP), and the Liberal Party. The DLP's poor relations with the non-East Indian population benefited the PNM as the largely white and mixed conservative business community began to swing behind Williams, especially after the passage of the ISA. At the same time, the largely black labor movement was not attracted to the DLP because of its distinctive East Indian and middle-class nature, although it was also widely felt that a vote for the smaller parties was wasted due to the racial structure of Trinidadian politics. While not excited by the PNM, many Afro-Creole workers continued to vote for that party fearing the possibility of an East Indian prime minister.

The WFP and the Liberal Party were shunted aside by the racial pattern of voting. The former was also hindered by the bad press it received, since there was only lukewarm public response to the radical policies advocated, such as extensive land reform and nationalization of the sugar and oil industries. Moreover, the government made public the Cuban ties of certain members and, in particular, emphasized that two candidates had participated in the Tricontinental Conference in Havana in January 1966. As Williams commented at a rally on September 14, 1966, "Go out and finish up with this Marxist ideology, which goes to Havana, Cuba and dares sit down and take part in subversive resolutions against the lawful Government of Trinidad and Tobago. To hell with Castro."[23] The prime minister's casting aspersions upon the candidates of the Workers and Farmers Party and his challenging their nationalism reinforced the major factors that strengthened the PNM campaign, which were the continuing concern over race and a brief upturn in the economy.

By mid-1966 the economy was in serious, though not critical, condition. The public debt had increased to over $50 million, while unemployment remained steady at 14 percent.[24] Despite these problems, the government continued to pursue its development plan, increasing the supply of services to the industrial community and building up the national infrastructure. Along these lines, a $31.5 million electric power station was opened in 1966, and loans were received from Canada to expand Trinidad's system of roads and increase water supply. Loans from the World Bank, totaling $8.5 million, also went to improve the nation's water supply.[25] Furthermore, a third vehicle assembly plant opened in Port of Spain in January 1966, providing some hope that the economic tide was turning.

On November 7, 1966, the PNM won a sweeping victory, taking 24 of 36 seats in the House of Representatives, while the DLP, with largely East Indian votes, won 12. Although voter turnout had declined from the 88.11 percent recorded in 1961, it was relatively high at 65.8 percent. In the popular vote the PNM received 52 percent, the DLP, 34 percent, the Liberal Party, about 7 percent, and the Workers and Farmers Party, close to 3 percent.[26] Capildeo insisted that the election was rigged due to the use of voting machines. The DLP leader, before retiring to the safety of London, instructed his party to adopt a policy of silence in Parliament and pledged that the DLP would not contest any new elections as long as voting machines were used. Parliament reconvened and the PNM, with a secure majority, continued to dominate the nation's political life.

THE DEEPENING ECONOMIC CRISIS

Without fear of attack from a self-muzzled opposition, Williams's government turned its attention to the economy. One of the negative side effects of the industrialization plan was that it was capital intensive, not labor intensive. In 1966, for example, the leading sugar producers received governmental approval for the purchase of combine harvesters, each designed to replace the labor of 80 canecutters.[27] In 1967 this situation grew worse as unemployment in the nation was estimated at 15 percent, and in Port of Spain, where many of the rural unemployed gravitated, it was over 17 percent.[28]

With an expanding population of over 1 million, the nation faced a severe crisis. As Thomas Mathews noted, the three major problems in the economy in 1967 were the retrenchment in the oil industry in which two companies in 1967 announced their intention of laying off almost 3,000 workers by 1969; a thinning out of government office workers to reduce overhead, thus qualifying for foreign loans; and the growing automation of the oil and sugar industries.[29] To its credit, the government attempted to safeguard the positions of workers as Williams proposed a new series of contracts and conditions for continued operation and expansion of the oil industry in Trinidad. Among these conditions were incentives for further drilling and exploring. Williams also announced a new short-term development program to supplement the Second Five-Year Development Program, which was due to end in 1968. Part of the new plan involved an additional investment of $11 million to bring three new tourist hotels to both islands and to construct six additional factories.[30] Furthermore, a $6.6 million loan from the Export-Import Bank of the United States was received for power-generating equipment, and a World Bank loan was acquired for highway construction.

As the government sought to remedy the economic situation, two elections took place. In January 1968 a by-election was held for Capildeo's seat in the House as it was declared vacant due to the DLP leader's prolonged absences. Bhadase Maraj won the election, bringing the People's Democratic Party back into the House, thereby challenging the DLP to abandon its policy of silence and to participate in the 1968 municipal elections under the leadership of Vernon Jamadar, who had become the leader of the opposition.

The municipal elections held on June 24, 1968, resulted in a PNM victory as that party captured 73 of 100 vacancies and gained control of all three municipalities and four of seven county councils. The DLP captured 23 seats, all of which were in areas where East Indians constituted a majority, while the remaining four seats went to independents. Although some observed the outcome as an indicator that the two-party system of democracy was functioning, only 30 percent of the eligible voters cast their ballot, a very low turnout.[31] Due to the poorly organized opposition party campaigns and dissatisfaction with the high level of unemployment, it was felt that the election would change little, hence the low turnout and general lack of interest. By 1968 economic affairs clearly overshadowed all other concerns in Trinidadian society, including elections in which the two major parties were acknowledged to be middle class in composition and pro-capitalist in their prescriptions for economic development.

In 1967 and 1968, 14 industrial disputes broke out, involving 3,129 workers, while unemployment remained constant at 15 percent, affecting some 54,000.[32] An increasingly concerned government sponsored a tripartite conference in July 1968 to discuss the impending cutbacks in the oil industry due to automation, declining production, and rising costs.[33] Representatives from the oil companies, the labor unions, and the government eventually reached an agreement: the companies would suspend layoffs until the government was able to provide other employment opportunities.

In 1969 Williams announced the government's Third Five-Year Development Plan (1969-73), which marked a change in development strategy. Hoping to silence his increasingly vocal critics from the left and right, the prime minister's new program was aimed at creating "a more diversified economy, with considerably more economic independence, and full employment."[34] Along these lines, the plan's other major objectives were to continue infrastructural improvements and to increase "the proportion of local ownership and participation in the economy."[35] Responding to a traditional criticism of overdependence on sugar, the five-year plan designated 1969 as the "Agricultural Year" and considered turning to the production of corn and soybean. The decision to decrease sugar production was also expedited by apprehension over the United Kingdom's entrance into the European Economic Community, which would adversely affect Trinidad's protected metropole market.

While the five-year plan sought to alleviate unemployment by housing, construction, and a number of other government-sponsored programs, one of the most significant actions in 1969 was the formation of the National Petroleum Company (NPC), which occurred when the government purchased all holdings of the British Petroleum Company.

This had been prompted by the company's announced intention of terminating its Trinidad operations, an action that would have displaced some 1,500 workers. Having the example of nationalizations in neighboring Venezuela and Cuba and considering the growing demands for national control of natural resources, the decision to take over British Petroleum was politically motivated, especially since the Oil Workers Trade Union had urged the government to do so.[36]

At the same time, the government entered the petroleum industry in a partnership with Tesoro of Texas. Concurrently, new petroleum legislation was enacted, of which the most important was a law that reduced the duration of leases from 30 years, with an option for 30 more, to 6 years and an additional 25.[37] The move into this sector was further reinforced by the discovery of major offshore oil deposits in May and September 1968.

The National Petroleum Company, part of the newly established Ministry of Petroleum and Mines, was from the very beginning plagued by bureaucratic infighting and the drain of competent personnel to the higher-paying foreign firms. Other government departments, such as Planning and Development or the Office of the Prime Minister, regarded the new organization either as a threat or a hindrance to their operations. Consequently, the NPC failed to attract the highest caliber personnel, and there was high turnover in the rank and file. As Farrell notes, the end result was that, "the staff of the Ministry of Petroleum and Mines is given to inessential tasks and is seriously demoralized and of low productivity."[38] As many of the measures undertaken in the oil industry were done at a rapid pace, the government's entry into the economy did not offset the downward spiral. Afro-Creole and mixed middle sector concern over the growing dimensions of the economic crisis had led to the expansion of the state sector in the national economy.

Part of the deepening crisis was related to the process of decolonization, undertaken by the government as part of the "national revolution" to destroy many of the structural manifestations of colonialism. In the course of decolonization, the party came to dominate the national bureaucracy but at the cost of creating a civil service that was unable to contend with the plethora of problems confronting a developing nation. Also, the party itself became more bureaucratic and less flexible. In many respects, the identity of the two organizations merged, and the result was not entirely conducive to the nation's developmental needs, nor did it project a democratic image for the government.

Gerand Chaliand has made the observation that a nationalist "revolution" that does not put its major stress on being simultaneously a social revolution is unlikely to yield results in the aftermath of independence.[39] These results, of course, in the case of Trinidad and Tobago were the survival of the democratic system and better economic distribution of the nation's wealth. Related to this, the real problem for nationalist movements, like the PNM, is the bureaucratization of the leadership. In Trinidad and Tobago the PNM sought to decolonize, hence seeking to avoid the ossification of the nationalist, in this case Afro-Trinidadian, "revolution." Unable to combine the social revolution with the national, the largely Afro-Creole PNM did not bring into realization a long-term political mobilization of the most economically oppressed segments of the population. Growth had been concentrated in the modern sectors of the economy and hardly touched the lowest income groups of the population, which, coincidentally, were East Indians living in the rural areas and tied to the traditional agricultural sectors.

Friction between administrative groups and the prime minister's authoritarian personality helped create a system increasingly marked by upward shifting of responsibilities and the centralization of power in a small core of ministers surrounding and dependent upon the head of state. In this scenario Williams dominated the national bureaucracy and the party, and, through these, the nation. As Michel Crozier notes, "Bureaucratic power, in this sense, implies the reign of law and order, but, at the same time, government without the participation of the governed."[40] Considering the politicking within the national bureaucracy, as exemplified by the difficult beginnings of the National Petroleum Corporation, it is easier to understand why the implementation of development programs did not always proceed smoothly nor always meet the demands of the citizenry. This situation was further complicated in the mid-1960s by the movement of competent civil servants from public service to the more lucrative private sector. For others unable to make the shift there was frustration, corruption, and the bucking of decisions upward. By the late 1960s the nation's leadership had become bureaucratized, and many had begun to wonder if middle sector democracy in Trinidad and Tobago had gotten lost in a bureaucratic maze.

CONCLUSION

From 1962 to 1969 Trinidad and Tobago's political-economic structure was dominated by Williams, who sought to implement his own distinctive blend of democratic capitalism. The economy was initially opened to foreign investment with generous incentives. Free market capitalism, however, did not prove entirely successful for the small nation, and the fluctuations of prices on the international market for Trinidad's major exports underscored the fragility of the economy to upward and downward price movements. As unemployment rose and labor unrest increased in the late 1960s, the government shifted away from a "hands off" policy regarding the economy, to the creation of public sector companies in the oil industry, which was the mainstay of the nation's finances. The shift was impeded by bureaucratic problems, and by 1969 the future of democratic capitalism was indeed hazy as the Afro-Creole middle class sought to find a path out of the growing economic crisis.

NOTES

1. Carl Stone discusses this development in Jamaica and suggests that in the more developed British Caribbean states the same could occur. See *Democracy and Clientelism in Jamaica* (New Brunswick, N.J.: Transaction Books, 1980), pp. 11-24.

2. A. N. R. Robinson, *The Mechanics of Independence: Patterns of Political and Economic Transformation in Trinidad and Tobago* (Cambridge, Mass.: M.I.T. Press, 1971), p. 59.

3. *The Year Book of the Commonwealth 1974* (London: Her Majesty's Stationery Office, 1974), p. 407.

4. Mahabir, *In and Out of Politics: Tales of the Government of Dr. Eric Williams from the Notebooks of a Former Minister* (Trinidad: Inprint Caribbean, 1978), p. 207.

5. Ibid.

6. Yogenda Malik, *East Indians in Trinidad: A Study in Minority Politics* (London: Oxford University Press), p. 144.

7. Ibid., p. 142.

8. Ibid.

9. Eric Williams, *Inward Hunger: The Education of a Prime Minister* (Chicago: University of Chicago Press), p. 307.

10. *Economic Survey of Latin America 1966* (New York: United Nations Economic Commission on Latin America, 1968), p. 236.

11. Ibid., p. 237.

12. Malik, *East Indians in Trinidad*, p. 150.

13. *Year Book of Labour Statistics 1972* (Geneva: International Labour Office, 1972), p. 427.

14. Williams, *Inward Hunger*, p. 311.

15. Malik, *East Indians in Trinidad*, p. 150.

16. *The Nation*, April 2, 1965, p. 3.

17. Williams, *Inward Hunger*, p. 311.
18. *Labour Statistics 1972*, p. 748.
19. Quoted in Malik, *East Indians in Trinidad*, p. 146.
20. The relationship between Maharaj and his fellow DLP members was hardly warm as exemplified by the former's comment in the House of Representatives: "I do not wish to unbalance this cordial relationship between the Government and certain hon. members of the Opposition." *Hansard*, session 1966, vol. 7, p. 559.
21. Malik, *East Indians in Trinidad*, p. 153.
22. S. N. Capildeo speaking on March 18, 1966, *Hansard*, session 1966, vol. 7, p. 254.
23. Williams, *Inward Hunger*, p. 335.
24. *Labour Statistics 1972*, p. 427; and Thomas Mathews, "Trinidad and Tobago," in *The Americana Annual 1967* (New York: Americana, 1967), p. 690.
25. Mathews, "Trinidad and Tobago," p. 690.
26. Williams, *Inward Hunger*, p. 336.
27. Mathews, "Trinidad and Tobago," p. 690.
28. Thomas Mathews, "Trinidad and Tobago," in *The Americana Annual 1968* (New York: Americana, 1968), p. 684.
29. Ibid.
30. Ibid.
31. Thomas Mathews, "Trinidad and Tobago," in *The Americana Annual 1969* (New York: Americana Corporation, 1969), p. 691; and *Trinidad Guardian*, June 25, 1968, p. 1.
32. *Labour Statistics 1972*, pp. 427, 748.
33. Ibid.
34. "Resume of Trinidad and Tobago's Third Five Year Development Plan" (Port of Spain: Government of Trinidad and Tobago, n.d.), p. 1.
35. Ibid. As Farrell notes, "Many of the policy measures, particularly in the late 1960s, were taken in desperation and in atmospheres of crisis, and this, combined with the government's philosophy of development and its sense of weakness, resulted in some very poor deals." Trevor Farrell, *The Multinational Corporations: The Petroleum Industry and Economic Underdevelopment in Trinidad and Tobago* (Ann Arbor: University Microfilms International, 1974), p. 352. The same situation developed in Argentina when the Peron government pushed the British companies to surrender the railroads. Consequently, the British sold the railways, but at inflated prices the government, caught by its own nationalistic rhetoric and policies, was bound.
36. Farrell, *Multinational Corporations*, p. 348.
37. Ibid., p. 349.
38. Ibid., p. 350.
39. Gerand Chalaind, *Revolution in the Third World* (New York: Penguin Books, 1976).
40. Michel Crozier, *The Bureaucratic Phenomenon* (Chicago: University of Chicago Press, 1964), p. 3.

8

The Shadow of Authoritarianism, 1969-76

In late 1969 and 1970 black power militants and labor leaders directed a powerful social movement aimed at toppling the government of Trinidad and Tobago. Had the government fallen, the political structure might have been destroyed in a radical revolution. "Real" revolutions, however, are historically rare. While a combination of factors was evident in this case, which has been evident in other cases where revolutions have been successful, Trinidad's political eruption failed to result in a rapid and basic transformation of its society's state and class structures. Like the financial imbroglio of the French monarchy and the calling of the Estates-General in 1787-89, the attempted social revolution in Trinidad and Tobago began with the overt political crisis of high unemployment and the government's inability to manage the economy for the benefit of all.[1] Most observers of revolution and political upheavals, such as Theda Skocpol and Juan Linz, have emphasized governmental ineffectiveness as one of the major factors that is likely to encourage illegitimate resistance to the state.[2] In Trinidad a disloyal extra-parliamentary opposition, strengthened by the support of the nation's intelligentsia, benefited from growing public discontent over the government's inability to resolve the economic crisis. The opposition's strongest argument under these circumstances was its claim to be able to solve the problems. The 1970-71 period, therefore, was characterized by riots, the rise of black power, and an almost successful military uprising. Trinidad's political system came very close to breaking down.

Linz has argued that "breakdown is precipatated by what the constitutional tradition calls 'states of emergency'—the need for extraordinary powers, the state of exception."[3] Pushed by the force of events, Williams turned to rule by emergency degrees and a marked personalization of power, which is a nondemocratic direction as dangerous as a left-wing revolution. The growing apprehension over the increased authoritarianism of Trinidad and Tobago's government was heightened in 1971 when most of the political parties sought to complete the delegitimization process begun by the failed social revolution of 1969-70 by boycotting the general elections. The PNM won every seat in Parliament, which ushered in a period of de facto one-party rule and put Trinidad's democratic system on the brink of complete breakdown. However, the Williams government and Trinidadian democracy survived the dark years of 1971-73: from 1973-76 the nation went from a situation of near bankruptcy, social unrest, and growing authoritarianism to fiscal recovery and political stability. The government involved itself, in a large scale, in the economy, and the threat of nondemocratic rule receded, especially with the holding of the general elections in 1976. The purpose of this chapter is to examine why the attempted social revolution in 1969-70 failed and what impact it had on the political and economic systems.

TRINIDAD AND TOBAGO'S TIME OF TROUBLES

For the Williams administration, the economy continued to be the major problem: although the unemployment rate was reduced to 13.5 percent in 1969 and 12.5 percent in 1970, over 45,000 remained out of work.[4] The number of strikes escalated from 9 in 1969, involving 2,767 workers, to 64 in 1970, involving 11,280.[5] The discontent in the labor movement, coincided with the importation of North American black power ideology. The rise of a militant black power movement, emphasizing the ills of racism and the need for black nationalism, took hold in the Anglo-Caribbean and added fuel to the fire. Although local politicians tended to ignore it as a "noisy and inconsequential phenomenon," it was an explosive new factor in the region's political economy, especially among the young.[6]

In Trinidad and elsewhere, black power activists argued that economic control remained in white hands or with small foreign minorities like the Chinese or Syrians in Trinidad. This neocolonial system of "exploitation" with its structural inequalities and personal debasement had to be terminated in light of the need for greater economic participation by the black population. Although much of black power ideology was hazy, it did place an emphasis on "black awareness" and the need to "liberate" the nation from North American imperialism in all its political, economic, and cultural forms.

By 1969 the black power movement had made some inroads at the University of the West Indies, St. Augustine, where a small group of social scientists of the John F. Kennedy Liberal Arts College found elements appealing. To them, it was a rejection of what Oxaal calls "the neo-colonial consumer-culture."[7] One of the more important spinoffs from the university scene was Tapia House, which was founded by Dr. Lloyd Best, a Cambridge-educated economist. At the time of its establishment, Best stated, "We have to stop being duped by personalities into forming now-for-now political parties. We have to discard the Westminster parliamentary model and design a form of government appropriate to our needs."[8]

The more radical voices of black power were Dave Darbeau and Geddes Granger, who were student leaders, and Alwin Primus, a leader of the local Black Panthers. Although influenced by U.S. black militants, there was no indication of outside financial or organizational support. Granger, however, had the most far-reaching solutions to Trinidad and Tobago's economic problems and the corruption that permeated its society. He advocated that "nothing but a complete change of the system, of our way of life could end this corruption."[9] In general, this radical group vilified local capitalists, especially the "Afro-Saxons" and the middle minorities, as the agents of foreign concerns and the plunderers of the popular sectors, while advocating socialist and populist alternatives to capitalism.

Trinidad's time of troubles began in 1969 when a number of interrelated events occurred in close sequence. The government, apprehensive over the black power movement and unrest at the University of the West Indies, banned Stokely Carmichael, a Trinidadian-born U.S. black power figure, from entering the country. During the same year, a number of West Indian students were arrested and put on trial in Canada for the occupation and destruction of a computer center at the University of Montreal. Arguing that those students had been discriminated against, students in Trinidad marched in protest. At the University of the West Indies, Geddes Granger and Dave Darbeau organized the National Joint Action Congress (NJAC), which had links to other radical groups on the island and attracted many unemployed and dissatisfied Trinidadians.

From the February 1970 Carnival, in which protest bands appeared carrying large portraits of Eldridge Cleaver, Malcolm X, and Stokely

Carmichael, a number of incidents occurred, polarizing Trinidadian society. These incidents included more student demonstrations, police crackdowns, and on March 4 a black power march through Port of Spain. An estimated 10,000 people went from Woodford Square to Shanty Town, mirroring the growing strength of the opposition movement.[10] In March the situation further deteriorated as individuals linked to the NJAC sought to disrupt the nation's life by conducting a bombing campaign: targets included the residence of the U.S. vice-consul as well as banks and shops. Nor were these attacks limited to those with light skin; they affected the mixed population and some of the "Afro-Saxons" involved in "black capitalism."

The element of violence polarized Trinidadian society. The conservative and moderate middle sectors largely sided with the government, which was on the defensive, while the Afro-Creole popular sectors sympathized with the multiheaded black power movement. That movement was especially attractive to the unemployed and frustrated youth who were usually without an effective political mouthpiece. The leadership of the Afro-Creole trade unions also found black power as a vehicle of power to challenge the ISA and what was regarded as a corrupt and declining PNM government. This perception was reinforced by Williams's television address of March 23 in which he announced a special 5 percent tax levy on foreign companies to help fight unemployment and warned the business community to "set its house in order" vis-à-vis any kind of discrimination in hiring procedures.[11] Although the prime minister acknowledged in his address "that the pace of change has been too slow" and that the PNM would attempt to rectify the situation, the opposition to the government felt that he had neglected to admit his own weakness.

Watching from the sidelines, the East Indian community regarded the struggle as Afro-Creole, although the poorer elements were either sympathetic to black power aspirations or participated in some fashion. By and large, however, the bulk of East Indians did not feel any unity with their "black brothers," and the DLP elite, in all likelihood, looked to the Afro-Creole middle sectors as possible allies if the situation deteriorated into outright revolution.

A new sequence of events almost brought Trinidad and Tobago to the brink of a full-scale revolution. On April 6 a NJAC supporter, Basil Davis, was shot and killed by the police in Port of Spain. Davis soon became a martyr and rallying cry for those seeking to topple the government. At his funeral black power groups lashed out at the "repressive" and corrupt nature of the government and the middle-class "sellouts" who worked for foreign companies. This was followed by the resignation of A. N. R. Robinson from the cabinet. Although he retained his seat in the House and his position as deputy political leader of the PNM, his action was highly symbolic, casting doubt upon the legitimacy of the administration. Regarded as the future successor of Williams and as leader of the PNM's liberal wing, his resignation made it appear that even the party's elite was fragmenting under the pressure of events and that the government would soon collapse. Next came a strike in the sugar belt, which involved East Indians. Armed with claims of racial and class unity, a general strike and march on the capital were planned for April 21-22. Many felt that the "revolution" would be launched since black power groups, sugar, oil, transport and electrical unions intended to bring the nation to a standstill.

Williams had long been inactive, but on April 21 he struck first. A state of emergency was declared, and the leaders of the movement were taken into custody.[12] Despite riots and arson in the capital, the police were able to control the situation and impose a dawn-to-dusk curfew. The opposition, offguard and poorly organized, crumbled in a matter of hours. The government's resolve, however, was almost shattered by the unexpected mutiny of the 800-man Trinidad Defense Force (also known as the Regiment). Sympathetic to the aspirations of the social movement, a number of soldiers attempted to rescue a group of the arrested popular sector leaders. Former Lieutenant Rex Laselle, one of the rebel officers (with lieutenants Raffique Shah and Michael Bazie), later commented that between 90 and 95 percent of the soldiers "felt a great sympathy with the people of the country because of the suffering they were experiencing. We understood their frustrations and we were part and parcel with it. And the clenched fist salutes we gave during the trial was an indication of this empathy and solidarity with the people."[13] Furthermore, though never proven, it was widely believed by some segments of the government that there was collusion between black power sympathizers in the military and the NJAC and that there was a conspiracy aimed at establishing a new revolutionary regime by coup.[14]

A coup was narrowly averted by the bombardment and blockage of the major road leading into Port of Spain, which, in effect, bottled the rebels up in the Chaguaramas peninsula north of the capital for five days while negotiations put an end to the crisis. In the event, the government had almost been toppled, and five people had been killed. Ultimately, what had saved the government was the lack of organization of the popular sectors' leadership and the absence of an opposing figure who could unite the masses.[15] The forces of the would-be social revolution also had not fully discredited the government which remained legitimate in the eyes of the majority of its citizens.

While Williams's left-of-center political ideas had raised the hope and awareness of the population, economic realities hindered the realization of a better society. The political system, dependent, in large part, on the infusion of foreign capital, was unable to accommodate the demands of the black-power- and labor-led popular sectors. Outright revolution and the toppling of the government had been averted, forcing Williams to rule forcibly while balancing the need to placate some of the popular sector demands for greater control over natural resources. The core issues for most Trinidadians remained improving the standard of living and reducing unemployment. However, the government's dependence on foreign investment and support was manifested in two ways: the gradual and sometimes haphazard movement of the state into the national economy, which will be discussed later in greater detail, and Williams's turn to the United States and Venezuela during the mutiny.

During Trinidad and Tobago's time of troubles, the United States' and Venezuelan governments watched with caution, the former because it did not want another "Cuba" and the latter because it now perceived that it had a regional role to play, especially considering that those two islands were just across the Gulf of Paria and that the government was democratically elected. Caracas had no desire to have a Castro-like regime on its borders. Consequently, when Williams asked for arms, the United States and Venezuela consented. Moreover, two British and six U.S. warships, including a helicopter carrier, entered Trinidadian waters, joining Venezuelan ships. Foreign troops were never officially landed, although there is the possibility that Venezuelan soldiers in civilian clothes were landed to help direct the flow of arms and supervise police in their training. Whatever may be the case, Williams was forced to purchase emergency military supplies from Washington and Caracas, a situation he did not entirely feel comfortable with.

THE AUTHORITARIAN TEMPTATION, 1970-72

With a nation wracked by labor-industrial strife, a militarizing radical fringe opposition, and antiwhite feelings publicly evident, the government was confronted by the problem of which policies to adopt.

Some felt that the PNM should have called for elections, hence acknowledging their loss of the popular mandate. For Williams the desire to remain in power overrode all others, even if it meant curtailing citizen's rights. The hardliners in the PNM, with the obvious support of the prime minister, moved to strengthen the state's control over the population. The authoritarian temptation, similar to that followed in Latin America, appeared to offer a solution for a beleaguered regime: the law and order approach would be maintained to continue the government's development programs, which were still highly dependent on outside, mainly North American, investors. In moving to authoritarian-like policies, the PNM brought out the entire question of whether economic development could be achieved within the democratic framework. In the 1970-72 period it appeared that the PNM government, with the support of conservative segments of the middle sectors, felt that certain democratic rights had to be sacrificed to protect the investment climate. Yet, at the same time, the democratic system could not be casually discarded, and the opposition to these measures was considerable. Many longtime PNM supporters were against the authoritarian laws considered and adopted; a certain degree of alienation occurred even in the middle sectors.

First of the government's new measures was the introduction into Parliament of the Public Order Bill on August 7, 1970. In a reactionary backlash to the political instability of the period, the government, pushed by hardliners, presented a piece of legislation that was to allow state control over public meetings, freedom of speech, and the right to bear firearms. Tremendous powers were placed in the hands of the police as exemplified by the fact that to hold public meetings the police had to be informed of the date, times, organizers, and all non-Trinidadian speakers, while also holding the authority to disallow or disperse any such meetings deemed harmful to public order.[16]

Drafted in large part by Attorney General Karl Hudson-Phillips, the Public Order Bill generated considerable opposition from all sectors of society, including the middle class and members of the ruling party.[17] few organizations and institutions, the Catholic Church excepted, supported the bill, hence forcing it to be withdrawn. Despite the government's insensitivity, the forces favoring democratic politics had triumphed on an important issue, which certainly could have led to an abandonment of such procedures and the establishment of an authoritarian regime. Interestingly, the middle sectors, which were still largely committed to the democratic system, were amongst those most opposed to the Public Order Bill, although their counterparts in Argentina, Brazil, and Chile favored military coups and such legislation to guarantee economic development conducive to the perpetuation of their lifestyles.[18] Moreover, the presentation of the Public Order Bill eroded much of the support the PNM had rallied in April, causing the leadership to reassess its policies.

Although PNM hardliners failed to pass the Public Order Bill, Karl Hudson-Phillips, supported by the majority in the party, advanced a new piece of legislation in early November 1970 called the Firearms Bill, which was intended to stop gun running into the country. The bill was passed and the new law required a person with firearms to have a license and gave the police the right to search for unauthorized weapons. The purpose of the Firearms Bill was publicly outlined by a PNM senator: "The Government are [sic] forced to take adequate measures to stamp out this tendency to violence, to arrest the spread of illegal arms in the country and restore a feeling of security and safety to all law abiding citizens."[19]

The Firearms Act, in many aspects, was a less encompassing version of the Public Order Bill. As one member of the opposition commented, parts of it were "taken directly and verbatim from the defunct Public Order Bill."[20] Its passage marked increased state control over public life, although its implementation was not without costs for the Williams government. Some concessions had to be made, at least on the surface for public consumption.

To a background of public discontent over the Firearms Act, continuous economic difficulties, and demands for nationalization of the national resources, the PNM attempted to demonstrate that it could change course and was democratically minded. Williams and the political elite badly needed to rebuild the party's image before the general elections in 1971. To indicate that the PNM had become less bureaucratic and inflexible, the state of emergency was lifted on November 19, 1970, and all political prisoners, except five, were released. Those five, the military men involved in the mutiny, were to stand trial for treason. At the same time, the lighter-skinned members of the PNM moved quietly to the background, allowing some of the more "black" members to have greater public exposure. Williams himself changed his appearance, shucking the traditional coat and tie for the open shirt and neckerchief, while visiting steelband yards and calypso tents. However, as Ryan notes, "In spite of this new 'mod' and 'Afro' -image, the power base of the Party had come to rest more and more on the old, the fair-skinned, the established. This silent minority made a special effort to turn out the vote for the PNM which they saw as the last defensible fortress against chaos and subversion."[21]

On December 1, 1970, governmental affairs were further complicated by the advancement of a no confidence motion in the Parliament. Although not a real threat, as the PNM held a two-thirds majority, it did reflect the growing loss of legitimacy of the ruling party. In attacking the inadequacies of the PNM's administration, Jamadar, the leader of the opposition, emphasized one of the major dilemmas confronting the political system at the time: "Obviously there is a great gap between parliamentary theory and parliamentary practice as we have experienced here."[22]

Criticism of the government went deeper as Jamadar attacked Williams's reliance on the white economic elite, calling them the "blue-eyed boys" who "encourage us to thrift whilst they blow money like water."[23] In particular, a number of whites close to the prime minister, Bruce Procope, Eldon Warner, Ellis Clarke, Joffre Eli Serrette, and Kenneth Julien, were criticized for having three or more jobs and blocking the advancement of others, by implication, who were nonwhite. Jamadar emphasized that Sir Alan Reece, an associate of Williams, was simultaneously on the Industrial Development Corporation, the Trinidad and Tobago Electricity Company (T and TEC), the Elections Commission, the Electricity Commission, and the Elections and Boundaries Commission.

What had evolved was a political-economic system presided over by a weak government led by a strong political leader. With an administration characterized by declining legitimacy in the eyes of the population, Williams had turned to an alternate system of dominance, that of "interlocking directorates."[24] The center of elite decision making had shifted from the PNM to a small group of business and public leaders who interacted through the expanding number of commissions established to investigate the plethora of problems plaguing the nation's public industries, such as the utilities.

In a very nondemocratic fashion, Williams had moved away from a reliance on the party, where he was anxious about possible challengers to his role as political leader. The departure of A. N. R. Robinson had been regarded as a betrayal and, in all probability, made the prime minister apprehensive over whom to trust. Simply stated, it was easier to rule through a handful of individuals on the interlocking directorates, who were directly dependent on him for their positions, than through the rank and file of the party. Moreover, as the process of delegitimization progressed, the tendency was to rely more heavily on interlocking directorates.[25]

Interlocking directorates emerged before 1970 when the state had created the National Petroleum Company and the Central Bank of Trinidad and Tobago, the latter having assumed the responsibility of banker to the Central Government in 1967. It should be emphasized, however, that it was not the pattern before 1972 to have the state actively manage the economy. Due to political pressures, caused by high unemployment, labor unrest, and a questioning of the ruling party's nationalism, the government moved into the public sector, but only on an ad hoc basis. Along these lines the government moved further into the banking sector in 1970, first by the passage of the Exchange Control Act, which sought to "regulate capital outflows and to control levels of payments for current goods and services," and, second, by the purchase of the Bank of London and Montreal's banking and finance companies.[26] Significantly, the owners of the foreign bank had decided to liquidate their holdings in the nation, which would have meant more unemployed and some currency loss. With great pomp and circumstance, the National Commercial Bank and Trust Company was opened on July 1, 1970, at the former premises of the Bank of London and Montreal. Moreover, the Workers Bank was created the same year to help the financial affairs of the traditionally pro-PNM Seaman and Waterfront Workers Trade Union.[27] Despite these ventures into the economy in the late 1960s and 1970, the government was not yet a major dynamic in the management calculus, and the interlocking directorates were in their early stages of development.

THE 1971 GENERAL ELECTIONS

On the eve of the May 1971 general elections, Eric Williams stated, "I'm the one who has power here. When I say 'come' you cometh. And when I say 'go' you goeth."[28] Reflecting this mentality, Williams had not released the date of the May 1971 elections until April, leaving the opposition parties little time to campaign.

Prior to the setting of the election's date, the opposition attempted to close ranks. The DLP, led by Jamadar, who had finally ousted Capildeo in the party convention of 1969, joined a coalition with the newly formed Action Committee of Democratic Citizens (ACDC). ACDC had been founded by Robinson shortly after he had left the ruling party in April and was composed of disgruntled Afro-Creole PNM members favoring constitutional changes. The ACDC was against overcentralization, corruption, economic mismanagement, the Public

Order Bill, and detention without charges. Like the DLP, Robinson's organization was aware of the population's disaffection with the established political process. Consequently, the ACDC and the DLP sought to form an electoral alliance capable of seriously challenging the ruling party. The DLP continued to be the preserve of the East Indian professionals but also had taken on a small number of Afro-Creoles, most notably Dr. E. C. Richardson, a founder of the PNM. After joining the DLP he had risen to the rank of deputy political leader, a position that, it was hoped, would emphasize to the public the multiracial nature of the organization.

The ACDC-DLP alliance collapsed when Robinson unilaterally withdrew from the contest, announcing a boycott. The DLP, although upset, and Tapia House and the UNIP (United National Independence Party, mainly composed of intellectuals at the University of West Indies) followed suit in the hope that such actions would bring the government down. It is probable that these parties realized that the PNM would not be defeated in the short term. The NJAC, however, contested the elections. With its radical stance, it had become isolated on the far left of Trinidadian politics, which was associated in the public mind with the violent politics of guerrilla attacks, arson, looting, and bombings.[29] After 1970 people either wanted positive messages or did not care, feeling their vote did little to change the situation.[30] Two other groups, the People's Liberation Party, a lackluster East Indian combination, and the little known African National Congress also contested the elections.

Discontent with this situation was evident: there were bombings of PNM headquarters and the homes of the commander in chief of defense forces and a PNM minister, while there were assassination attempts on a state prosecuter and the commander in chief of the coast guard. However, in May 1971 the PNM, unopposed in eight constituencies, captured all 36 seats in the House. Of 400,000 eligible voters, less than 100,000 had cast ballots, of whom 90 percent voted for the PNM.[31] The alienation from the political system had reached an all-time high, as total voter turnout had decreased from 88.1 percent in 1961 and 65.8 percent in 1966 to 33.1 percent in 1971. Voter turnout in the East Indian areas had been particularly low, and, in general, that community was the most alienated from the nation's political system, as reflected by the fact that the People's Liberation Party received only 4.2 percent of the vote. The PNM won the elections because of the opposition's inability to unite and continued middle sector support for Williams, built on the perception that he would keep the nation out of a revolution.

Opposition to the government continued: there were strikes and in late 1971 a new group came on the scene, The National Union of Freedom Fighters, which believed in guerrilla warfare and Marxism-Leninism, helping push the government to adopt tougher measures. Unhindered by any opposition in the House, the ruling party soon took action by imposing its second state of emergency. Even Carl Hudson-Phillips admits, "These powers, admittedly, on paper appear wide. . . ."[32] The motion, not surprisingly, passed unopposed. The OWTU, constantly a difficulty for the government, was forced back to the bargaining table and conceded on a number of issues.

By 1972 democracy was neither alive or well in Trinidad and Tobago, nor was it dead. Economic and political development was unbalanced: while the nation's gross domestic product grew, the distribution of income was skewed, and the ownership of the means of production remained largely in foreign hands despite some government entry into the economy. Agricultural production continued to slide, unemployment remained almost unmanageable, and public borrowing from international agencies increased. On the political side, stability had gradually given way to violence, union militancy, and an abortive coup, while the ruling party had become a de facto one-party state. Most evident was the lack of a broad consensus on national goals and strategies, which was reflected by the divergent political and economic demands of the population; this situation was made critical by the inability of the opposition to unify or even make an imprint on the national decision-making process. Furthermore, the population as a whole held no unifying concept of the national community, while trust in others and support for the system of government were at all-time lows. The cleavages in society were especially evident as the largely black labor movement drew closer to the East Indian sugar workers and the middle sectors of all races moved closer together in a national alliance founded on class interests. In all likelihood, the middle sectors, which were not a majority, had the greatest sense of Trinidadian "nationalism" and, with such a belief, relied increasingly on the strong political personality of Eric Williams to restore order and progress. In turn, Williams increasingly relied on interlocking directorates to rule the nation, while seeking to maintain some middle-class support.

THE MIDDLE SECTORS AND LOCALIZATION OF THE ECONOMY, 1972-76

The fracturing of Trinidadian society affected the middle sectors as the complacency of being a privileged group was badly shaken. More importantly, there was some fragmentation of middle-class consensus, which was most evident in the early 1970s as three groups emerged: the hardliners who felt that a strong government along authoritarian lines was needed to restore order and economic progress; the right-of-center moderates who felt that democracy should be maintained only as long as it did not jeopardize their way of life, namely the capitalistic system; and the liberals who argued that democracy should be maintained regardless of the circumstances and were appalled by the curtailment of personal liberties in the 1970-72 period. These divisions also cut across occupational and racial lines, as the "new middle class" of public managers, technocrats, and "modern sector" financial leaders drew closer to the state as the state moved deeper into managing the economy. Moreover, the East Indian bourgeoisie quietly supported what was regarded as an Afro-Creole-dominated government. The difficult financial situation had caused, in part, a polarization along class lines, displacing, to a certain extent, racial polarization, which had previously dominated the nation's politics.

By 1972 the middle sectors in Trinidad and Tobago had managed to remain in the leadership position vis-à-vis the working classes and the traditional elites (i.e., the merchants and planters). The latter group, in the wake of the troubled years at the close of the 1960s, had gradually come to support Williams, while the former, in its frustration at the lack of meaningful changes, had moved leftward and into open opposition. The states of emergency in 1970 and again in 1971, which removed many militants from public life, and the absence of an official opposition party in the Parliament made the unions the most important and best organized force outside the formal political system. This position was enhanced by the fact that the larger unions, especially in the oil industry and the sugar belt, could bring the nation to a standstill through striking.

For the government to survive in the dark years of 1972-73, when unemployment remained above 15 percent and the number of strikes rose from 32 in 1972 to 84 in 1973, Williams and the PNM were forced to accommodate the labor unions and adopt visible new policies toward foreign investment, which was the major source of controversy.³³ Simply stated, the ruling party had to acknowledge that the economy, above all else, was the number-one political issue. It was recognized that tied to national economic survival were the needs of continued socioeconomic development and the reduction of unemployment. Seeking to regenerate the economy and to silence critics, the PNM moved to localize control over many of the nation's key financial sectors as well as furthering its penetration into the industrial and agricultural sectors. The most prominent feature of the 1972-76 period, therefore, was the entry of the government into the economy on a major scale.

In early 1972 George Chambers, then the finance minister, presented the government's new foreign investment rules, which would be modified to varying degrees in the following years. According to Chambers, from 1972 onward joint ventures, diversification of foreign investment, higher taxation on foreign oil companies, greater equity available for local nationals from foreign-owned companies, and control of capital outflow were to be enforced. Other steps included: nationals would be promoted and trained to work in local banks and insurance firms; no new 100 percent foreign-owned ventures would be allowed in "key" sectors of the economy; and foreign investors were to be excluded entirely from certain sectors reserved for locals.³⁴

Although individual bargaining continued and the language concerning key sectors remained ambiguous, the government signaled to the companies that the door would remain open to them as long as they continued to contribute to national goals, which for the oil companies meant higher taxes. The heavier taxing of the oil industry certainly was not excessive considering that Trinidad and Tobago's treasury received U.S. $.69 per barrel compared with Kuwait's $1.29, Libya's $2.03, and Venezuela's $1.56.³⁵ These changes served notice to foreign investors and the Trinidadian public that the nation had embarked upon an economic policy aimed at the localization of controls and eventual economic independence, while bringing up the standard of living and reducing unemployment.

The government's relations with the foreign companies over localization proceeded with relatively few problems, since the approach was gradualistic and did not aim at total control. Early in 1972 the Royal Bank of Canada sold 51 percent of its equity to local nationals on a five-year payment scheme, becoming, by this transaction, the Royal Bank of Trinidad and Tobago. Barclays followed suit on April

14, 1972, and the Bank of Nova Scotia on May 1, 1972, as did a number of insurance firms.[36] To avoid a drain on national reserves, all banks were required by law to keep 75 percent of the proceeds of the sale of their stock for at least five years.[37]

In the oil industry, Trinidad gradually increased the level of taxation and, despite advice from Venezuela and Iran to quicken the pace of nationalization, worked to resolve any major misconceptions with the major companies that might have occurred. Discovery of offshore oil in 1972 provided some hope that increased output would benefit all. Since cooperation with the companies was needed to tap these resources, the government's programs were flexible enough so as not to frighten away foreign investors. Despite criticism from the left, labor, and within the party, foreign control over certain sectors of the economy remained substantial, if not dominant.[38] Simply stated, the Williams government, in response to a lack of legitimacy in the eyes of the population, pushed the foreign companies for some benefits and profit sharing with the state, but could not push so hard as to drive them from the country since their departure would greatly complicate the situation. In this scenario the government's relations with labor remained tension filled, as the unions, which represented less than one-third of the total workforce, opposed government suggestions to cut overtime and install a double shift system to reduce unemployment.

By 1972 the policy of diversification of production through import substitution had made some headway against the unemployment situation, but the kind of industries developed most rapidly were those that contributed little to the solution of joblessness. At the same time, in pursuing the localization of controls over the economy, as outlined in the 1969-73 development plan, government holdings increased. By mid-1972 the public sector owned assets in productive enterprises, public utilities, and the mining sector to a value of U.S. $85 million.[39] The government also sought to reorient the educational system to provide the necessary skills for localization in banking, sugar, petroleum, and manufacturing plants.

While there were some improvements during the 1971-72 period, economic development in 1973 was profoundly influenced by the unsettled nature of the international economy. The problems of an uncertain world monetary situation, the inflationary tendencies and sharply rising interest rates in the advanced nations, along with domestic shortages of some basic commodities seriously undermined overall economic expansion and once again threatened Trinidad and Tobago's political stability.[40] Banking and finance activities of which the government had sought to gain local control showed little or no increase during 1973, since these sectors suffered severely from interest rates and spiraling inflation of the industrialized countries as well as a domestic credit squeeze. All these factors combined cast a gloomy picture for the nation's future economic development.

In 1973 the country was again afflicted by considerable unrest and Williams's base of support had eroded considerably, as those who had left the ranks included most trade unions, the younger Afro-Creoles, and a growing number of middle-class professionals.[41] There were even considerable problems within the PNM concerning its validity at representing the nation, a situation confused by the prime minister's announced intention to resign as political leader and the discussions involving constitutional reform. Both of the latter derived from Williams's attempt to halt the process of delegitimatization.

Constitutional reform was aimed at creating a more open political system with additional checks and balances on the powers of the prime minister, especially his ability to declare a state of emergency. The size of the Parliament was also expanded to 72 seats to provide for a wider field of representation. Despite these measures, serious doubts remained that a numerical increase in Parliament would be a sufficient bulwark against a strong executive.[42]

At a party convention in 1973, Williams turned on his own party and lambasted it for colossal incompetence and corruption. He declared that his hopes for Caribbean unity were exceedingly doubtful and announced that the "national movement" (that is, the PNM) in Trinidad was like Carnival.[43] Offering his resignation, the prime minister left the convention.

This action shocked the party and unsettled Trinidadian society. The PNM leadership attempted to find a successor, narrowing the candidates to two men, former Attorney General Karl Hudson-Phillips and Kamluddin Mohammed. A vote was held and Hudson-Phillips emerged as the heir-apparent with 224 votes to Mohammed's 24.[44] It appeared that the PNM was not ready for an Indo-Trinidadian prime minister. Williams, however, was not ready for a new prime minister as he changed his mind saying that he would remain in office until the end of the year. This action was taken only after the leaders of the various churches met with him and pleaded that he stay at the nation's helm in the interest of "stability." Returning in late 1973 to the party, Williams quickly reasserted his control, forcing Hudson-Phillips and a number of others to leave the PNM.

At the close of 1973 the Trinidadian economy reached a new nadir, and there was apprehension that the government would not be able to pay its employees. The Treasury was nearing bankruptcy, and the terms of trade continued to decline. Moreover, the offshore oil finds had not yet brought in substantial new revenues, and cutbacks of Middle East oil led to considerable reduction in local refining because less crude was available. However, this reduction of crude proved to be a blessing to the government.

As the Arab oil embargo gained momentum in November and December 1973, the world price for oil quadrupled.[45] Before the embargo the United States was importing 1.2 million barrels of Arab oil a day. By February 1974 it was down to 18,000 barrels, and U.S. companies began looking to alternative sources. Although the bonanza of petrodollars was not immediately felt, Trinidad-Tobago was to benefit from the rise in prices, especially as the United States had become its chief customer for petroleum products. While the economies of most surrounding nations, with the exception of Venezuela, contracted, the inflow of petrodollars stimulated a long-awaited and badly needed economic boom in Trinidad and Tobago. At the same time, the West Indian nation fulfilled its traditional role as a safe source of oil for the West.

Throughout 1974 and 1975 the state moved further into the economy. In 1974 Shell's operations on the island were taken over with compensation, and in the following year Williams announced that all of Texaco's gas stations were to come under Trinidadian ownership.[46] National Petroleum became the sole domestic marketing company, including the distribution of aviation and bunker fuel, as well as controlling all supplies of domestic gas. By 1975 the government was quickly becoming the nation's major employer.

THE NEW MIDDLE CLASS AND INTERLOCKING DIRECTORATES

Coinciding with the government's large-scale entry into the economy was the emergence of a "new bourgeoisie" as the nation's dominant class stratum. This ascendant class element had and continues to have its primary base of support in the country's crucial petroleum sector and in related industries. What has occurred is a fractionalization of the middle sectors between those associated with the modern, internationally linked capitalist sector and others that remained rooted in the traditional national sectors—agriculture, small-scale manufacturing, and much of the service economy. As David Becker notes of the same process in Peru, "Fractionalization enables the state to attain a larger amount of 'relative autonomy' with respect to civil society."[47] He also notes that while the state was able to benefit from the divisions within the middle sectors, "state technocrats tend to share values and interests with private-sector managers, both domestic and foreign."[48] Furthermore, the objectives the state's managers desired, in large part, depended on the modern sector of the economy, and "that its health in turn depends on continuing imputs [sic] of capital and technology from abroad."[49]

In Trinidad and Tobago, as in Becker's study on Peru, a triad of state officials, multinational corporate managers, and domestic manager-entrepreneurs captured the core of the political economy, having the support of those members of the middle sectors who consumed the products that the multinational corporations produced and "who aspire to upward mobility into the managerial-technocratic bourgeois stratum."[50] At the same time, the traditional middle class, comprised of the old white commercial elite that did not move with the changes in the international economic system and, to a lesser extent, some elements of the professional middle class (doctors, lawyers, and other nonindustrial high-finance actors), and the working class were pushed into opposition. The former groups were simply unable to compete in terms of capital base and market ranges, while the latter were unable to afford many of the new luxuries the new bourgeoisie enjoyed.

As Becker and others have argued, the temptation to resort to authoritarian political systems is a clear-cut pattern in Latin America and the Third World. In Trinidad and Tobago the triad that emerged in the mid-1970s did not resort to authoritarian government. Instead, Williams and the new bourgoisie maintained middle sector domination through interlocking directorates. As already mentioned, this system had emerged before 1970, and it was not until 1973 that it became a more pronounced political pattern. According to Parris, between June 1973 and December 1979 no fewer than 11 commissions were established in Trinidad "to investigate the condition of the utilities and public enterprises, aspects of tenure of building land, alleged misuse of public funds, sports, disaffection among magistrates."[51] As each commission led to another, the entire scope of national socio-economic affairs fell under the observation of a "directorale" elite composed of chairmen from the modern sector of the economy.

Combined with Williams's strong political personality, the system of interlocking directorates operated above and outside of the party system.

Although these commissions were multiracial, having a representation of the middle minorities, whites and East Indians, the majority of those in the interlocking directorates were Afro-Creoles. Furthermore, the same pattern repeated itself in the evolution of the new bourgeoisie. What made Williams turn to this group and the system of interlocking directorates?

By 1973 Eric Williams had lost confidence in the PNM, a factor that became more evident in 1974 and 1975. The earlier "betrayal" of A. N. R. Robinson had rankled him, and the challenge of Karl Hudson-Phillips had made Williams wary of the party's general council and vice versa. In response, Williams, feeling increasingly isolated within the party, sought to centralize power into a small group of trusted individuals who, in turn, could coordinate the triad of state officials, multinational corporate managers, and domestic manager-entrepreneurs. In turning away from the party, Williams placed more power in the cabinet, and it was not irregular for a minister to hold two or more portfolios. Williams himself was not only the prime minister and political leader, but usually held at least one of two other portfolios, including that of finance minister. While perceiving the party as an impediment to his governing, Williams was also concerned about a "take-over by technology," led by "a small ambitious minority of civil servants."[52] Acting through various commissions, most notably the Public Services Commission, the prime minister sought to curtail the independence of certain civil servants and guarantee his control over the nation's leading political and economic decision-making centers.

DEVELOPMENT OF A NEW OPPOSITION

Despite the fact that 1974 ended with a positive balance of payments and no out-of-control deficit and that the GDP grew 3.2 percent in 1975, unemployment remained close to 15 percent, inflation increased from 14.8 percent to 32 percent in 1974, and wages rose only 10 percent.[53] Moreover, there was considerable depreciation of the Trinidadian dollar due to its links to the English pound, which was badly hit by the energy crisis.

To the background of unbalanced economic development, a new opposition formed, spearheaded by the labor movement. Following the events of 1969-70, labor leaders sought to create an alliance between the economy's two major sectors, oil and sugar. As John Humphrey, one of the leaders associated with this development, comments, "Oil and sugar united controls the country. But it does more than that; it united Indian workers and African workers."[5][4] The need to create a unified political opposition was made even more urgent by the existing array of small and largely ineffective parties such as the NJAC and UNIP. The DLP, under the weight of personal rivalries, had fragmented into two factions in 1972, and as an alternative to the PNM it could offer little.

Since the economic situation was grim in 1972 and 1973, the working class placed their faith in the unions. In late 1974 it became evident that the nation's financial problems were easing, and union leadership began to demand better distribution of income and increases in wages. In the oil sector the Oil Worker's Trade Union under George Weekes led the way. It was in the sugar industry, however, that the economic situation was most serious and the struggle between government-private-sector-run companies and East Indian workers became increasingly acrimonious. Since 1971 the sugar belt had been wracked by a number of strikes during which two men emerged as leaders, Raffique Shah and Basdeo Panday. The former was one of the 1970 military mutineers, who upon his release from prison had set out to organize the Indo-Trinidadian cane farmers. Shah organized the cane farmers into the Trinidad Islandwide Cane Farmers' Union (TICFU), which was involved in an unsuccessful strike in 1974.

On February 8, 1975, members of the OWTU met with members of the All-Trinidad Sugar Estates and Factory Workers' Trade Union and the TICFU at a rally at Skinner Park, San Fernando. The rally's objective was the pledge of support for sugar workers who had decided to strike against Caroni Ltd. since the company refused to discuss profit sharing with the employees. The meeting of these unions was highly symbolic as it marked the birth of the United Labour Front (ULF) and the unification under one banner of Indo-Trinidadian and Afro-Creole workers. Led by Weekes, Shah, and Panday, the ULF quickly became a focal point of the discontented elements in Trinidadian society.

The government, feeling threatened by a class-based movement, increased police scrutiny of labor leaders. In a growing atmosphere of confrontation in early March, the OWTU called out workers from the oil and petrochemical companies to participate in a march on Port of Spain on March 18 for "bread, justice and peace."

On March 18, 1975, a large gathering prepared to move on the capital. Amongst the ranks were DLP leader Jamadar, Weekes, Shah, Panday, and a number of UWI professors. The police eventually teargassed the procession and, with clubs flying, broke it up. It was felt that the marchers would disrupt Port of Spain's traffic and commerce, although the fundamental reason for police action was the attempt to preclude a possible repeat of the marches on the capital that occurred in 1970. While the march was a failure in its objectives of reaching Port of Spain, it was highly successful in giving the United Labour Front national coverage and drawing a degree of sympathy to its harassed position. A public inquiry was called for by the Journalists Association of Trinidad and Tobago, and a resolution was sent to the commissioner of police, the prime minister, the governor general, and the minister of national security. Although the government was generally silent on the issue, the entire affair drew considerable criticism of the PNM, helping set the stage for the 1976 general elections.

THE GENERAL ELECTIONS OF 1976

As Ryan comments, "The 1976 General Elections in Trinidad and Tobago were characterized by a great deal of confusion and uncertainty."[55] Rumors abounded that if elections were held the ULF would win, in which case a "Chile-style" action would be conducted with U.S. support. The public in general was left wondering about what issues would be the most important, such as race or the ideology of the United Labour Front. By the time the dates were set for May 1976, the campaigning was centering on the ideological slant of the ULF.

By 1976 the United Labour Front had become the party of the trade unionists and left-of-center intellectuals, its leadership including Panday and Weekes. Campaigning with the slogan "Let those who labour hold the reins," the ULF advocated populist alternatives to PNM conservatism, urging national land reform and greater Trinidadian control of the commanding heights of the economy, barring foreign ownership, completely nationalizing foreign trade and Trinidadian branches of multinational firms in oil, petrochemicals, construction, banking, and insurance, as well as increasing worker participation in management.[56] The ULF leaders felt that their chances of success were high and that class perceptions would triumph over race, especially when the working class struggles in 1969-70 and 1975 were considered.[57]

The ULF's major area of support was the south of Trinidad where the oil and sugar industries were situated. In the north the ULF remained a question mark, since people did not fully understand what the new party represented. As Ryan notes, "In the absence of firm knowledge, rumours spread that the ULF was communist and atheistic."[58] These perceptions, bolstered by the press and the outcry of other politicians such as Stephen Maharaj, led the Indo-Trinidadian business and professional community either to abstain from voting or to vote PNM rather than having a "socialist" or "communist" East Indian government elected. The East Indian middle class, in general, felt that a ULF victory would be a disaster to the nation, as the stability and viability of the economy would be jeopardized.

In the Indo-Trinidadian community, there was a hope that the East Indian elements of the ULF would leave the Marxist and black power factions and form an alliance with what was left of the old Democratic Labour Party. The "unofficial" faction of the DLP under Vernon Jamadar had continued for a time under that name, but eventually reorganized itself into the Social Democratic Party (SDP). By 1976 the fortunes of this group had declined considerably, and, although they sought to appeal to the East Indians, their appeal was limited, especially when considering that the ULF had attracted much of the community's working class. Although some in the Indo-Trinidadian community had hoped for an alliance between the old DLP politicians and the Indian wing of the ULF, the prospects were never promising. In fact, many of the old DLP politicians joined the fray against the ULF's alleged "communist" stance.

As the campaign gained momentum, the attacks on the ULF mounted, and that party's leadership realized that the national mood was anticommunist and feared anything resembling it. Put on the defensive, ULF leaders were forced to emphasize their adherence to the democratic system and disavow that they intended to establish a Marxist state. However, the press hinted that communist funds were reaching the ULF, and the party's position with the electorate was gradually undermined. The PNM quickly exploited the situation as Williams attacked socialism by relating his state visit to Cuba in 1975. At a rally the prime minister "clarified" the differences between the ULF and his party by saying, "the PNM does not intend planning to take away anybody's land; it does not intend to take away the cane farmers' land; as far as the PNM is concerned, the cane farmer is the man of the future in the sugar industry, and so long as the PNM is the government, the cane farmers are safe."[59]

As election day approached two other factors undermined the ULF—the racial issue and politicking to form an electoral alliance against the PNM. The former was brought back into the picture when the Indian cricket team came to Trinidad. The question of East Indian loyalties surfaced when a number of ugly incidents occurred between Afro-Creoles and Indo-Trinidadians. To the former, East Indian support for the Indian team was close to treason. Moreover, the East Indian loyalty to the motherland gave some indication as to how their loyalties would be divided on election day. Despite all of the ULF's work to create a multiracial slate, based on working-class solidarity and focused on economic issues, race had once again become an important factor in the two-island nation, especially with the popular sectors. This also proved to be part of the reason for the failure of the ULF and A. N. R. Robinson's Democratic Action Party (DAC) to form an alliance. Another important reason was that the DAC was much more capitalist oriented and regarded the ULF as too far to the left.

Compared to the campaigns of the past, the 1976 general election was relatively peaceful. With a field of nine parties, the major issues were economic in nature, focusing on the ownership of the means of production, unemployment, and government mismanagement. As the population went to the polls, it was certain that the PNM would lose a number of seats to the ULF, Tapia House, DAC, and a new DLP formation. Although it was felt that the PNM would win, the contest was expected to be keen. Also expected by some observers was a strong showing by Tapia House, which appeared to have made gains in the weeks before the vote, presenting itself as a moderate alternative to the ULF and the PNM, favoring localization over nationalization. Having become less radical and having participated in the 1971-76 government with four appointed senators, Tapia House had become a reformist party with intellectual and middle-class leadership, appealing to the younger white creole community, segments of the civil service, and the intelligentsia.[60]

The election results showed that the PNM still had a degree of popularity and that the opposition remained a weak force due to its divisions. Of 36 seats, the PNM won 24, the ULF 10, and DAC 2. Tapia House and the other parties failed to gain a single seat, and many candidates lost their deposits. Although up from 1971, only 55.8 percent of the total electorate went to the polls. A sizable part of the population still remained alienated from the political process.

The PNM benefited from two years of the oil boom, which was gradually improving Trinidad and Tobago's financial position. It had also worked on the creation of a new constitution, which aimed at being more representative, and had allowed elections to be held. As one Trinidadian commented, "By 1976, the ruling party was again standing firm on its record of investment in democratic institutions, mass education, economic enterprise, subsidies to help the weak, or inefficient, and leadership by a man now considered to be the senior politician in the region."[61] In many respects, the authoritarian temptation had been curbed as the threat of a one-party government receded, which was one reason among many for the PNM's victory. The return of an opposition in the Parliament was a healthy indication that democracy had survived as an institution in the political development of Trinidad.

The 1976 elections reflected several important transformations in the nation's political economy. While Trinidadian capitalism, supported and projected into the economy by the state, had survived, new threats had emerged. First and foremost was the ULF, which had won 26.8 percent of the popular vote. Although it is probable that it was illegally deprived of victories in two districts, the ULF secured the "Hindu Heartland" against the PNM and all other parties, and only in one case was there a close contest. The ULF had become, in many respects, the new East Indian party, and one of the major reasons for its inability to win the national election was its failure to make inroads into the urban Afro-Creole popular and middle sector votes. Its weakness in the north of Trinidad had not been helped by a last-minute campaign blitz that had made public the extent of its East Indian following. The fear of an East Indian prime minister functioned to split the popular sector vote along racial and geographical lines, a pattern similar to the 1971 period. Simply stated, the rhetoric had changed, but the actors had remained the same, with the PNM being the party of the Afro-Creoles, the mixed sectors, and the white creoles, and the ULF replacing the DLP as the Indo-Trinidadian party. A major difference, of course, was the shift of middle-class East Indian votes to the PNM. The ULF's ideology also appealed to the lowest rungs of Trinidad's socioeconomic pyramid, the majority of whom were East Indians tied to agricultural production. Other parties, such as the Tapia House, were caught in the return to ethnic-based politics.

The PNM faced a challenge of a different sort from the DAC. The Democratic Action Congress had won the two Tobago seats. On Trinidad's sister island, race was not a variable; economic and political development were. Discontent with Port of Spain's administration was clearly evident, and there was some discussion of secession. Although prosecession advocates lost their deposits in the election, those who won favored greater autonomy and access to the nation's resources. As Ryan notes, "Tobagonians resented the fact that almost everything was controlled in Port of Spain and that they had to undergo the cost and inconvenience of going to Trinidad to get things such as land title deeds, approval for building plans, birth or death certificates, or to attend to any official matter."[62] There were also complaints over the poor state of the island's infrastructure, educational facilities, and high cost of food.

To the PNM, the DAC victory represented a "rebellion." The situation was made even more bitter as one of the DAC victors was A. N. R. Robinson, whom Williams regarded as a "traitor." Only two weeks after the election Williams commented, ". . . I said it in Tobago: If you want to go, go. We are not holding you. I'm not going to send any Coast Guard or ship or army there to hold them back. What for? They want to go, go!"[63] The prime minister's attitude was that of sour grapes as the DAC had never advocated leaving the unitary state, only asking for self-government within that context. Furthermore, Williams's attitude was offensive to Tobagonians, especially those who had voted for the PNM. The problems between the two islands would be one source of friction in the post-1976 period as Trinidad's standard of living increased at a much more rapid pace than in Tobago due to the oil wealth.

CONCLUSION

The 1969-76 period was pivotal for Trinidad and Tobago. From the brink of political and economic collapse, the government had managed to recover its authority, stay in power, hold elections, and take advantage of the world oil crisis. Significantly, the authoritarian temptation of 1970-72 had been resisted, and a right-wing dictatorship was never imposed. At the same time, however, the elected government of Williams had demonstrated certain authoritarian tendencies, and the prime minister, in particular, had a tendency to act in an autocratic fashion. This, in part, was a reaction to his uneasiness with the party and his tendency to rule through the cabinet and interlocking directorates. In this context, middle sector support to the PNM continued to be essential, especially since that party had the loyalty of not only the Afro-Creoles and white and mixed middle segments, but increasingly the East Indian bourgeoisie. Other sections of the middle sectors turned to the smaller parties such as the DAC and Tapia House as they searched for alternatives to what they regarded as the PNM's economic mismanagement and corruption. The new bourgeoisie, allied to the state and part of the dominating triad, also regarded the PNM with a critical eye but were aware of their dependence on the state and feared what a government under the ULF would bring. The three major political groupings, the hardliners, moderates, and liberals, continued to move further apart politically as the last were increasingly dissatisfied with the PNM. Some discontent existed within the hardliners also, but as of 1976 the conservative forces remained within the fold, having no alternative charismatic leader to follow. Only the moderates were relatively content as the PNM continued to be their base of power. Capitalism, albeit state capitalism, held sway and proved beneficial to them.

NOTES

1. Theda Skocpol, *States and Social Revolutions: A Comparative Analysis of France, Russia, and China* (Cambridge: University of Cambridge Press, 1979), p. 24.
2. See ibid., pp. 47-111. Also see Linz, *The Breakdown of Democratic Regimes*, p. 50. As he comments, "Such crises are the result of a lack of efficacy or effectiveness of successive governments when confronted with serious problems that require immediate decisions."
3. Linz, *Democratic Regimes*, p. 54.
4. *Year Book of Labour Statistics 1972* (Geneva: International Labour Statistics, 1972), p. 427.
5. Ibid., p. 748.
6. "Dreaming of a Black Christmas," *The Economist*, December 27, 1969, p. 34.
7. Ivar Oxaal, *Race and Revolutionary Consciousness: An Existential Report on the 1970 Black Power Revolt in Trinidad* (Cambridge, Mass.: Schenkman, 1971), p. 66.
8. Quoted from *Tapia*, November 29, 1970, in Selwyn Ryan, *Race and Nationalism in Trinidad and Tobago: A Study of Decolonization in a Multiracial Society* (Toronto: University of Toronto Press, 1972), p. 470.
9. Granger in Oxaal, *Race and Revolutionary Consciousness*, p. 66.
10. Ibid., p. 23.
11. Williams quoted in ibid., p. 23.
12. "Trinidad: Black against Black," *The Economist*, April 25, 1970, p. 25.
13. "Interview with Rex Lasalle," *People Monthly*, October 1981, p. 41. For more on the mutiny, see S. Hylton Edwards, *Lengthening Shadows: Birth and Revolt of the Trinidad Army* (Port of Spain: Inprint Caribbean, 1983).
14. Ryan, *Race and Nationalism*, p. 463.

15. As James notes, "In Trinidad, people felt that Dr. Williams ought to go. They had had enough of him and the People's National Movement (PNM). After 1970 they were having nothing from him. But there was no opposing figure whom they could look to, and we in the Caribbean have been trained by the colonial government in terms of a leading figure." C. L. R. James, *Walter Rodney and the Question of Power* (London: Race Today, 1983), p. 11.

16. *An Act to Make Provision Respecting Public Safety, Public Order and Defense of Trinidad and Tobago* (Port of Spain: Government Printery, 1970), pp. 2-3.

17. Ryan notes, "The outcry against the bill was vehement and overwhelming with criticisms coming not only from radical militants, but establishment lawyers, doctors, the unions, the official opposition, university students and the established press." *Race and Nationalism*, p. 467.

18. This refers to the coups in Brazil in 1964, Argentina in 1966, and Chile in 1973. In each case the military took power with the support of the middle sectors, which were exceedingly apprehensive over the rising power of populist or Marxist forces in their respective nations and the deteriorating economic situation. See Paul E. Sigmund, *The Overthrow of Allende and the Politics of Chile, 1964-1976* (Pittsburgh: University of Pittsburgh Press, 1977); Gary Wynia, *Argentina in the Postwar Era: Politics and Economic Policy Making in a Divided Society* (Albuquerque: University of New Mexico Press, 1978); and Frederick C. Turner and José Enrique Miguens, ed., *Juan Peron and the Reshaping of Argentina* (Pittsburgh: University of Pittsburgh Press, 1983).

19. Debate on the "Firearms Bill," in Parliamentary Debates (Senate), *Hansard*, vol. 10, session 1970-71, November 10, 1971, p. 11.

20. Ibid., p. 20.

21. Ryan, *Race and Nationalism*, p. 482.

22. Parliamentary Debates (House of Representatives), *Hansard*, vol. 14, session 1970-71, December 1, 1970, p. 316.

23. Ibid., p. 330.

24. The literature on interlocking directorates is relatively new and has been largely limited to sociological and business studies and, in analysis, has focused on large and medium-sized industrialized nations. See T. Koenig and R. Gogel, "Interlocking Corporate Directorships as a Social Network," *American Journal of Economics and Sociology* 40 (1981): 37-50; B. Mintz and M. Schwartz, "Interlocking Directorates and Interest Group Formation," *American Sociological Review* 46 (1981): 851-69; M. Useem, "The Social Organization of the American Business Elite and Participation of Corporation Directors in the Governance of American Institutions," *American Sociological Review* 44 (1979): 553-72; and W. L. Warner and D. Unwallo, eds., *The Emergent American Society* (New Haven: Yale University Press, 1967). For this phenomenon in Trinidad and Tobago, see Carl D. Parris, "Personalization of Power in an Elected Government, Eric Williams and Trinidad and Tobago, 1973-1981," *Journal of Interamerican Studies and World Affairs* 25 (may 1983): 171-99.

25. As Ryan notes, "The small size of the community and the dominant position of the public sector in the creation of jobs or opportunities for amassing wealth for private sector operations also helped augment his power." Selwyn Ryan, "The Limits of Executive Power," *Journal of Caribbean Studies* 3 (Spring/ Autumn 1982): 14.

26. *History of Banking and Currency in Trinidad and Tobago* (Port of Spain: Central Bank of Trinidad and Tobago, 1974), p. 37.

27. Ibid., pp. 45-46.

28. "Trinidad-Tobago, Hollow Victory?" *Newsweek*, June 7, 1971, p. 52.

29. Ryan, *Race and Nationalism*, p. 468.

30. "Hollow Victory?" p. 52.

31. Ryan, *Race and Nationalism*, p. 483.

32. "Emergency Powers Debate" (House of Representatives), *Hansard*, vol. 15, session 1971-1972, October 22, 1971, p. 197.

33. *Year Book of Labour Statistics 1981* (Geneva: International Labour Office, 1981), p. 678.

34. "Trinidad Sets Foreign Investment Rules," *Business Latin America*, January 27, 1972, p. 31.

35. Ibid.

36. *History of Banking*, pp. 48-49. Bank acquisitions were done under the Bank Amendment Act, 1972, of April 8, 1972, Act No. 10 of 1972.

37. "Foreign Bank in Trinidad Takes in Local Equity," *Business Latin America*, February 24, 1972, p. 58.

38. "Trinidad's Program for Its Natural Gas Shows Flexible Dealing With Companies," *Business Latin America*, November 30, 1972, p. 378.

39. *Economic Survey of Latin America 1971: Latin America and the World Economy, Prospects and Trends* (New York: United Nations, 1973), p. 157.

40. *Economic Survey of Latin America 1973* (New York: Economic Commission for Latin America, United Nations, 1975), p. 267.

41. Parris, "Personalization of Power," p. 173.

42. "Trinidad's Constitutional Reform," *Business Latin America*, June 21, 1973, p. 195.

43. Raoul Pantin, "In Trinidad the Natives Are Getting Restless Again," *Caribbean Contact* 2 (September 1983): 5.

44. "Trinidad's Political Scene: The Effect of Williams' Move," *Business Latin America*, December 5, 1973, p. 389.

45. Pantin, "Natives Getting Restless," p. 5.

46. Anthony Sampson, *The Seven Sisters: The Great Oil Companies and the World They Shaped* (New York: Bantam Books, 1975, 1979), p. 301.

47. *The Energy Crisis 1973-1974, 4 Addresses by Dr. Eric Williams, Prime Minister of Trinidad and Tobago* (Arima: Trinidad and Tobago Printing and Packaging, 1974), p. 3.

48. David G. Becker, *The New Bourgeoisie and the Limits of Dependency: Mining, Class, and Power in "Revolutionary" Peru* (Princeton: Princeton University Press, 1983), p. 9.

49. Ibid.
50. Ibid.
51. Ibid.
52. Parris, "Personalization of Power," p. 174.
53. *Economic Survey of Latin America 1974* (New York: Economic Commission for Latin America, United Nations, 1976), pp. 347-48 and *Labour Statistics 1981*, p. 367.
54. Owen Baptiste, ed., *Crisis* (Trinidad: Inprint Caribbean, 1976), p. 20.
55. Selwyn Ryan, "Trinidad and Tobago: The General Elections of 1976," *Caribbean Studies* 19 (April-July 1979): 5.
56. C. Miceal Henry, "Trinidad and Tobago," In Robert J. Alexander, ed., *Political Parties of the Americas: Canada, Latin America and the West Indies* (Westport, Conn.: Greenwood Press, 1982), p. 665.
57. Ryan, "General Elections," p. 7.
58. Ibid.
59. *Express*, April 26, 1976; *Trinidad Guardian*, July 4, 1976, quoted in Ryan, "General Elections," p. 10.
60. Ryan, "General Elections," p. 18.
61. Pantin, "Natives Getting Restless," p. 5.
62. Ryan, "General Elections," p. 19.
63. J. G. Davidson, *Tobago Versus P.N.M.* (Port of Spain: Beacon, 1979), p. 4.

9

The Middle Classization of Trinidad and Tobago, 1976-83

In many ways Trinidad and Tobago's society drew closer from 1976 to 1983 as the middle stratum opened to new groups seeking upward mobility. The wealth generated by oil revenues stimulated a consumer boom accompanied by the "middle classization" of the upper echelons of the working class, while the general prosperity of the period allowed Williams to continue ruling through interlocking directorates, supported by the triad of state officials, domestic manager-entrepreneurs, and multinational corporate managers. The revolution in Grenada in 1979 caused some concern but was not a major issue to a nation seemingly secure in its economic development with improving distribution of income, health facilities, and social services. Although problems existed, the nation appeared to absorb them. Beneath the surface, serious problems lurked, which became apparent with Williams's death in 1981 and the appointment of his successor, George Chambers.

Although the PNM won the 1981 general elections, new problems of an economic nature emerged due to the world oil glut and U.S. hostility to Trinidadian steel production. By the time of the PNM defeat in the 1983 municipal elections, the political and economic situations had changed, and middle sector fragmentation became more pronounced over a number of issues ranging from large-scale corruption to the government's response to the U.S.-led invasion of Grenada in October 1983. The purpose of this chapter is to examine how the developmental process affected the middle sectors: did the national bourgeoisie, inclusive of the upwardly mobile unionized modern sector workers, continue to regard the democratic system as the correct path? Moreover, did the middle classization of the nation, that is, the attitudinal perception of being middle class and being able to purchase those consumer goods wanted (which, in some cases, meant going to Miami or New York to get them), mean a more democratic system and an acceptance by the majority that capitalism was a necessary evil?

TRINIDAD'S ECONOMIC MIRACLE

Between 1974 and 1980 Trinidad and Tobago underwent an "economic miracle." Real output grew by 7 percent, and unemployment gradually declined, reaching the 8.8 percent mark in 1980. While 1974 and 1975 witnessed a tremendous inflow of foreign exchange, which was linked to the oil industry, benefits for the nation on a widespread basis were not felt until 1976 when the government began to arrest price increases, particularly of goods catering to the needs of low-income group consumers. This was accomplished by a two-pronged strategy of increasing supply of such goods and raising subsidies to dampen price expectations.[1] Furthermore, per capita GNP (at market prices) increased from U.S. $1,231 in 1973 to $3,168 in 1978, a substantial improvement.[2] By 1979 per capita income inched to $3,390. Other indicators of the economic boom were the shrinkage of the gross public debt, considerable expansion of the manufacturing, government, and construction sectors in terms of productivity and employment, a surplus of foreign exchange reserves, and growth of public expenditure. As one Trinidadian commented, "The Republic was literally awash in money."[3] Williams himself is known to have remarked, "Money is no problem." Although taken out of context, it became a slogan of the boom years.

The major focus of government activities in the 1976-80 period was the capture of an increasing proportion of the GDP as revenues were needed to mobilize the resources necessary for restructuring the economy by the creation of heavy industries and the transfer of technology.[4] Part of this developmental scheme was the improvement of education as a massive school-building program was implemented as well as an overall upgrading of the state's responsibilities for its citizens. The latter was emphasized by increased old age pensions and provisions for food stamps.

By mid-1978 the government's investment in 50 companies stood at $190.1 million. These enterprises encompassed 23 that were completely state owned, 14 majority owned, and 13 of minority interests.[5]

Many of the government's wholly owned companies were in the oil, natural gas, aviation, agriculture, public utilities, and financial sectors. Moreover, there was the 1,754-acre Point Lisas Industrial Estate where the Iron and Steel Company of Trinidad and Tobago Limited (ISCOTT) was established. Initiated under Williams, the rationale stemmed from "the country's endowment of substantial reserves of natural gas and the imperative to utilize this basic raw material for the country, and ... from a conscious decision to reduce the exclusive dependence of the economy on oil."[6] By 1983 the total capital expenditure of establishing ISCOTT on an operating basis was $443.3 million, and trade had been opened with the United States and Brazil.[7]

Substantial state penetration of the economy was not without interrelated political developments. Prior to 1976 the system of interlocking directorates was already established, although during that year the pattern became even more pronounced with the creation of the National Advisory Council (NAC). Referred to as Williams's "think tank," the NAC included "academics and high-powered representatives of various important groups" within the business community, the technocratic elite, and trusted government officials, usually cabinet ministers.[8]

Williams's distrust of the party led him to create a new supraorganization that appropriated planning from the national bureaucracy. With this shift the responsibility for economic operations was moved, as Parris notes, into "the hands of a group of individuals wholly selected by the prime minister and wholly responsible to him."[9] Parris also feels that Williams regarded the council "as a device to enlarge his executive by recruiting individuals who, for one reason or another, could not be drawn into the more obvious political arena through the Senate."[10] In such a fashion, the prime minister sought to take direct control of the nation's economic development, thus bypassing what had come to be regarded as a corrupt and somewhat inefficient bureaucracy. At the same time, Williams attempted to halt the delegitimazation process and regain some standing with the popular sectors. This was pursued with the creation of the Development Environment Works Division (DEWD), which, together with government subsidies, provided a buffer for the lowest economic groups. DEWD's particular function was to create jobs, although it was known as part of the PNM government handing out the dole to curry political support.

Williams's tendency to concentrate decision-making authority into interlocking directorates was further advanced by the establishment of a number of new committees, ad hoc councils, inquiries, and commissions, including Corporation Sole, the Inter-Ministerial Enterprises Committee, the International Marketing Organization (IMO), and the Advisory Committee for the IMO. The Inter-Ministerial Enterprises Committee, in particular, was powerful and sometimes referred to as the "Inner Cabinet."[11] Moreover, the accumulation of office holding and functions continued, as exemplified by Errol Mahabir who was minister of petroleum and mines, a minister in the Ministry of Finance, the general manager of the Trinidad and Tobago Industrial Development Corporation, and IMO's chief executive and accounting officer. George Chambers, minister of agriculture, lands and fisheries was also minister of commerce. Therefore, by the time of his death in 1981, Eric Williams sat at the helm of a government run by interlocking directorates all linked to and dependent on the Office of the Prime Minister. Personal interface with a selected elite had replaced the concept of a functioning public service.

THE CONSUMER REVOLUTION, CORRUPTION, AND THE CRISIS IN AGRICULTURE

One of the major offshoots of the economic miracle was the consumer "revolution."[12] As the former editor of the *Trinidad Express* commented on this phenomenon, "An apparent non-stop consumer boom has put a car in at least one home in every two, electronic equipment in almost every house, refrigerators and stoves in most kitchens and vacation travel to North America within reach of increasing numbers."[13] In this context merchandise imports rose from U.S. $860 million in 1977 to $1,748.9 million in 1980, a substantial upward leap.[14] *Business Latin America* notes that "Trinidadians seem to have an unlimited appetite for consumer goods."[15] Furthermore, between 1970 and 1979 the growth in electricity consumption per capita kilowatt hours in Trinidad and Tobago was 169 percent, in contrast to 164 percent in Venezuela, 144 percent in Canada, and 133 percent in the United States.[16] As of 1979, energy consumption per person (4,272 in kilograms of coal equivalent) was considerably higher than most Caribbean nations, including Venezuela and Mexico and comparable to that of France, Austria, and Romania.[17] In many aspects North American consumer culture had come to permeate Trinidad and Tobago by the close of the 1970s, a point further brought home by the construction of suburban shopping malls north of Port of Spain and in the vicinity of San Fernando, the nation's two largest urban centers.

While "ultramodern" enclaves appeared and access to consumer goods created a society increasingly accustomed to a high standard of living by Caribbean standards, serious problems existed, one of the foremost being corruption. Corruption was fairly widespread, permeating all levels of the economy. In a bureaucracy where decisions were often made on a case-by-case basis, frequently needing cabinet-level deliberation, the result was delays. Moreover, government agencies were bogged down by red tape and the somewhat self-important attitude of many bureaucrats. In this atmosphere bribes were and are common, and middle-level officers prefer to pass the buck rather than make a decision, since they are fearful of being overruled by a superior.[18]

One of the more notorious cases of corruption has been the Water and Sanitary Authority (WASA), which is responsible for the delivery of water and the maintenance of sanitation. In various neighborhoods wealthy government officials, with contacts within WASA's hierarchy, are able to have water delivered twice a week and sometimes daily in certain outlaying areas; everyone else has it once a week, although it may be needed more often. In other areas phone calls for water have gone unheeded, unless, of course, someone was willing to pay a little extra. As WASA is a public utility, financed by the government and not a private enterprise operating on a profit motive, many Trinidadians have been annoyed that "the little extra" is expected and casually accepted. As one resident comments, "If you want anything done you have to pay for it."[19]

Other public utilities, such as the Trinidad and Tobago Telephone Company Ltd., have had an equally bad reputation. In 1978, as telephone services worsened, it was estimated that only one call in ten got the number dialed.[20] By the time of Williams's death in 1981, other problems continued to plague the country.

As the construction industry became increasingly involved in heavy projects, such as Point Lisas and private housing work, government housing projects for the lower-income stratum were given less priority and funding.[21] The nonunionized popular sectors and those on fixed incomes were also hit by rising consumer prices due to a rise in inflation in the 1973-80 period. In 1978 inflation was 10 percent, but in 1979 it had jumped to 16.1 percent.[22] As David Renwick notes of this situation, "While the expanding middle class and the unionized working class have successfully managed to keep ahead of these increases, as the figures for average earnings show, the same is not true of non-unionized workers, pensioners and those receiving various forms of public assistance."[23]

In all probability one of the most evident shortcomings of the PNM government in the late 1970s and early 1980s was in agriculture. Not only had the situation arisen that good agricultural land lay unused; Trinidad and Tobago increasingly, throughout the 1970s, imported foodstuffs it could grow. By the 1980s well over two-thirds of the nation's food came from overseas producers such as Belize or the United States. In 1977 alone, U.S. $125 million worth of food was imported.[24]

Nowhere was the decline in agriculture more marked in Trinidad than in the sugar industry. Although sugar had benefited from high international prices in the early 1970s and maintained its exports to Canada, the United States, and the European Economic Community, the industry was in serious trouble by the mid- and late 1970s as production declined to 173,111 tons in 1977, a decline of 13.6 percent from the 1976 level.[25] Consequently, Caroni Limited, the largest sugar operation, lost a considerable amount of money in 1977 and 1978. The following years were not much better. Like the cocoa and coffee enterprises, the sugar companies found it difficult to retain an adequate workforce as the construction boom offered better wages and more social prestige than working the land. In 1978 the importance of the agricultural sector fell further as sugar production declined to its lowest level in 25 years.[26] The economy's growth continued to depend on the oil industry and the manufacturing, government, and construction sectors. Simply stated, agriculture was in crisis, and its overall importance to the economy had declined considerably from the days when King Sugar ruled.

The government's efforts to revive the sugar industry were futile, as were attempts to promote private sector food production. To encourage the East Indian farmers to remain on the land, government subsidies were given. From this situation another scam arose as a number of Indo-Trinidadians grew vegetables near swamps, and, when the swamps overflowed, the government provided compensation. The farmers then sold the water-logged produce to the stores, almost doubling their original investment, which was usually government financed also. Although all East Indian farmers have not done so, this practice has not helped in the overall decline of agriculture, nor does it inspire others to toil.

THE LAST YEARS OF THE DOCTOR, 1980-81

As the government's revenues from the oil sector rose from U.S. $33 million in 1972 to $1.58 billion in 1980, and its foreign reserves multiplied from $28 million in 1973 to close to $2.7 billion in early 1981, the last years of Eric Williams were not marred by an economic crisis. The major concern of the Williams government in the 1980-81 period was the need to arrest the process of delegitimization, which eroded the regime's support on a number of fronts ranging from problems with Tobago, official corruption, and the questioning of the political system's viability, stemming, in part, from a new wave of revolution in the Caribbean Basin.

After the 1976 general elections Tobago's two members of Parliament were in the opposition. One of them, Robinson, continued to push for greater local self-government, and, despite Williams displeasure at "losing" Tobago to the DAC, he was forced to concede some form of local government in Scarborough. On September 12, 1980, the House of Representatives approved the Tobago House of Assembly Bill, which proposed a 15-member elected body with responsibilities for financial affairs, economic planning, programming, and development of resources, and infrastructural improvement.[27] There was considerable criticism that the bill did not go far enough since it left many responsibilities in the hands of Port of Spain, such as communication and water supply.[28] With the bill's passage in the Senate, the Tobago House of Assembly came into being as a compromise between DAC self-government adherents led by Robinson and a hostile central government in Port of Spain. Williams clearly intended, by keeping some controls, to maintain some leverage on Tobago. This attitude was blantantly obvious when after a long delay the government charted a car ferry for the Port of Spain-Tobago run at a cost of U.S. $7,000 a day. On its first run it was met by demonstrators in Tobago who regarded the timing of the charter as an election gimmick.[29]

As elections were to be held every four years for the Tobago House of Assembly for 12 positions, 3 being appointed by the winning party, polling took place on November 24, 1980. The continued process of delegitimization was evident as the PNM failed to win control of the house. The Democratic Action Congress won eight seats, in addition to the right to appoint three additional members. Robinson, as the leader of the DAC, was shortly elected as the assembly's chairman although he had to resign from Parliament to stand in Tobago.

Unlike the previous elections in 1971 and 1976, voter turnout in Tobago was high as nearly 63 percent of the 40,000 island's eligible voters cast their ballots.[30] The DAC captured 52.7 percent and the PNM 44.9 percent, while the DAC splinter group of Winston Murray, the Fargo House Movement, won only 2.3 percent.[31] The non-PNM forces triumphed and Williams appeared to have grown weary of Tobago's affairs. This lack of interest helped diffuse the atmosphere of confrontation that had been building since the 1976 general elections when the DAC had won both seats and Williams had dismantled the Ministry of Tobago Affairs in an attempt to punish the "rebellion." At the same time, the government made it clear that the DAC's $625 million ten-year plan aimed at converting Tobago into a productive, self-reliant ministate was not going to be considered, especially after the outcome of the local elections. Instead, Port of Spain provided the Scarborough assembly with an operating budget and a capital budget of $59.7 million after discussions with Robinson.[32] The central government also served notice that it would improve Tobago's airport while embarking upon a highway from Crown Point, the airport, to Scarborough.

Williams's problems with Tobago were increasingly overshadowed by problems with corruption in the government. In July 1980 the "DC-9 Scandal" made the headlines, as well as other deals involving the awarding of contracts for a large racing complex and the charter to Tobago. The first-mentioned appeared to involve high officials in the government airline, British West Indies Airways (BWIA, also referred to as Between Walk If Able). It also opened the door to other aviation corruption cases as there was a probability that questionable payments accompanied the sale of two 1011-500 Tristars to the national airline by Lockheed and the purchase of Sikorsky helicopters for the national security ministry. Allegations were given additional probability when Lockheed's principal agent in Trinidad and Tobago, who admitted earning U.S. $1.3 million from the Tristar sales, resigned in November 1980 as chairman of the Trinidad Tesoro Oil Company and other government appointments, referring to what he called "an agonizing reappraisal" of his position.[33]

At the opening session of the PNM's twenty-second annual convention on September 26, 1980, Williams took notice of the erosion of popular support, hinting that there were "enemies within" the nation who wrote anonymous slogans and innuendos (about corruption) in an attempt to create racial disunity. These enemies within also sought to drive a wedge between workers by artificially creating a class called "managers." Moreover, Williams contended it was the trade union movement that was the source of many of the society's problems. The most dangerous "enemy" was the one who blamed the government for all the dilemmas confronting Trinidadian society. As Williams comments, "If there is a tropical storm and if it floods, it is the government; if two private companies get together and attempt, and perhaps succeed in defrauding the government, it is the government. All evils begin and end with the government."[34]

At the convention Williams also sought to emphasize that the PNM had maintained its pledge to continue democratic government. Though not mentioning the Grendadian revolution by name, nor discussing the political instability in St. Lucia, St. Vincent, and Dominica, nor the installation of a military regime in Suriname, Williams said that as long as the PNM was in power "there will not be the slightest signs of dictatorship."[35] Furthermore, he notes, "the Westminster model spells democracy and not dictatorship." He also adds, regarding the militarization in the Eastern Caribbean, "we don't stand for that in Trinidad and Tobago, not even from the Head of State, far less from the Head of Government. . . . I would like a damn fool in any military uniform."[36] Despite Williams's attempt to shift the blame of corruption from the government to "enemies within" and emphasize the PNM's commitment to democracy, he was forced to concede that "We cannot be a Toronto or a Miami in a matter of years," thus serving notice that economic development would proceed at a slower pace than the rise of expectations.

The government's base of support continued to erode despite the creation of new commissions of inquiry, the holding of public meetings at which the boards and management of the utilities were made responsible to the citizen, and the filing of libel suits against *The Express*. In a poll conducted by Selwyn Ryan in January-February 1981, only 6 percent of those interviewed felt that the government was revealing to the nation all it knew about the DC-9 scandal, while 69 percent of the survey believed the government was "stonewalling" on the issue.[37] Of those believing in a cover-up, 49 percent felt that the prime minister was covering for persons in the party or the cabinet, and 39 percent believed that he was covering for himself and others. As Ryan notes, "Whatever the truth of the matter in a legal sense, and no guilt is presumed, the fact remains that on this as well as other issues, the credibility of the government was in serious question by large numbers of people, many of whom had come to believe that nothing which the government said or promised could be taken at face value."[38] This was further supported by the fact that 50 percent of the sample felt that Williams should resign, making room for a successor, in contrast to a similar poll conducted in November 1979. Nor was discontent limited to one ethnic community, as 54 percent of Indo-Trinidadians and 45 percent of Afro-Creoles surveyed felt that Williams should "take a rest."

Prior to and during the period of Ryan's survey, late 1980 and the beginning of 1981, Trinidad and Tobago witnessed a number of labor disputes. A weeklong protest by senior port officials left Port of Spain's waterfront in a chaotic situation, as well as being badly congested.[39] A new commission of inquiry was created to investigate the matter and concluded that "nobody seems to take responsibility for anything." Labor unrest and discontent with the status quo were also manifested by teachers seeking union recognition, state lawyers, workers at Federation Chemicals, bus workers, junior air traffic controllers, electricians, and postal officials.

At the PNM's twenty-fifth anniversary in January 1981, Williams sought to rally the party and set the stage for elections to be held later that year. He blamed the nation's frustration on "problems resulting from the rapid pace of our development."[40] Although conceding that there was inefficiency, delays, bureaucratic bottlenecks, and mismanagement, the prime minister refused to place any responsibility on the government, hinting that part of the societal malaise was caused by "sabotage" and "unvarnished hostility from vested interests at home and abroad."

On March 29, 1981, as the nation prepared for elections, which had not yet been announced, Eric Williams died alone in his house of complications stemming from acute diabetes. In his last months he appeared disillusioned by his inability to arrest the process of delegitimization and had become more isolated, traveled nowhere, saw few people, and refused interviews.[41] Having become increasingly ill in March, he refused to see even many of his closest associates, who urged him to call a doctor. The seriousness of his condition was known only to a small circle, and his death, therefore, came as a shock to the nation. His demise, however, was followed by a smooth succession as George Chambers became Trinidad and Tobago's second prime minister within 12 hours of Williams's death.

Chambers was relatively unknown to the public and was described as "a low-key, low-profile figure, uncontroversial and cool."[42] He first entered politics in 1966 when he won the St. Ann's seat for Parliament and served in various capacities, ranging from minister of public utilities to minister of finance, planning and development. Having carefully bided his time and lacking any major foes, he was the ideal compromise for the various factions in the PNM over Kamaluddin Mohammed, then health minister, and Errol Mahabir, then energy minister.

Also to be considered was that Chambers was an Afro-Creole, and the latter two, though better known to the public, were East Indians. As Chambers consolidated his position as prime minister and political leader, it became clear that the PNM would not be led by an East Indian, nor would there be any radical policy changes. Furthermore, the new prime minister faced what many expected would be a difficult election later in 1981 and growing problems with the economy.

In May Chambers declared, "What is wrong must be put right."[4][3] This was one of his first promises of reform aimed at wooing a disgruntled public. Situated as the new leader in the old one's shadow, he halted two of the more controversial projects, namely the horse-racing complex and a housing project in East Trinidad. He also served notice to the public that there would be decentralization of decision making, less corruption, reform of public services, and better relations with Tobago.

Chambers changed little despite the fanfare of a cabinet reshuffle, announcements of intended reform, and the halting of a few controversial projects. Except for the departure of John O'Halloran, a white Creole businessman and close associate of Williams, the cabinet's membership was the same. Furthermore, O'Halloran was increasingly implicated in a number of major scandals, and it is possible that he was asked to leave before he became an embarrassment to the new government. There was growing pressure to call elections from the opposition parties and public organizations, which further complicated the situation for Chambers.

One of the few changes noticeable was Chambers' more relaxed style in tackling the nation's problems. Realizing that he was largely unknown to the public, the new prime minister decided to wait until the last moment to call elections and followed this with a swift, sudden campaign that was well organized and aggressive. Moreover, he sought to make his face better known to the public while seeking to resolve many of the industrial disputes plaguing the nation. Moving quickly, he treated the local press to scotch and chicken at the Trinidad Hilton, undertook an electioneering tour of Trinidad's industrial belt, and settled wage disputes in key sectors of the economy. By the time he announced elections on October 11 for November 9, 1981, Chambers had enjoyed some favorable press coverage, calmed a troubled industrial sector, and managed to overcome his nearest competitor in the opinion polls. Called the "Doctor's Shadow," Chambers had, with few changes, made a smooth transition for the nation into the post-Williams era. In many aspects the PNM under Chambers offered "more of the same," a safe choice for many Trinidadians.

THE 1981 GENERAL ELECTIONS: MIDDLE SECTOR FRAGMENTATION

One of the major offshoots of the economic miracle of the 1970s was the expansion of the middle class and the development of a modern sector working class. The latter was more skilled and secure in its conditions of employment, far better organized, and somewhat more active politically than was the case a decade or so before. Becoming increasingly bourgeois, this group became affiliated with the capitalist societal consensus in exchange for material benefits, namely consumer goods, and the opportunity of some upward mobility. Political participation in Trinidad and Tobago, for this upper stratum of the popular sectors, was a given and had a long tradition dating back to the 1930s.

In Becker's study on Peru, it was noted that the emergence of an "upper class" of workers from the ranks of the popular sectors does not concur with the general assertion "that corporate enterprise in the Third World subsists on the basis of exploitation of cheap labor; that the highly capital-intensive production methods introduced there by transnational firms are designed to simplify tasks so as to reduce job skill requirements; and that, given low skills, wages are held down by the existence of a huge 'industrial reserve army' of urban marginals"[44]

In Trinidad and Tobago 30 percent of the labor force in 1978 was unionized, and its leadership politically active in obtaining work and better wages.[45] Topping the list of business difficulties for foreign firms operating in Trinidad in the late 1970s was that "unions have tremendous clout and control the vital sectors of oil, sugar, construction and transport." In controlling these sectors, the unions had become exceedingly competitive amongst themselves and even more so with any new "small unions" or nonunion labor. This trend was noticed even by Williams who commented in September 1980, "Indeed, one is tempted to say as well, that there will be no room for the small trade union."[46] Unionized labor demanded and got a portion of the large inflow of petrodollars that occurred after 1973 and, in doing so, placed itself above the rest of the popular sectors. Interestingly enough, the majority of ULF supporters in 1976 were East Indians, many of whom were tied to the production of sugar and nonindustrial activities.

Among the urbanized Afro-Creole workers, who were tied to the modern sector of the economy, the tendency in many cases was to vote for the PNM, especially in the north. As the 1981 general elections neared, the modern sector working class became an important electoral element, especially as the three groupings within the middle class had drifted further apart and were casting about for allies through their respective parties.

The liberal group of the middle sectors was the most badly divided as its loyalties went to the ULF, DAC, and Tapia House. Each of these parties continued to attract a following, with Tapia being reformist in nature, centered around the University of the West Indies, and the most top-heavy with bourgeois intellectuals, while the DAC had become identified with Tobagonian issues.

The ULF was a largely popular sector party attracting the East Indian sugar workers and cane farmers and a small segment of the modern sector workforce in the southern oil belt. Having captured the traditional seats held by the DLP, with the exceptions of Pointe-à-Pierre and Nariva, ULF "territory" encompassed most of east central Trinidad and part of the southern oil belt but had failed to make inroads into the nation's leading urban areas such as Port of Spain, San Fernando, and Arima. Simply stated, the ULF was geographically limited, and important labor votes eluded it in the north and south.

Why did the party of labor fail to win all the labor votes? While the racial factor was important, in that many Afro-Creoles, whether they were middle class or workers, did not want to see an East Indian prime minister, the lack of unity and poor leadership of the ULF elite went far in discouraging possible voters. In August 1977 the ULF's Central Committee removed Panday as party leader in favor of Shah, who was perceived as more radical and had the support of Weekes, still the president of the OWTU. Moderate elements in the ULF, however, rallied behind Panday and had him reinstated in early 1978. A key factor in the internal party struggle was that Panday was able to gain the support of the ULF members of Parliament. The decline of the radical faction was further reflected in a local municipal by-election in Shah's parliamentary district in September 1978 when the nominee supported by Panday won and Shah's candidate came in a dismal fourth.[47] Despite Panday's hold over the party, it was far from being a unified organization.

Panday's leadership of the ULF from 1978 to 1980 was a continued tale of uneasy factional relations. After a crushing PNM victory in local elections in April 1980, the East Indian laborite resigned. His reelection a few months later did little to improve his or the party's reputation, nor did it unify the ULF, especially when Panday made such comments as: "I would only stand if the membership and the people as a whole reconsidered their mistakes and re-affirmed their confidence in me."[48] When comparing Panday to Williams, which many Trinidadians have done, the former does not appear to be an inspiring leader, a very negative factor in the politics of the two-island nation.

As elections neared the ULF, DAC, and Tapia formed the National Alliance, which was advertised as a social democratic political force. In July 1981 it finally managed to initiate a campaign, although it had no agreed leading candidate and little press coverage. The National Alliance position had been weakened when Robinson, probably the best known politician among the new organization's leadership, opted to remain in Tobago as chairman of the House of Assembly rather than return to national politics in a bid for the prime minister's seat. This brought forth the question as to whether the nation would accept an Indian prime minister as Panday appeared as the National Alliance's leader. The only other contender was Lloyd Best, Tapia's leader, who had little support from the electorate. To complicate matters further, the ULF was now challenged in the sugar belt by the PNM and the conservative Organization for National Reconstruction (ONR).

In early 1981 the Organization for National Reconstruction was formed with Karl Hudson-Phillips as its leader. At both of its first public gatherings, a rally in Woodford Square and its first party convention in the Chaguaramas Convention Center, the turnout was sizable, and the composition was ethnically balanced with members of all racial communities present.[49] Most of the crowd at both occasions was middle class with a small working-class representation. As one observer comments: "The 16 candidates in general reflect the composition of the party following—middle class, ethnic diversity and comparatively young."[50] Of the candidates presented at the second meeting, 13 had university degrees, 1 was an oil worker, 1 a teacher, and 1 a public servant, while 8 were Afro-Creoles, 7 East Indians, and 1 of mixed Chinese extraction. The line of attack followed by Hudson-Phillips was that the PNM government had reduced the people of Trinidad and Tobago into a "state of defeat and corruption."[51]

Vowing to reform the government, Hudson-Phillips outlined the ONR's purpose as the "elimination of poverty and want."[52] To accomplish this, the government's development programs had to be reexamined, land reform was necessary, and decentralization measures would be enacted in a number of sectors, especially agriculture. Hudson-Phillips also lamented the lack of unity among the nation's trade unions and declared the reason for disunity to be "preoccupations with ideological positions to the detriment of the worker" as well as "continuing inter-union rivalry, poaching and posturing."[53] As an attraction to the modern sector working class, he also proposed tax relief for workers. Finally, in seeking to leave no stone unturned, the ONR leader called for greater cooperation between church and state, vowed to create a ministry of women's affairs, advocated a revaluation of contacts with the revolutionary government of Grenada, and supported a long overdue CARICOM summit.

The ONR, attacking the government on corruption and inefficiency, appeared to be the greatest challenge to the PNM, especially as the National Alliance was without a clear leader. To many in the middle sectors, in particular those conservatives disillusioned with the corruption of the PNM administration, Karl Hudson-Phillips appeared as a dynamic new leader who could put the nation "back on the right track." Campaigning with the slogan, "We must do better," the ONR mounted a serious challenge to the ruling party as it even went to the extent of hiring Sabo Associates, the U.S. public relations firm that helped Edward Seaga's Jamaica Labour Party to power in 1980.

Chambers's ability to resolve some of the nation's problems and his low-key approach helped him gradually overtake Hudson-Phillips in the opinion polls conducted by *The Express* in June and published in July. The prime minister was favored by 35 percent of the respondents, as opposed to his new rival's 14 percent. Moreover, 29.2 percent said they would vote for the PNM and only 10.9 percent for the ONR, which in an earlier poll had been favored by 29 percent.[54]

The emergence of a party to the PNM's right was not taken lightly by the ruling party, which increasingly relied on the support of the moderate segment of the middle sectors. This grouping was multiracial, encompassing East Indian professionals and businessmen fearful of the ULF and some of the urban Afro-Creole professional groups as well as part of the mixed community. Additional support came from those middle sector elements linked to the international economy, the technocrats, state managers, and those employed by the multinational firms, as well as some segments of the Afro-Creole modern sector working class that was disillusioned with the internecine struggles in the ULF. One factor, however, that made the ONR such a threat to the PNM was that it was founded by PNM defectors and challenged the ruling party for many of the same people: moderate and conservative middle-class voters, with some support from Afro-Creole labor groups, especially those located in the north around Port of Spain and in the south around certain urban areas.

Benefiting from a low voter turnout of 54.7 percent, the PNM won a stunning victory, gaining 2 seats from the ULF to give it a total of 26 of the 36 parliamentary seats.[55] The ULF remained the major opposition party, but lost 2 seats in Caroni East and Princes Town. The ONR, with 91,704 votes and 22.1 percent of the popular vote, failed to win a single seat even though it obtained more votes than the National Alliance's 87,572.[56] Tapia won no seats and the DAC was limited to the 2 Tobago seats.

A combination of factors explain the PNM's victory. The fact that the majority of the nation's population had experienced some noticeable improvement in the standard of living may be regarded as a major reason.[57] Related to this was the fear of the unknown, as neither the National Alliance or the ONR had ever been in office. One of the major PNM tactics had been to play on the public perception that the ULF represented a leftist threat, headed by radical East Indians, while the ONR stood for right-wing reactionism and a possible reduction of traditional freedoms. In the game of perceptions, the PNM once again won control of the 18 urban- and Afro-Creole-dominated constituencies around Port of Spain and the second city, San Fernando. However, of the total electorate, including the 45.3 percent who did not cast their ballot, the PNM was the choice of only 29.8 percent.[58]

THE 1983 MUNICIPAL ELECTIONS: A WAVE OF THE FUTURE?

Although Chambers won an important victory, his government was confronted by a plethora of problems, some old, some new. Of the former, cases of corruption implicated former members of the government, friction resumed with Tobago, and unrest marked industrial relations. Of the latter, the government risked a balance of payments deficit, took unpopular measures concerning the removal of squatters on the outskirts of Port of Spain, and the international economic system was increasingly causing difficulties in the marketing of oil due to an emerging oil glut and a fall in prices. Most serious for the Chambers administration was that the boom years were over as reflected in the findings in the *1981 Central Bank Report*. In that report it was acknowledged that, while agriculture was in a severe slump and the export of sugar was becoming a faint possibility, the oil industry was also in decline. In 1980, 212,066 barrels per day were produced, which declined by 11 percent in 1981 to 189,487 barrels per day, as well as a 23 percent fall in productivity in refinery output.[59]

Dwindling oil revenues forced the Chambers government in 1982 to reduce subsidies, welfare spending, government employment, and development projects.[60] Regarding the development projects, the government announced that a number of them, in particular, those being implemented as joint ventures with foreign governments, had been plagued by problems including cost overruns, delays in completion, and an absence of technology transfers. These government-to-government projects commenced under Williams and had been with the United Kingdom, France, Sweden, Luxembourg, Japan, the Netherlands, Belgium, Finland, Italy, and Switzerland, ranging from road and harbor repairs to hospital and airport development. The severity of the situation was also underscored by the arrival of a joint team from the World Bank and the International Monetary Fund to advise the government on financial management and control.

By mid-1982 the Trinidadian economy was once again heading into troubled waters, although the scope of its problems was relatively lighter than those facing many other Caribbean states such as the Dominican Republic and Jamaica. Despite real GDP growth of 4.8 percent in 1980, a fall in inflation of 11.4 percent from 14.3 percent in 1981, and a decrease in unemployment to 10.3 percent, real GDP growth slowed to 0.3 percent in 1981 and 0.4 percent in 1982.[61] Moreover, foreign exchange reserves fell from $3,196,700 in 1981 to $1,881,500 in 1983.[62] There was also a sharp reversal in the current account balance of payments from a $283 million surplus in 1981 to a $909 million deficit in 1982 due to declining oil exports and earnings.[63] Oil production continued to decline, and the government turned to higher rates for electricity, water, telephones, and public transport.

One of the biggest problems facing Chambers was public sector employment. By the early 1980s the government accounted for two-thirds of all jobs in the nation, which meant that a substantial bureaucracy existed, complete with unions. In 1982 Chambers conceded to several demands for close to 52,000 public employees, allowing a public sector pay award that helped push government expenditure up by 76 percent.[64] This action was, in many aspects, exceedingly political as the PNM was looking ahead to the municipal elections and needed as much support as possible.

One of the groups most afflicted by the changing economic picture was the modern sector working class. The industrialized oil belt, in particular, became a tense region as the large firms began retrenching personnel in an effort to cut costs. To meet the deteriorating situation, the OWTU formed a "war chest" in mid-January 1983 to protect the national interest against multinational corporation domination and Texaco in particular. In April 1983 the OWTU was forced, after long negotiations, to agree to lower the retirement age at Texaco Trinidad from 65 to 60, which immediately involved 700 workers and a further 400 in the next two years. In return the company withdrew 400 notices issued in March and undertook to give 60 days notice of further retrenchment. Weekes, still the OWTU president, announced that further layoffs in the oil industry would be met with the "maximum amount of resistance." As the modern sector working class was forced on the defensive, the oil industry was not alone since the manufacturing workers also felt the increasingly difficult financial pinch as exemplified by the jailing of 11 workers and 3 union officials for defying to end their occupation of a biscuit factory where 60 workers had been dismissed.

Plagued by another scandal, once again including former cabinet member John O'Halloran, and the poor state of the economy, Chambers postponed local elections, hoping that something positive would occur. The new prime minister was also increasingly criticized for being a copy of Eric Williams and for creating a cabinet that was "a mixed bag of old, weary faces and fresh talent from outside politics."[65] Along these lines, the same pattern of interlocking directorates and the personalization of power continued from Williams to Chambers with little interruption. Not only was Chambers the nation's chief executive; he also maintained control over the all-important Finance and Planning Ministry and was the political leader of the PNM. Furthermore, of the eight newcomers to the cabinet, seven were nonelected and, therefore, dependent on Chambers for their jobs and futures in the government.

To deal with the situation, the Chambers government created a 14-member team of well-known economists from inside and outside of the public sector, headed by William Demas, the Trinidadian president of the Caribbean Development Bank based in Bridgetown, Barbados. According to Chambers, the purpose of the Demas Task Force was to prepare a "framework for national action over the next three years within a long term development perspective for the country."[66]

The report of this special task force was then to be placed before the National Economic Planning Commission for consideration prior to its submission to the cabinet and to the Parliament. In essence, Chambers's mistrust of the national bureaucracy appears to have been inherited from Williams as the Demas Task Force, dependent on the prime minister for its existence, superceded some of the functions usually performed by the Ministry of Finance and Planning. This pattern was also reinforced by the government's turn to the IMF for advice on the management of the economy.

From 1982 onward the Chambers administration sought to tighten the national budget, generate new sources of revenue, and put ceilings on the various ministries' spending. Although the public sector had enough financial leverage not to "press the panic button," the fall in oil prices in late 1982 and 1983 and declining productivity in that sector cast some shadows of doubt over the future financial solvency of the government and over the advancement of the standard of living for all societal levels. An additional problem was the inflow of illegal aliens from the smaller islands, such as Grenada, St. Vincent, and St. Lucia, to Trinidad where the standard of living and access to health and education services were considerably better.[67] In many aspects, the flow of "illegals" into Trinidad is similar to the situation between the United States and Mexico in that children born in Trinidad are citizens and thereby entitled to all the services that the government provides. With the emergence of shantytowns on the outskirts of Port of Spain and San Fernando, the government has had to divert some of its resources to either the eviction of the squatters or the extension of social services, while having some difficulty in managing the inflow of "illegals."

By the August 8, 1983, local elections, discontent with the Chambers government was evident on many levels. Significantly, the conservative ONR had made an "accommodation" with the left-of-center National Alliance to dislodge the PNM from its long control of all county councils and municipalities. In the former bodies, the ONR-National Alliance combination captured majorities in St. George East, St. Patrick, Caroni, Victoria, Nariva/Mayaro, and St. Andrews/St. David. In Victoria the National Alliance accounted for ten seats, the ONR, one, and the PNM, one, due to a default, reflecting a strong rejection of the ruling party in one district.[68] In the municipalities the PNM was able to maintain control of the nation's major urban areas, although the ONR made substantial inroads in Port of Spain, capturing 4 of 12 seats, in Arima, winning 3 to the PNM's 4, and in San

Fernando, with 3 to the PNM's 6. Only in Port Fortin in the south did the ruling party win all the seats excluding the opposition. Of the total seats voted for, the PNM won 54 and the ONR-National Alliance accommodation gained 66, giving the opposition its first victory since 1958, when the DLP won the federal elections.

Regarded as a "national referendum" by the opposition, the 1983 local elections were indicative of several patterns. First and foremost was that the PNM's support had eroded further, as the process of delegitimization continued. In the predominantly East Indian rural areas in south and central Trinidad, the ruling party's decline in popularity was most evident, while the defection of a segment of the urban Afro-Creoles was equally significant. The ONR, a largely middle sector party, made particularly strong showings in Arima and San Fernando, traditional PNM strongholds. Although the importance of the opposition's victory should not be overstated, Trinidad and Tobago's political arena had become more fluid. A. N. R. Robinson comments, "The whole politics of the country has opened up, the pattern has changed and new trends set up. The PNM cannot reverse these new trends unless there is dramatic change and recovery. And the PNM is incapable of such change."[6][9]

Considering the entire breakdown of seats, the PNM led with 54, the ULF followed with 38, the ONR with 26, and Tapia with 2. The National Joint Action Congress failed to win any seats due to its radical stance and racial nature. The ULF, led by Panday, continued in its role as the leader of the opposition, although the ONR's showing indicated that conservative and urban middle sector elements could also make a serious demonstration of anti-PNM strength.

The most significant dimension of the 1983 local elections was that they took place and that the opposition was allowed to win. Although distasteful for the ruling party, it had to admit defeat and did not resort to military or extraconstitutional means to nullify the results. Despite the corruption in government, possible excesses of police action in the past, and the tendency of the prime minister to personalize power and rely upon interlocking directorates, democracy, Trinidad-style, did exist.

CONCLUSION

The relationship between politics and economics was amply demonstrated by the defection of an element of the middle sectors to the ONR, as that societal group had come to perceive the PNM as a party increasingly unable to maintain or advance the middle sectors' way of life. This analysis would also help explain the ONR's accommodation with the National Alliance, despite obvious ideological differences. A portion of the modern sector working class also came to regard the government as incapable of advancing the economy. This unlikely alliance of the conservative and urban multiethnic middle-class party with the left-of-center parties representative of the rural East Indians and segments of the modernized Afro-Creole popular sectors and intellectuals increasingly characterized Trinidadian politics in the early 1980s.

The new bourgeoisie and the modern sector working class did not find the early 1980s as a period of political unity, and the triad of state officials, multinational corporate managers, and domestic manager-entrepreneurs lost the all-important consensus of shared interests. The emergence of the ONR tended to pull a number of those in the triad out of the PNM orbit, aligning them with the traditional national middle sectors linked to agriculture, small-scale manufacturing, and the service economy as well as those elements of the professional group involved in nonindustrial activities such as medicine and law. Support for the PNM, while being predominantly urban, also continued to attract some segments of the middle sectors, especially sections of the modern sector workforce and the lower middle class, which was dependent on the government for jobs in the national bureaucracy. Although political loyalties were divided, the commitment to the continuation of the democratic system appeared to have widespread acceptance.

NOTES

1. Central Bank of Trinidad and Tobago, *Annual Report for Year Ended 31st December 1976* (Port of Spain: College Press, 1977), p. 11.

2. Ramesh Ramsaran, "The Growth and Pattern of Public Expenditure in Trinidad and Tobago, 1959-1979," paper presented at the Sixth Annual Conference of the Caribbean Studies Association, St. Thomas, U.S. Virgin Islands, May 27-30, 1981, p. 3.

3. Raoul Pantin, "In Trinidad the Natives Are Getting Restless Again," *Caribbean Contact* 2 (September 1983): 5. Also see *Financial Times*, October 4, 1978, p. iii: "... international finance flocked to lend it money, its credit-worthiness is high, and its political stability proved."

4. Central Bank of Trinidad and Tobago, *Annual Report for Year Ended 31st December 1977* (Port of Spain: College Press, 1978), p. 13.

5. "Marketing Organization Will Change Role of IDC," in John Badd, Elizabeth Chang, and Colin Richards, "Profile of Trinidad and Tobago," reprinted from *Caribbean Business News*, December 1978, p. 2.

6. "Independence Address by Prime Minister George Chambers," *Newsletter*, Embassy of Trinidad and Tobago, Washington, D.C. (August/September 1983), p. 6.

7. Ibid., p. 7.

8. "Special Report Trinidad and Tobago," *The Times*, October 4, 1978, p. i.

9. Carl D. Parris, "Personalization of Power in an Elected Government, Eric Williams and Trinidad and Tobago, 1973-1981," *Journal of Interamerican World Affairs* 25 (May 1983): 180.

10. Ibid.

11. *Caribbean Business News*, December 1978, p. 2.

12. This view was taken in *Business Latin America*, September 6, 1978, p. 285: "Soaring per capita income is carrying the momentum into the consumer goods field."

13. David Renwick, "Trinidad and Tobago," *Latin America and Caribbean 1983* (Saffron Walden, Essex, England: World of Information, 1983), p. 261.

14. International Monetary Fund, *International Financial Statistics, December 1984* (Washington, D.C.: International Monetary Fund, 1984), p. 458.

15. *Business Latin America*, September 26, 1978, p. 285.

16. Renwick, "Trinidad and Tobago," p. 265.

17. *The World in Figures* (London: The Economist, 1981), p. 13.

18. "Sunny Business Climate in Trinidad Has a Few Shadows," *Business Latin America*, September 6, 1978, p. 287.

19. Interview with the author, June 6, 1982, in Trinidad.

20. *The Times*, October 4, 1978, p. 1.

21. Ibid.

22. *Latin America Regional Reports Caribbean*, October 31, 1980, p. 6.

23. Renwick, "Trinidad and Tobago," p. 261.

24. *Caribbean Business News*, December 1978, p. 5.

25. Ibid.

26. Central Bank of Trinidad and Tobago, *Annual Report for Year Ended 31st December 1978* (Port of Spain: College Press, 1979), p. 13.

27. *Caribbean Monthly Review* 14 (September-October 1980): 19-20.

28. See W. D. Moore, "That Tobago House of Assembly Is a Glorified County Council," *The Express*, September 21, 1980, p. 1.

29. *Latin America Regional Reports Caribbean*, October 31, 1980, p. 5.

30. Ibid., December 5, 1980, p. 6.

31. Ibid.

32. Ibid., January 16, 1981, p. 4.

33. Ibid., December 5, 1980, p. 6.

34. *Caribbean Monthly Bulletin* 14 (September-October 1980): 16.

35. Ibid., p. 15.

36. Ibid.

37. Selwyn Ryan, "The Church That Williams Built: Electoral Possibilities in Trinidad," *Caribbean Review* 10 (Spring 1981): 12.

38. Ibid.
39. *Latin America Regional Report Caribbean*, January 16, 1981, p. 4.
40. Ibid., February 20, 1981, p. 4.
41. "Dr. Eric Williams, Dominant Role in the Life of Trinidad and Tobago," *The Times*, March 31, 1981. Also see Ramesh Deosaran, *Eric Williams: The Man, His Ideas and His Politics: A Study of Political Power* (Port of Spain: Superservice Printing, 1981), pp. 158-71.
42. *Latin America Regional Reports Caribbean*, May 8, 1981, p. 9.
43. Ibid., June 12, 1981, p. 4.
44. David G. Becker, *The New Bourgeoisie and the Limits of Dependency: Mining, Class, and Power in "Revolutionary" Peru* (Princeton: Princeton University Press, 1983), p. 5.
45. *Business Latin America*, September 6, 1978, p. 285.
46. *Caribbean Monthly Bulletin* 14 (September-October 1980), p. 16.
47. Henry, "Trinidad and Tobago," in Robert J. Alexander, ed., *Political Parties of the Americas* (Westport, Conn.: Greenwood Press, 1982): p. 666.
48. *Latin America Regional Report Caribbean*, January 16, 1981, p. 4.
49. Ric Mentus comments, "those who turned out to give support to the party constituted such an even mix of the nation's multiplicity of ethnic origins that the gatherings could be considered a true reflection of what a racial callaloo Trinidad really is." *People Monthly*, October 1981, p. 29.
50. Ibid.
51. Ibid.
52. Ibid.
53. Ibid., p. 32.
54. *Latin America Regional Report Caribbean*, August 21, 1981, p. 4.
55. Jacqueline A. Braveboy-Wagner, "Trinidad and Tobago," in Jack W. Hopkins, ed., *Latin America and Caribbean Contemporary Record Vol. 1: 1981-82* (New York: Holmes and Meiers, 1982), p. 623.
56. Renwick, "Trinidad and Tobago," p. 261.
57. Ibid. Also see *Latin America Weekly Report*, November 27, 1981, p. 2.
58. *Latin America Weekly Report*, November 27, 1981, p. 2.
59. *Latin America Regional Report Caribbean*, May 7, 1982, p. 8.
60. "Trinidad gov't shelving 18 projects," *Advocate-News* (Barbados), June 17, 1982, p. 3.
61. International Monetary Fund, *International Financial Statistics, December 1984*, p. 458.
62. Ibid.
63. *Latin America Regional Report Caribbean*, May 13, 1983, p. 4.
64. Jeremy Taylor, "Trinidad's '83 Budget," *Caribbean Contact* 10 (February 1983): 16.
65. *Latin America Weekly Report*, November 27, 1981, p. 8.

66. "Independence Address by Prime Minister George Chambers," *Newsletter*, Embassy of Trinidad and Tobago, Washington, D.C. (August/September 1983), p. 5.

67. Based on personal observations and interviews with Trinidadian teachers involved in primary school education in the Port of Spain area and the south of Trinidad.

68. "Shake-up for PNM," *The Express*, August 9, 1983, p. 1.

69. "ANR: They Can't Treat Councils as Assembly," *The Express*, August 10, 1983, p. 1.

10

Conclusion

By the early 1980s Trinidad and Tobago's political and socioeconomic systems had changed considerably from the colonial period as the middle class became the dominant elite and guided the nation along the lines of democratic capitalism. In many respects, the Trinidadian middle-class perception of development is best summarized by B. L. C. Johnson: "Development means change; it implies betterment. The word carries a sense of optimism and confident expectation of progress for society, and improvement in the human condition."[1] Development, however, has not proven to be like the analogy of an airplane (the nation) taxiing for takeoff on the "onwards and upwards forever" approach.[2] As Gerald Heeger notes, "Social change, far from being inevitable and ultimately modernizing, is sporadic, erratic, and unpredictable in its consequences."[3] This has been the case in Trinidad and Tobago as the Afro-Creole middle sectors took the nation to independence and sought to form a "nation-state" founded upon Creole culture and Afro-Trinidadian nationalism after a long period of formative colonial rule in which the Westminster tradition was instilled.

When the East Indians, the last societal group tied to the land, became active in politics, the direction of the nation under the PNM was questioned. Racial and ethnic tensions were particularly troublesome as the nation moved to independence in the late 1950s and early 1960s. The democratic capitalism of the middle class formed an important core ideology upon which the nation was to launch itself into independence. Along these lines, what helped diffuse the racial situation, unlike neighboring Guyana where democracy was shunted aside by racial confrontation, was the emergence and expansion of the East Indian middle sectors, who increasingly had more in common with their Afro-Creole counterparts than with their own lower classes. Moreover, this group also regarded the Westminster parliamentary system as the rules of the game.

When economic growth slowed in the mid-1960s and the DLP grew apart from the needs of the majority of poorer East Indians, the national middle sectors, both East Indian and Afro-Creole, drew closer. This trend was accelerated by the DLP's gradual fragmentation, the lack of any political alternatives for the Indo-Trinidadian middle class, and the turmoil of the late 1960s and early 1970s. For the continuation of capitalism, the national middle sectors drew closer together than previously, providing the support for Eric Williams and the ruling party. From this socioeconomic accommodation, the prime minister was to draw the needed personnel for the interlocking directorates and the supportive triad of the new bourgeoisie, the state managers, and corporate agents. The system of rule by interlocking directorates evolved in the face of the government's erosion of support from elements of the middle and popular sectors.

The end of the economic boom in the early 1980s has once again brought out a questioning of the direction of the nation similar to that of the mid-1930s and late 1960s and early 1970s. The questions raised over the continuance of the nation's advancement in economic development were emphasized in Chambers's address on August 31, 1983. The prime minister claimed that the citizens "have an inescapable responsibility to adjust our style of living since Trinidad and Tobago could not continue to insulate itself from the reality of the harsh economic conditions in the world at large."[4] The "harsh economic conditions in the world at large" certainly has some impact on the domestic situation as reflected by the reduction of subsidies for various consumer items as well as the PNM's poor performance at the polls in 1983.

In all probability, the fragmentation of the PNM's base of support, linked in part to the negative GDP growth of 5.2 percent in 1983 and 7.4 percent in 1984, will continue.[5] In November 1984 this trend was evident as mirrored by the elections for the Tobago House of Assembly: the Democratic Action Congress took 11 out of 12 seats and received 11,090 votes to the PNM's 8,130 votes and 1 seat.[6] The DAC had previously held 8 seats, gaining from a decline in PNM support. Moreover, the loss of 3 of their 4 seats was a considerable setback to the PNM's political leader and prime minister, Chambers, who had been active in the campaign. With the two-island nation caught in a serious recession, there has been increasing grumbling that the party's leaders mismanaged the oil wealth of the previous decade. This was further underscored when George Chambers announced on July 9, 1985, that the nation intended to borrow more from international financial markets to help develop its indigenous resources, notably natural gas.[7]

By the next parliamentary elections in 1986, depending on economic conditions and Chambers's ability to project himself as a strong leader, the opposition parties could possibly gain ground. Looking ahead at those elections, Ryan comments, "The bottom line is that there's a good chance that the opposition could emerge as triumphant."[8] It is important to emphasize, however, that the PNM has demonstrated tremendous staying power and that the ONR and the National Alliance have substantial ideological differences, especially in their approaches to the management of the economy. The former advocates government divestment and greater private sector management, and the latter favors complete nationalization of all major industries. Considering such differences, the viability of an ONR-National Alliance coalition winning in 1986 and forming a government would present a situation possibly fraught with governmental breakdown and parliamentary stalemate.

The ONR-National Alliance coalition is limited, in terms of leadership, by the conservative stance of Hudson-Phillips and the leftist stance of Panday. The former is often regarded as too authoritarian and linked to the draconian public order acts in the early 1970s, while the latter is sometimes perceived as a weak leader and a "communist." The only real compromise politician with nationwide renown is Robinson of the DAC. The question is whether he could hold an accommodation government together. Although a pragmatist, his skills would clearly be taxed to maintain the union of middle-class Afro-Creoles and East Indians, white Creole merchant and corporate interests, agricultural and working-class East Indians, unionized Afro-Creole oil workers, and idealistic intellectuals.

The remaining possibilities would be a new economic boom, which would give the PNM the necessary success to be victorious at the polls in 1986, or a coalition government between the ruling party and the most ideologically compatible of the opposition, the ONR. Throughout the period before the elections in 1986, the pressure will be greater on the opposition to maintain the accommodation as the PNM is the party in power and enjoys much greater consensus of opinion and objectives. One last consideration is that the threat of a military coup is remote.

Johnson's observations, albeit modified considerably, clearly deserved a second look as Trinidad and Tobago's middle sectors have been the key factor in the development of democratic capitalism. Public education has been pushed, the economy has been increasingly industrialized, the state has actively intruded in the social and economic areas, and the political party has become the norm in the political system. Trinidad and Tobago's political system is based on the Westminster parliamentary tradition, and the following have been upheld: equality before the law; freedom of association, religion, and speech; and independence of the judiciary and the press. The opposition has largely been allowed to participate in the political process unhindered, and there have been no political prisoners, let alone the disappearances of people, which have occurred in both authoritarian and communist regimes. While certain aspects of the British colonial structure left a tradition of strong, if not sometimes autocratic, chief executives, the Westminster model has been relatively successful, especially as internal conflicts have been contained without the massive use of coercive force and the loss of life. Moreover, class has gradually come to weigh more than race, although that factor can never be completely discounted.

The underlying reason for the existence of democratic pluralism (and also democratic capitalism), therefore, has been the emergence of a national middle class, bound by commitments to the Westminster system and to capitalism with its linkages to the larger world economy. This has not meant, however, that the Trinidadian middle class "sold out" national development for short-term material gains. The state's role in the economy, the continued existence of a sizable private sector, and industrialization have had the result of putting Trinidad and Tobago in competition with some of the major capitalist nations, the United States, the United Kingdom, West Germany, and Japan in the steel market—not an indication of a socioeconomic and political system totally dependent on the metropolitan nations. There is a dependence on the global economy, but that is a dependence shared by all nations including the Soviet Union, Eastern Europe, and the People's Republic of China. In some ways, Trinidad's dependence may be greater than Brazil's or Mexico's, although that is more a result of geographical size and limited resources rather than a stronger desire of the national middle class to prostitute itself to the joys of Western consumerism. Unlike many nations, there has been some meaningful distribution of national wealth, and basic human needs have been met. This is not to say that poverty no longer exists in Trinidad and Tobago, but that improvements have been made in the standard of living strong enough to attract immigrants from the poorer neighboring islands and help maintain a belief that the Westminster model is viable.

Ingrained with a sense that the political system works, although it is not perfect, the Trinidadian middle sectors underscore that the nation should develop along a capitalist path and that the political party should be the primary vehicle of political expression, not the barrel of a gun. The Trinidadian experience poses a strong counterpoint to the dictatorial regime of Forbes Burnham in Guyana and, of course, Grenada under the New Jewel Movement. In both Grenada and Guyana, the gun has been used and still is being used in settling matters in the political arena. Moreover, the middle sectors in those nations were small and never as effective as their Trinidadian counterparts, perhaps a crucial factor in each country's different paths of development. It also indicates crucial historical differences in each nation's evolution and, perhaps, argues the uniqueness of Trinidad and Tobago's political and economic experiment.

As of the mid-1980s the Westminster model, supported by a capitalist economy, functions in Trinidad and Tobago, and the middle class continues to be the nation's leadership elite. It is very probable that Trinidadian democratic capitalism will continue to dominate the nation's direction. It is not probable that Trinidad and Tobago will turn into a Grenada or Guyana. Trinidad's future lies in its ability to balance between democracy based on the Westminster tradition and economic development based on a distinctive Trinidadian form of capitalism. For one to work, so must the other. In the past Trinidad–Tobago has been able to resolve its problems as the leadership elite has usually exercised sound judgment. It is hopeful that the middle sector leadership of the 1980s will rise to the occasion and sort out the nation's current development problems.

NOTES

1. B. L. C. Johnson, *Development in South Asia* (New York: Penguin Books, 1983), p. 15.

2. Frederick C. Turner, "The Study of Development in the 1980s," paper prepared for the International Conference United States (ICUS) workshop on the developmental experience in East Asia and Latin America, held at the Mayflower Hotel, New York City, May 27-29, 1983, p. 4.

3. Gerald A. Heeger, *The Politics of Underdevelopment* (New York: St. Martin's Press, 1974), p. 5.

4. "Independence Address by Prime Minister George Chambers," *Newsletter*, Embassy of Trinidad and Tobago, Washington, D.C. (August/September, 1983), p. 3.

5. Canute James, "Search Is on for Crutches," *Financial Times Survey*, July 8, 1985, p. iii.

6. Embassy of Trinidad and Tobago, "Tobago Local Elections," *Newsletter*, November 26, 1984, p. 3.

7. Peter Montagnon, "Trinidad to Step up Borrowing," *Financial Times*, July 10, 1985, p. 13.

8. Quoted in Joseph B. Treaster, "Party in Trinidad Seen as Slipping," *New York Times*, April 11, 1985, *Information Services Latin America*, 1985, p. 267.

Selected Bibliography

BOOKS

Alexander, Robert. *Today's Latin America*. New York: Garden Press, 1962.

Almond, Gabriel, and James Coleman. *The Politics of Developing Areas*. Princeton: Princeton University Press, 1960.

Axline, Andrew. *Caribbean Integration: The Politics of Regionalism*. New York: Nichols, 1979.

Becker, David G. *The New Bourgeoisie and the Limits of Dependency: Mining, Class, and Power in "Revolutionary" Peru*. Princeton: Princeton University Press, 1983.

Beckford, George. *Persistent Poverty: Underdevelopment in Plantation Economies of the Third World*. New York: Oxford University Press, 1972.

Basdeo, Sahadeo. *Labour Organization and Labour Reform in Trinidad 1919-1939*. St. Augustine: University of the West Indies, 1983.

Binder, Leonard, et al. *Crises and Sequences in Political Development*. Princeton: Princeton University Press, 1971.

Blanshard, Paul. *Democracy and Empire in the Caribbean: A Contemporary Review*. New York: Macmillan, 1947.

Brereton, Bridget. *A History of Modern Trinidad*. London: Heineman Educational Books, 1981.

_____. *Race Relations in Colonial Trinidad, 1870-1900*. New York: Cambridge University Press, 1979.

Chaliand, Gerand. *Revolution in the Third World*. New York: Penguin Books, 1976.

Chilcote, Ronald H. *Theories of Comparative Politics: The Search for a Paradigm*. Boulder: Westview Press, 1981.

Crozier, Michel. *The Bureaucratic Phenomenon*. Chicago: University of Chicago Press, 1964.

Davidson, J. G. *Tobago Versus P.N.M.* Port of Spain: Beacon, 1979.

Dalton, George. *Economic Systems and Society: Capitalism, Communism and the Third World*. New York: Penguin Books, 1978.

De Lima, Arthur. *The De Limas of Frederick Street*. Trinidad: Inprint Caribbean, 1981.

Demas, William. *The Economics of Development in Small Countries with Special Reference to the Caribbean*. Montreal: Centre for Developing-Area Studies, 1965.

Deosaran, Ramesh. *Eric Williams, The Man, His Ideas, and His Politics: A Study of Political Power*. Port of Spain: Superservice Printing Company, 1981.

Deutsch, Karl. *Nationalism and Its Alternatives*. New York: Alfred A. Knopf, 1969.

———. *Nationalism and Social Communication: An Inquiry into the Foundation of Nationality*. New York: John Wiley and Sons, 1953.

De Verteuil, Fr. Anthony. *The Years Before*. Port of Spain: Inprint Caribbean, 1981.

———. *The Years of Revolt: Trinidad 1881-1888*. Port of Spain: Paria, 1984.

Edwards, S. Hylton. *Lengthening Shadows: Birth and Revolt of the Trinidad Army*. Port of Spain: Inprint Caribbean, 1983.

Erisman, H. Michael, and John D. Martz, eds. *Colossus Challenged: The Struggle for Caribbean Influence*. Boulder: Westview Press, 1982.

Fanon, Frantz. *The Wretched of the Earth*. New York: Grove Press, 1968.

Farrell, Trevor M. A. *The Multinational Corporations, the Petroleum Industry and Economic Underdevelopment in Trinidad and Tobago*. Ann Arbor: University Microfilms International, 1974.

Frank, André Gunder. *Lumpen-Bourgeoisie; Lumpendevelopment: Dependence, Class and Politics in Latin America*. New York: Monthly Review Press, 1972.

Froude, J. A. *The English in the West Indies or, The Bow of Ulysses*. New York: Charles Scribners and Sons, 1888.

Furtado, Celso. *Obstacles to Development in Latin America*. New York: Anchor Books, 1967.

Gomes, Albert. *Through the Maze of Colour*. Port of Spain: Longman Caribbean. 1974.

Hirschman, Albert O. *Essays in Trespassing: Economics to Politics and Beyond*. New York: Cambridge University Press, 1981.

———. *Latin American Issues: Essays and Comments*. New York: Twentieth Century Fund, 1961.

Huntington, Samuel P. *Political Order in Changing Societies*. New Haven: Yale University Press, 1968.

Jacobs, W. Richard. *The Trial of Uriah Butler: A Study of Colonial Injustice*. Trinidad: Longman Caribbean, 1974.

James, C. L. R. *Walter Rodney and the Question of Power*. London: Race Today Publications, 1983.

Johnson, John J. *Political Change in Latin America: The Emergence of the Middle Sectors*. Stanford: University of Stanford Press, 1958.

Joseph, E. L. *History of Trinidad*. London: Frank Cass, 1838, New Impression, 1970.

Lewis, Gordon K. *The Growth of the Modern West Indies*. New York: Monthly Review Press, 1968.

Lewis, W. Arthur. *The Evolution of the International Economic Order*. Princeton: Princeton University Press, 1978.

Lloyd, T. O. *Empire to Welfare State: English History, 1906-1967*. London: Oxford University Press, 1976.

Mahabir, Winston. *In and Out of Politics: Tales of the Government of Dr. Eric Williams from the Notebooks of a Former Minister*. Trinidad: Inprint Caribbean, 1978.

Malik, Yogenda. *East Indians in Trinidad: A Study in Minority Politics*. London: Oxford University Press, 1971.

Manning, Helen Taft. *British Colonial Government After the American Revolution 1782-1820*. Hamden, Conn.: Archon Books, 1966.

Millette, James. *The Genesis of Crown Colony Government, Trinidad, 1783-1810*. Curepe, Trinidad: Moko Enterprises, 1970.

Misra, B. B. *The Indian Middle Classes: Their Growth in Modern Times*. London: Oxford University Press, 1961.

Mordecai, John. *The West Indies: The Federal Negotiations*. Evanston, Ill.: Northwestern University Press, 1968.

Naipaul, V. S. *A Flag on the Island*. London: André Deutsch, 1967.

_____. *Guerrillas*. London: André Deutsch, 1975.

_____. *The Loss of El Dorado*. London: André Deutsch, 1969.

_____. *The Suffrage of Elvira*. London: André Deutsch, 1958.

Norton, Robert. *Race and Politics in Fiji*. New York: St. Martin's Press, 1977.

Novak, Michael. *The Spirit of Democratic Capitalism*. New York: An American Enterprise Institute/Simon and Schuster Publication, 1982.

Organski, A. F. K. *The Stages of Political Development*. New York: Alfred A. Knopf, 1965.

Ottley, C. R. *The Story of Port of Spain*. Diego Martin, Trinidad: Crusoe, 1962, 1970, 1978.

_____. *The Story of Tobago*. Trinidad and Jamaica: Longman Caribbean, 1973, 1979.

_____. *The Trinidad Callaloo: Life in Trinidad From 1851-1900*. Diego Martin, Trinidad: Crusoe, 1978.

Oxaal, Ivar. *Black Intellectuals Come to Power: The Rise of Creole Nationalism in Trinidad and Tobago.* Cambridge, Mass.: Schenkman, 1968.

———. *Race and Revolutionary Consciousness: An Existential Report on the 1970 Black Power Revolt in Trinidad.* Cambridge, Mass.: Schenkman, 1971.

Payne, Anthony J. *The International Crisis in the Caribbean.* Baltimore: Johns Hopkins University Press, 1984.

———. *The Politics of the Caribbean Community, 1961-1979.* New York: St. Martin's Press, 1980.

Payne, Anthony J., and Paul Sutton, eds. *Dependency Under Challenge: The Political Economy of the Commonwealth Caribbean.* Manchester, England: University of Manchester Press, 1984.

Pelling, Henry. *A History of British Trade Unionism.* Harmondsworth, Middlesex, England: Penguin Books, 1977.

Prebisch, Raúl. *The Economic Development of Latin America and Its Principal Problems.* New York: United Nations, 1950.

Pye, Lucian W. *Politics, Personality, and Nation Building: Burma's Search for Identity.* New Haven: Yale University Press, 1962.

Robinson, A. N. R. *The Mechanics of Independence: Patterns of Political and Economic Transformation in Trinidad and Tobago.* Cambridge, Mass.: M.I.T. Press, 1971.

Rodney, Walter. *How Europe Underdeveloped Africa.* Washington, D.C.: Howard University Press, 1974.

Rostow, Walt W. *The Stages of Economic Growth: A Non-Communist Manifesto.* Cambridge: Cambridge University Press, 1960.

Ryan, Selwyn. *Race and Nationality in Trinidad and Tobago: A Study of Decolonization in a Multiracial Society.* Toronto: University of Toronto Press, 1972.

Rustow, Dankwart A. *A World of Nations: Problems of Political Modernization.* Washington, D.C.: Brookings Institute, 1967.

Sigmund, Paul. *The Overthrow of Allende and the Politics of Chile, 1964-1976.* Pittsburgh: University of Pittsburgh Press, 1977.

Silvert, Kalman H. *Expectant Peoples: Nationalism and Development.* New York: Random House, 1963.

Skocpol, Theda. *States and Social Revolutions: A Comparative Analysis of France, Russia and China.* Cambridge: University of Cambridge Press, 1979.

Smith, Anthony. *The Ethnic Revival in the Modern World.* Cambridge: Cambridge University Press, 1981.

Solomon, Patrick. *Solomon: An Autobiography.* Port of Spain: Inprint Caribbean, 1981.

Stepan, Alfred. *The Military in Politics: Changing Patterns in Brazil.* Princeton: Princeton University Press, 1971.

Stone, Carl. *Democracy and Clientelism in Jamaica.* New Brunswick, N.J.: Transaction Books, 1980.

Szulz, Tad. *Twilight of the Tyrants.* New York: Anchor Books, 1959.

Thomas, J. J. *Froudacity.* London: New Beacon Books, 1889, 1969.

Ward, Robert E., and Dankwart A. Rustow, eds. *Political Modernization in Japan and Turkey.* Princeton: Princeton University Press, 1964.

Weller, Judith Ann. *The East Indian Indenture in Trinidad.* Rio Piedras: University of Puerto Rico, 1968.

Wiarda, Howard J. *Critical Elections and Critical Coups: State, Society and the Military in the Processes of Latin American Development.* Athens, Ohio: Ohio University Center for International Studies, 1978.

_____, ed. *Rift and Revolution: The Central American Imbroglio.* Washington, D.C.: American Enterprise Institute for Public Policy Research, 1984.

Williams, Eric. *Capitalism and Slavery.* New York: Capricorn Books, 1944, 1966.

_____. *From Columbus to Castro: The History of the Caribbean 1492-1969.* London: Andre Deutsch, 1970.

_____. *History of the People of Trinidad and Tobago.* London: Andre Deutsch, 1964.

_____. *Inward Hunger: The Education of a Prime Minister.* Chicago: University of Chicago Press, 1971.

Wood, Donald. *Trinidad in Transition.* London: Oxford University Press, 1966.

Wynia, Gary. *The Politics of Latin American Development.* Cambridge: Cambridge University Press, 1978.

ARTICLES

Beloff, Nora. "COMECON Blues." *Foreign Policy,* no. 31 (Summer 1978): 159-79.

Blanksten, George. "In Quest of the Middle Sectors." *World Politics,* no. 2 (January 1960): 324-26.

Campbell, Carl. "The Rebel Priest: Francis DeRidder and the Fight for Free Coloureds' Rights in Trinidad, 1825-32. *Journal of Caribbean History* 15 (1981): 20-40.

Casella, Alexander. "Dateline Vietnam: Managing the Peace." *Foreign Policy,* no. 30 (Spring 1978): 170-91.

Cross, Malcolm. "On Conflict, Race Relations and the Theory of the Plural Society." *Race* 12 (1981): 23-56.

Deosaran, Ramesh. "Some Issues in Multiculturalism: The Case of Trinidad and Tobago in the Post Colonial Era." *Ethnic Groups* 3 (1981): 199-225.

Elkins, W. F. "Black Power in the West Indies: The Trinidad Longshoremen's Strike of 1919." *Science and Society* 33 (1969): 20-42.

———. "Hercules and the Society of Peoples of African Origin." *Caribbean Studies* 2 (January 1972): 47-59.

Frank, Andre Gunder. "Sociology of Development and Underdevelopment of Sociology." *Catalyst* 3 (Summer 1967): 20-73.

Glazier, Stephen. "Research Report: Cultural Pluralism and Respectability in Trinidad." *Ethnic and Racial Studies* 6 (July 1983): 16-29.

Horowitz, Irving Louis. "Democracy and Development: Policy Perspectives in a Postcolonial Context." In *The Newer Caribbean: Decolonization, Democracy and Development*, edited by Paget Henry and Carl Stone, pp. 221-34. Philadelphia: Institute for the Study of Human Issues, 1983.

Jacobs, W. Richard. "The Politics of Protest in Trinidad: The Strikes and Disturbances of 1937." *Caribbean Studies* 17 (1977): 23-28.

Johnson, Caswell L. "Political Unionism and Autonomy in Economies of British Colonial Origin: The Cases of Jamaica and Trinidad." *American Journal of Economics and Sociology* 39 (July 1980): 240-60.

Joseph, C. L. "The British West Indies Regiment, 1914-1918." *Journal of Caribbean History* 2 (May 1971): 94-124.

La Guerre, John G. "The General Election of 1946 in Trinidad and Tobago." *Social and Economic Studies* 21 (June 1972): 186-96.

Laurence, K. O. "The Evolution of Long-Term Labour Contracts in Trinidad and British Guiana." In *The Caribbean in Transition*, edited by F. M. Andic and T. G. Matthews, pp. 170-83. Rio Piedras: University of Puerto Rico, 1965.

MacDonald, Scott B. "The Future of Foreign Aid in the Caribbean After Grenada: Finlandization and Confrontation in the Eastern Tier." *Inter-American Economic Affairs* 38 (Spring 1985): 59-74.

MacDonald, Scott B., and Albert L. Gastmann. "Mitterand's Headache: The French Antilles in the 1980s." *Caribbean Review* 13 (Spring 1984): 19-21.

Pantin, Raul. "In Trinidad the Natives Are Getting Restless Again." *Caribbean Contact* 2 (September 1983): 5.

Parris, Carl D. "Personalization of Power in an Elected Government, Eric Williams and Trinidad and Tobago, 1973-1981." *Journal of Interamerican Studies and World Affairs* 25 (May 1983): 171-99.

Ramasar, M. "The Impact of the Indian Immigrants on Colonial Trinidad Society." *Caribbean Quarterly* 22 (1976): 14-24.

Ryan, Selwyn. "The Church that Williams Built: Electoral Possibilities in Trinidad." *Caribbean Review* 10 (Spring 1981).

———. "The Limits of Executive Power." *Caribbean Studies* 3 (Spring/Autumn 1982).

———. "Tobago's Quest for Autonomy: From Colony to Ward to . . . ." *Caribbean Review* 14 (Spring 1985): 7-9, 38-40.

———. "Trinidad and Tobago: The General Elections of 1976." *Caribbean Studies* 19 (April-July 1979).

Samaroo, Brinsley. "C. P. David: A Case in the Emergence of the Black Man in Trinidad Politics." *Journal of Caribbean History* 3 (1971).

———. "The Trinidad Workingmen's Association and the Origins of Popular Protest in a Crown Colony." *Social and Economic Studies* 21 (June 1972).

Stockwell, A. J. "Hugh Clifford in Trinidad 1903-1907." *Caribbean Quarterly* 24 (March/June 1978): 9-16.

Wiarda, Howard J. "At the Root of the Problem: Conceptual Failures in U.S.-Central American Relations." In *Central America: Anatomy of Conflict*, edited by Robert S. Leiken, pp. 259-78. New York: Pergamon Press, 1984.

GOVERNMENT AND OTHER PRIMARY LITERATURE

Commodity Yearbook 1939. New York: Commodity Research Bureau, 1940.

Commodity Yearbook 1941. New York: Commodity Research Bureau, 1941.

Economic Commission for Latin America. *Economic Survey of Latin America 1966*. New York: United Nations, 1968.

The Economist. *The World in Figures*. London: The Economist, 1981.

Government of Trinidad and Tobago. "Independence Address by Prime Minister George Chambers." *Trinidad and Tobago Embassy Newsletter* (August/September 1983): 2-14.

———. *Trinidad and Tobago Report on the General Elections of 1961*. Port of Spain: Prepared by the Supervisor of Elections, 1965.

Inter-American Development Bank. *Economic and Social Progress in Trinidad and Tobago 1979 Report*. Washington, D.C. Reprinted from the Inter-American Development Bank's 1979 *Economic and Social Progress in Latin America*.

International Monetary Fund. *Direction of Trade Statistics Yearbook 1984*. Washington, D.C.: International Monetary Fund, 1984.

U.S. Department of State. *Democracy in Latin America and the Caribbean*. Current Policy No. 605 (August 1984).

Year Book of Labour Statistics 1966. Geneva: International Labour Office, 1966.

Year Book of Labour Statistics 1972. Geneva: International Labour Office, 1972.

Year Book of Labour Statistics 1980. Geneva: International Labour Office, 1980.

The Year Book of the Commonwealth 1974. London: Her Majesty's Stationery Office, 1974.

Index

Action Committee of Democratic Citizens, 170-171

Becker, David G., 6, 178
Betancourt, Romulo, 10, 122
black power, 8, 162-166
British Guiana (see Guyana)
Butler, T. U., 57-60, 76, 80-83, 109

Caribbean Socialist Party (CSP), 80-81
Capildeo, Rudrunath, 151-154
Capildeo, Simbhoonath, 152
Castro, Fidel, 154
Césaire, Aimé, 8
Chambers, George, 174, 215-216
China, 27
Cipriani, Captain Arthur A., 50-60
cocoa, 28
Crown Colony, evolution of, 24-26, 61-62

Demas, William, 16
Democratic Action Congress (DAC), 215
Democratic Labour Party (DLP), 113, 116-118, 151-152, 170-171, 180
dependency theory, 11-13
De Ridder, Francis, 33
Dubois, W. E. B., 8
Destroyers-for-Bases Deal, 63

East Indians, arrival of, 27-28
East Indian National Congress (EINC), 48
Elections, (1925) 53-54, (1946) 72-75, (1950) 80-83, (1956) 105-111, (1958) 118-120, (1961) 130-135, (1966) 153-154, (1968) 155,

[Elections]
(1976) 181-185, (1981) 200-205, (1983) 205-209, (1984) 215

Federation, Caribbean, 114-116
Fiji, 27

Gomes, Albert, 62, 71, 74, 79, 84-85, 90, 92, 109-110
Grenada, 190, 198
Guyana (formerly British Guiana), 7-9, 27, 86, 214-215

Hudson-Phillips, Karl, 176

Inter-Ministerial Enterprises Committee, 193
Iron and Steel Company of Trinidad and Tobago (ISCOTT), 192

Jamadar, Vernon, 169-170, 182
James, A. P. T. "Fargo", 109
James, C. L. R., 123
Johnson, John J., 2-5, 9-10, 217-218
Joseph, Roy, 73-74, 84, 109

Kumar, Ranjit, 79-80

Liberal Party, 154

Maharaj, Stephen, 150, 152, 182
Mahabir, Errol, 193
Maraj, Bhadase Sagan, 107-108, 155
Mauritius, 27
Mercantilism, 15-16
Moyne Commission, 61-62

National Advisory Council (NAC), 192
National Joint Action Congress (NJAC), 163-164
New World Group, 12
Nyerere, Julius, 8

O'Connor, Quinton, 73
Oil, 46-47
Oil Workers Trade Union (OWTU), 62, 150, 180
Organization of National Reconstruction (ONR), 216

Panday, Basdeo, 180
Party of Political Progress Group (POPPG), 109-110
Philip, John Baptiste, 33
Peoples Democratic Party (PDP), 107-109
Pioneer Industries Ordinance, 87
Pitt, David, 73
plantation economy, 23-28
Progressive Democratic Party (PDP), 72
Political Education Group (PEG), 103
Prebisch, Raúl, 10
Public Order Bill, 167-168

Ratepayers Association (RPA), 38-40
Réunion, 27
Rienzi, Adrian, 62, 73
Robinson, A. N. R., 165
Rodney, Walter, 11

Sanatan Dharma Maha Sabha (SDMS), 107-108

Shah, Raffique, 180-181
Socialist Party of Trinidad and Tobago, 73
Solomon, P. J., 74, 78
Spain, 22-24
sugar, 23-24, 27, 45, 195
Suriname, 7-9, 27

Tang, Norman, 82, 84
Teachers Economic and Cultural Association (TECA), 103
Tobago, early history of, 29-30
Trinidad and Tobago Telephone Company Ltd., 194
Trinidad Labour Party (TLP), 50-61, 109
Trinidad Workingmen's Association (TWA), 40-42, 51

United Labour Front (ULF), 181-182
United States occupation of Trinidad and Tobago, 63-66

Venezuela, 166, 174

Water Riot of 1903, 39-40
Water and Sanitary Authority (WASA), 194
Weekes, George, 150, 180-181
West Indian National Party (WINP), 73-74, 80
white supremacy, 30-32
Williams, Eric, 98-102, 179, 192-193, 196-199
Workers and Farmers Party (WFP), 153

About the Author

Scott B. MacDonald is the international and specialized industries' unit manager at Connecticut National Bank in Hartford, Connecticut and a consultant on Caribbean and Latin American affairs. He is also a director of the North American Friends of the School of Oriental and African Studies. Before his current position at Connecticut National, he was the senior country risk analyst, covering Africa, Asia, Europe, Latin America, and Canada.

Dr. MacDonald is a member of the Association of Political Risk Analysts, the International Political Scientist Association, and the Latin American Studies Association. He has travelled extensively and has lived overseas. He has published articles in the *Caribbean Review*, the *Latin America and Caribbean Contemporary Record*, *Inter-American Economic Affairs*, *The Financial Times* (London), *The Times of the Americas*, and is currently editing a book on Grenada's implications for the Caribbean Basin. His major interests are Latin American debt, sugar, trade policy, and commodities.

Dr. MacDonald received his Ph.D. from the University of Connecticut in Political Science in 1985, his M.A. in International Relations in the Far East from the University of London's School of Oriental and African Studies in London, and his B.A. in History and Political Science from Trinity College in Hartford, Connecticut. He achieved honors at Trinity in Political Science, and while at the University of Connecticut he was presented the Stein Rokkan Travel Award by the International Political Science Association. This was given to an outstanding graduate student and allowed him to attend the congress held in Rio de Janiero. He is a native of the Hartford area and his wife, Kateri, is a Canadian specialist and is of English and French nationalities.